CREATIVITY
AND LEARNING

THE DÆDALUS LIBRARY

Each of these volumes is available as a Beacon Paperback.

CREATIVITY
AND LEARNING

EDITED AND WITH AN
INTRODUCTION BY
JEROME KAGAN

BEACON PRESS   BOSTON

CONTENTS

Documents

JEROME KAGAN

Introduction

CONCEPTUAL MAN abhors insufficient differentiation as nature resents a vacuum. Man seems to prefer a small number of reasonably homogeneous categories; when one becomes both too large and heterogeneous, he searches for an intellectual trick that will allow semantic mitosis and the creation of two where originally there was one.

The last decade has developed a fetish for what was once a perfectly legitimate word, *creativity*. Where previous centuries saw fit to apply this label with some caution and in single units, our generation exuberantly assigns its adjective form every day to hundreds of young people. The intellectual priests of earlier generations assigned the label after the proof was in; our contemporaries wish to predict it, as if creativity resembled life expectancy, rather than number of children, to which it bears a closer conceptual tie. This change in fashion takes its nurture from several sources. When society boasted only a few intelligent people, one word—or one word with a superlative—was sufficient to categorize them. Today we have so many that an additional category of kind is required to accumulate the overflow at the top. *Creative* is as good a word as any.

The press to invent strategies to predict creativity rather than to name creative people comes primarily from the educational estate. College and industry complain that traditional tests of mental prowess are less valid than they used to be. It is now more difficult to guess who will produce talented ideas from test scores alone. Young people have learned how to be intelligent by what appears to be the absorption of "instant knowledge." Since our shared premise about genius is that it is born not made, we will do anything that will allow us to retain this belief, and we often wrap a Pollyannish and semireligious cloak about the word *creativity*. The empirical model that we have adopted for discovering potential creativity has been borrowed, unfortunately, from the paradigm developed for intelligence. There is a tendency to confuse capacity for creativity with the creative man, where we never would confuse fertility with number of children.

Let us be clear about the issues. *Creativity* refers to a product, and if made by a man, we give him the honor of the adjective. Philip W. Jackson and Samuel J. Messick state it well—novelty, appropriateness, transformation, and condensation characterize the creative product. The attributes that define a creative invention are multiple and include, at a minimum, its novelty and appropriateness, as well as its structural relation to an existing matrix of ideas. What is required for the simultaneous brewing of these attributes? A rich reservoir of knowledge is, of course, mandatory. Transformations of old notions require a rich set of concepts and experiences to be transformed. A creative idea can hardly be born if there is no rich medium in which it can grow.

The novelty that is a defining attribute of the creative work owes its allegiance to two forces—the availability of diverse possibilities and, equally important, the desire to surprise. The wish to produce a unique idea sets the compass of the mind in an oblique direction and leads it to search in out-of-the-way places for a course to pursue.

A creative product is actively sculpted, not passively generated. This is a less romantic view of creativity than we ordinarily like to hold but perhaps a more honest one. The suggestion that the creative product derives from a need for its expression demands that we consider motivational processes as sharing the burden of explanation with traditional intellective factors. Contemporary testing procedures in school or industry typically limit assessments of creativity to the originality of a set of associations, to the uniqueness of some thought structure, and *pari passu* assign a subordinate role to the more dynamic motivational levers that make potential creativity kinetic. One current attitude toward predicting creativity in a child or adolescent rests on the premise that a large collection of unusual hypotheses is sufficient. Possession of bizarre ideas is sometimes regarded as necessarily linked with creative action. This presumption of causality between quality of thought and a class of behavior by the scientist concerned with creativity has its counterpart in the behavioristic assumption that action is a necessary prerequisite for the acquisition of new knowledge. Both attitudes reflect an erroneous premise. Man can be defined in the most abstract sense as consisting of two parallel hierarchical organizations—a conceptual apparatus that translates experience and a set of actions. The conceptual and active domains touch in many places but usually out of choice, not out of necessity. If a rich network of conceptual ideas is forbidden exit into the world of public events, then our prediction of creative products will be in gross error. Motivational forces can block expression of a new brew of symbols. These forces are often difficult to overcome, and the educational and social institutions in our community have as much responsibility to tutor the creative act as they do to teach aesthetic and conceptual rules. Creative, artistic, theoretical, or empirical work by female students or mature women scientists is far below that to which we are entitled, given their rich store of knowledge. But the girl is taught from the earliest age to covet similarity to her peer and to flee from disagreement. Moreover, the desire to be different often draws some nurture from a relatively hostile component that is satisfied by the novel act. It interprets *different* as *superior*. Despite the questionable validity of this translation, it is more likely to occur among men than among women. The young girl is carefully taught to place strong curbs on hostile feelings and overtly aggressive behavior. The consistency and duration of this training produces strong inhibitions on acting out any desire to "outdo" a peer.

Donald W. MacKinnon's classic studies of creative architects and mathematicians furnish a more human profile of the creative professional. He is less concerned than most with the pleasant security of positive peer regard. The possibility of a harsh evaluation or direct rejection by the social community is not cause for personal alarm. He may be either completely free of the addictive quality of social acceptance or well defended against this motive, but he is not constrained to censor thought or product. He is freed from checking his conclusions with the confining reference that the community cherishes. He is free to believe that the earth rotates around the sun, that things that cannot be seen, heard, smelled or touched have a poisonous existence, that the energy in a piece of wood consumed in flame is never lost, or that a bizarre and inchoate dream has a personal and coherent meaning. Such freedom is not born. It is made in the pain of adolescent loneliness, the isolation of physical handicap, or, perhaps, the smug superiority of inherited title. The freedom that permits "generation of possibilities," to use Michael

Wallach's phrase, is the beginning of a creative product. The enemy of this fluid process is a severe attitude toward error. The fear of being incorrect, which represents the fear of disapproval by the social community, acts as a permanent insulation against the discovery of new mental combinations.

Too many of our schools behave as if they believed that the task of education was to teach pieces of correct information and to eliminate mistaken ideas. The child views education in this light, for the typical eight-year-old will reply to the question, "Why do you go to school?" with a reasonable answer, "To learn." We give too little concern to a second goal: that of convincing the child that he can produce possible solution hypotheses, even though each might contain a little error. We do not devote enough energy to teaching the child that he can think. It is certainly easier to teach facts than to train thinking, and machines can perform the former task with a far greater elegance and efficiency than a bright woman with a Bachelor's degree in education. But there is a clear danger in persuading the child that "facts" are the heart of the intellectual enterprise. To know is not to think; and to think is not to act. To teach the child to generate possibilities in the face of a problem and to reduce his anxiety over expressing actions that do not match those of the majority peer group are difficult but central missions of education.

The papers in this volume touch most of the vital social, educational, political and psychological issues bearing on creativity. Each author speaks to a different theme, but there is a general unanimity on one proposition: each is worried and wary about the deadening effect of group pressure and the negative sanctions that are placed on a deviant response. Jerome Wiesner argues:

There must be encouragement and stimulation of imaginative and un-conventional interpretation of experience in general; this is particularly true in problem-solving activities. It is important, especially in childhood and early youth, that novel ideas and unconventional patterns of action should be more widely tolerated, not criticized too soon and too often.

He suggests that this might be facilitated by associating "the prospective scientist with a person who has demonstrated both his creative ability and the capacity to transfer his spirit to youngsters."

David Hawkins, in a similar vein, urges adoption of an eclectic and pluralistic view of knowledge acquisition:

What each individual knows that he can use in this way is, at any moment, a highly individual affair. In reducing our experience to order, the distance we must travel to achieve any component of this order is not a well-defined quantity; for there are many paths to a goal of understanding, and along any path there are *many* available important goals . . . Patterns of optimal learning are highly individual . . . Since there are so many important things to be learned, the direction of exploration is not critical. What is learned will add to the power of later learning. What is important is the confrontation with materials which play can exploit and incorporate—absorption in fresh subject matter!

The decades of the forties and fifties witnessed a zealous concern with group adjustment, an evangelical fervor to bring the child on the sidelines into the center. The lack of tolerance for heterogeneity quickly cripples the generative process and the sculpting of creative adolescents. As our increasing population density reduces group differences and mechanical aids impose similar norms for thousands of children, there is a need to maintain some balance with a vector that protects and encourages heterogeneity, even at the cost of awesome efficiency.

CREATIVITY AND LEARNING

PHILIP W. JACKSON AND
SAMUEL MESSICK

The Person, the Product, and the Response: Conceptual Problems in the Assessment of Creativity[°]

THE ULTIMATE concern of the psychologist is the human mind and its inventions. Although there are many ways to describe man's mental complexity—and particularly to depict his cognitive strengths—the two terms "intelligence" and "creativity" seem to have the greatest summary power. It is this concentration of meaning that explains the endurance of these two words in the layman's language and their continued use in professional discussions.

Typically, efforts to distinguish empirically between creativity and intelligence have concentrated on demonstrating that tests requiring the production of unusual responses involve somewhat different abilities than do conventional tests of intelligence. But as Golann quite correctly points out in his review of studies of creativity,

".... these data are in a sense arbitrary: intelligence is not performance on a test; creativity is more than test performance or being judged as creative. What is needed for the understanding of the relationship between creativity and intelligence is not only data at the correlational level, but conceptual reorganization as well."[1]

The Evaluation of Intellectual Performance

The exercise of a person's cognitive powers is often the occasion for evaluation. People are continually being informed that they have done well or poorly on intellectual tasks, and the variety of

° This article is reprinted, with minor additions and emendations, from the *Journal of Personality*, 1965, Vol. 33, with the kind permission of the editor and the Duke University Press.

forms these judgments may take is almost as great as the variety of behaviors being judged. The wide assortment of evaluative comments can be crudely classified, however, into two overlapping categories. On the one hand, there are those judgments having to do with the "correctness" or "rightness" of a person's response. These evaluations deal with the degree to which certain objective and logical criteria have been satisfied. These criteria of correctness tend to be categorical: They usually admit only one answer, or a relatively restricted set of solutions, with all other responses regarded as incorrect or in error. On the other hand, there are judgments having to do with the worth or "goodness" of a person's response. These evaluations deal with the degree to which certain subjective and psychological criteria have been satisfied. The criteria of goodness tend to be continuous: They admit a wide range of responses that vary in the degree of their acceptability. Although, as has been suggested, these two classes of evaluations overlap (and some kinds of behavior satisfy both sets of criteria), the two are nonetheless distinguishable and the distinction between them has important implications for the conceptual separation of intelligent and creative responses.

In the simplest terms, the adjectives "correct" and "good" apply differentially to the terms "intelligent" and "creative." Intelligent responses are correct; they satisfy objective criteria; they operate within the constraints of logic and reality and thus may be considered right or wrong, true or false. Creative responses, in contrast, are "good"; they satisfy subjective criteria; although they may not necessarily be limited by the demands of logic and reality, they are responsive, as we shall see, to a wide variety of judgmental standards. Always, though, in the assessment of a response's creativeness or "goodness" we are aware of the humanness required to make the judgment. As Santayana puts it, ". . . for the existence of good in any form it is not merely consciousness but emotional consciousness that is needed. Observation will not do, appreciation is required."[2] And only man, not machine, is capable of appreciation.

The distinction being made here between the correct and the good is contained, at least implicitly, in many other discussions of the creative process. Guilford, for one, is particularly aware of it when he says, "There are different bases or criteria by which a product is judged. One is its logical consistency with known facts. Another is its less-than-logical consistency with other experiences."[3] Guilford goes on to imply that logical criteria are applied primarily to scientific products whereas artistic products are evaluated by less-than-logical standards. In the present distinction no such separation between the evaluation of scientific and artistic products is implied. A piano solo may be as incorrect as the solution to a mathematical equation. A scientific theory may be as good as a great novel. The poet's attempt to write a Spencerian sonnet may be both incorrect and poor, as may the engineer's design for a bridge.

In many of the tests currently proposed to assess creative ability, the failure to differentiate between correct responses and good responses leads to unnecessary confounding. Take as an instance the Remote Association Test developed by Mednick.[4] In this test the subject is presented with three words, such as "rat," "blue," and "cottage," and is required to supply a fourth word to serve as a kind of associational link between them. For the example given the answer is "cheese." Now it is argued that this answer reflects a degree of creativity because it is "remote" and "useful," at least in the sense of meeting specified requirements. We would insist that the answer reflects an aspect of intelligence because it is correct. To further illustrate his point, Mednick maintains that the answer 7,363,474 to the question "How much is 12 and 12?" is original but not creative because it is not useful. What seems more important, however, is not that the answer lacks usefulness, but that in the absence of a special formal system to justify it, it is wrong. As we use the term, there are no creative answers to the question, "How much is 12 and 12?" The constraints of reality implied in the question only allow for correct or incorrect responses.

Mednick introduces the concept of usefulness because he realizes, as do most researchers in this field, that the criterion of unusualness or originality is not enough. These qualities, as Guilford's work has so brilliantly demonstrated, do take us beyond the confines of correctness in evaluating cognitive performance. But, as Guilford and others also recognize, the identification of the unusual is, at best, a first step in trying to understand the good.

Creative Products and Appreciative Responses

Frequency and Fit. No matter what other positive qualities it might possess, we generally insist as a first step that a product be novel before we are willing to call it creative. Indeed, the conjoining of novelty and creativeness is so deeply ingrained in our thinking that the two concepts are sometimes treated as synonymous. The result is that novelty often comes to be used as the most common and, in some of our current paper-and-pencil tests of creativity, the only measure of a product's creativeness.

The application of the criterion of unusualness requires a two-step operation: a comparison of the product in question with other products of the same class and a counting of those comparisons that yield similar or identical products. Further, if such a relative frequency criterion of unusualness is to be applied consistently, some standard must be established to decide how few is few.

The collection of objects with which the judged object is compared also requires definition. Typically the judgment of unusualness is made not in terms of *all* other objects of a general class, such as all paintings in existence, but in terms of a greatly restricted subset. When we say, for example, that a child's painting contains an unusual representation of three-dimensional space, our standard of comparison most frequently includes other paintings by children. We likely would not make the same judgment if adult work were the standard. When we consider the potential populations against which the unusualness of a particular object might be judged, it becomes apparent that the relative rareness of the object depends on what it is compared with. With a shift in frame of reference, the same product could be unique in one population and common in another. Clearly, the choice of an appropriate baseline or norm group against which to judge a creative work is of utmost importance in applying the standard of unusualness. In short, the infrequency of a response is relative to *norms*, which thus serve as a judgmental standard for evaluating unusualness.

Although the judgment of uniqueness or infrequency is a logical first step in evaluating the creativeness of a product, if we proceeded no further, the total set of products nominated as creative would make a strange collection. It would include, among other things, all of the products that are simply bizarre or odd. Somehow the mere oddities must be weeded out. This task requires the application of a second criterion, *appropriateness*.

To be appropriate a product must fit its context. It must "make sense" in light of the demands of the situation and the desires of the producer. Further, in the case of complex products, the internal elements of a work must also blend together. Thus, both internal and external criteria of appropriateness may be distinguished. Indeed, two separate critical stances arise from the relative emphasis on internal or external views of appropriateness.

The major role of the appropriateness criterion, as it is used here, is to help eliminate from the set of unusual products those that are simply absurd. As a criterion of creativeness, it is used conjointly with unusualness rather than independently. Appropriateness without unusualness would be merely cliché. At fairly low levels of creative production—as, for example, in paper-and-pencil tests of divergent thinking—the criterion of appropriateness is not too difficult to apply. When a person is asked, for instance, to think of different uses for a common object such as a paper clip and he responds, "Eat it," the inappropriateness of his response is obvious. When a person is asked to write captions for cartoons and responds by giving the names of colors, again there is little question about the inappropriateness of his reaction. Note, however, that both of these illustrative responses would probably be unusual, if not unique, in a statistical sense. In those cases where the product has to meet some "reality tests" the application of the appropriateness criterion does not appear to be too difficult.

As products become more complex, however, and more responsive to the needs of the producer than to the demands of the situation, the determination of appropriateness also becomes more complex. There are times, of course, when the judgment is still fairly easy to make. It does not require much aesthetic training to realize that the meter of a poem beginning "Death is here / Death is there / Death is lurking everywhere / . . ." is inappropriate to the theme being treated. Yet at higher levels of creation the entanglement of sense and nonsense can become so involved that the judgment of appropriateness requires a detailed examination by a highly trained person. Even then there is always the chance that the creator, who is often more aware of the demands that gave rise to his product than is the critic, will disagree with the judgment. As Bruner[5] has pointed out, "It takes a tuned organism, working with a certain kind of set, to recognize the appropriateness of an idea."

As the term is used in the judgment of creative products, appropriateness deals with much more than the logical fit of the product within its context or of the product's elements with each other (although this kind of fit would be the dominant question in many applications of the criterion). At times a product violates conventional logic but somehow manages to hang together and to have a logic of its own. Illustrations of this phenomenon abound in modern literature and art. Thus, although the judgmental standard for evaluating appropriateness is the *context* of the response, this context must be interpreted psychologically as well as logically and should include the producer's intentions as well as the demands of the situation.

Finally, appropriateness is a continuous quality, not a discrete one. It exists in degrees rather than completely or not at all. In its lower forms, we recognize the appropriateness of a product that is merely "responsive"—that bears a clear relation to the environment or to the internal motivations of its producer. In its higher forms, we marvel at the way in which the product reflects not only the massive forces that went into its making, but the more subtle influences as well. At low levels of appropriateness we speak of a product as being "about right," given its sources, the avowed purpose of its maker, and the like. At higher levels we speak of a product as being *just* right." Indeed, at the very highest level of appropriateness we may experience almost a sense of recognition when we come upon the product. Things are so right they look almost familiar. One critic described such products as having "the handprint of necessity upon them instead of the quickly tarnished sheen of the merely novel, the fetchingly precious, the different."[6] When he comes upon these "handprints of necessity," the viewer may sometimes feel as if his expectations have been fulfilled, whereas what has really happened is that the product has made him aware of what his expectations should have been. Again quoting Bruner, "What makes something obvious is that at last we understand it."[7]

The Transcendence of Constraint. Although unusualness and appropriateness may be necessary criteria for limiting the class of potentially creative products, are they sufficient for making required distinctions in quality and level within the class? Among the products that are considered to be both unusual and appropriate some are surely at a higher level of creative excellence than others. One property present in some products but absent, or less obvious, in others is the power to transform the constraints of reality. Some objects combine elements in ways that defy tradition and that yield a new perspective. They literally force us to see reality in a new way. These products involve a *transformation* of material or ideas to overcome conventional constraints. The question of how much transformation power a product has can serve, then, as a third criterion of creativeness. Just as the unusualness of a product is judged relative to norms and its appropriateness relative to the context, the transformation power of a product would be judged relative to the strength and nature of the *constraints* that were transcended.

The criterion of transformation is more difficult to define than are those of unusualness and appropriateness. At first glance it might seem to be nothing more than an extreme example of unusualness. But it is unusualness with a difference. It is a type of aggressive unusualness that attacks conventional ways of thinking about things or viewing objects. In its most dramatic forms a transformation involves a radical shift in approach to a subject—the kind of shift, for example, caused by the introduction of the heliocentric theory or Freud's earliest propositions.

The difference between a merely unusual product and a transformation may be approached in another way. Things are often unusual in the purely quantitative sense—in the sense of being the most or the least, the largest or the smallest of a pre-existing class of objects. (The objects and events described in the *Guinness Book of Superlatives* offer fine examples of this sort of unusualness.) Products that are unusual in this "record-breaking" sense need not, and usually do not, qualify as transformations. Transformations are not merely improvements, however unusual, on pre-existent forms. Rather, they involve the creation of new forms.

The distinction between the concepts of transformation and unusualness requires that a further distinction be made between an object that represents a transformation and one that is merely new. If transformation demanded only a new combination of elements, almost any unique collection of things, however derived, would qualify. Mechanical techniques for supplying these fortuitous combinations could be devised, as in the story of the popular writer who obtained the plots of his novels by spinning a set of wheels on which were written adjectives, nouns, verbs, and the like. Generally, however, these new combinations do not qualify as transformations because they are low in heuristic power. They terminate rather than generate thought. They are the occasion for surprise and laughter, but not for reflection and wonder.

The possibility just alluded to—that the presence of a transformation may be determined in part by its effect on the viewer—raises the interesting question of whether the other two response properties, unusualness and appropriateness, might also have distinguishable effects upon the person who experiences them. Are there, in short, types of aesthetic responses that somehow parallel the criteria of creativeness? This intriguing possibility occurred to us at approximately the stage in the development of criteria for creativeness to which the writing has progressed so far. Although recognizing that the job of identifying the criteria was not complete, we decided to delay that task for a time while we attempted to distinguish among possible dimensions of aesthetic response and to relate them conceptually to dimensions of creative performance. In order to give the reader some idea of how the present scheme came into being, we will retrace in the exposition of our ideas the same path that was followed in their development. Thus, for a time, we will put aside the search for more criterion response properties and focus on how the criteria we have already discussed might strike the viewer. The development thus far is summarized in Table 1, which lists the three response properties of creative products and the judgmental standards associated with each.

TABLE 1

Response Properties	Judgmental Standards
unusual	norms
appropriate	context
transformed	constraints

The Impact of the Product. Confrontation with an unusual object or event characteristically evokes *surprise* in the viewer. The unusual is attention-getting, it "catches our eye," its unexpectedness may shock or amaze us. By definition we cannot be prepared for it, except in a very general way. The impact of first exposure creates surprise and requires a period of adaptation during which the unusual object or event is assimilated into the viewer's experience.

Reaction to the unusual is at its maximum immediately upon exposure and diminishes rapidly thereafter. Though surprise may occur more than once in response to the same object, the second and subsequent exposures never quite match the impact of the first. Objects and events whose value is derived almost solely from their unusualness—such as freaks in side shows or *New Yorker* cartoons—rarely warrant continued viewing.

In this connection it is well to point out that improbability is itself not a sufficient condition for the occurrence of surprise. Most of the events we experience daily are improbable in the sense of being composed of unusual combinations of elements that will rarely be exactly repeated. George Miller points out that a mediocre bridge hand is just as rare, in a statistical sense, as a perfect hand. But the latter surprises us while the former does not.[8] In order for surprise to occur, there must be improbability, to be sure, but improbability that violates the viewer's expectations.

The quality of appropriateness calls forth in the viewer a reaction, which we will call *satisfaction*, that is akin to the general condition of comfort. This feeling of satisfaction would seem to have two major sources. First, there is the recognition that the demands of the creator, the material, and the milieu have been responded to and that, as was mentioned before, the response is not only right, but is "just right." There is a recognition of inevitableness about the product, given the context in which it is embedded. Second, there is the recognition that the product is not only "right" but is complete or sufficient. The first source of satisfaction focuses on the qualitative aspects of appropriateness (i.e., on how *well* the demands are met); the second source of satisfaction focuses on what might be considered the quantitative aspects of appropriateness (i.e., on how *completely* the demands are met). The satisfied viewer's answer to the first criterion is "just right," his answer to the second is "enough."

Bruner describes something close to the meaning intended here in his discussion of what he considers the prime property of the creative act—effective surprise. He states, "What is curious about effective surprise is that it need not be rare or infrequent or bizarre and is often none of these things. Effective surprises . . . seem rather to have the quality of obviousness to them when they occur, producing a shock of recognition, following which there is no longer astonishment."[9]

Products embodying a transformation are likely to be *stimulating* to the viewer. The primary value of such products resides in their power to alter the viewer's conventional way of perceiving or thinking about his world. Whereas confrontation with the unusual requires the viewer to assimilate the product, to make it part of his world, confrontation with a transformation requires that he revise his world. The new element is not only the product itself but the changed environment which has been caused by the product. Metaphorically, a transformation is something like a stone dropped in water. To a person standing on shore the object of interest is not the stone, which quickly disappears from sight, but the waves it produces. A transforming object invites the viewer to move out, intellectually, in new directions—it stimulates him to consider its consequences.

In review, the first three criteria of creativeness—unusualness, appropriateness, and transformation—may possibly be the source of three types of aesthetic responses, which may be summarized by the key words: surprise, satisfaction, and stimulation. The possibility that different types of aesthetic responses might be isolated gives rise to two important questions that can only be posed here. First, can the aesthetic responses themselves be used to indicate the presence of the qualities that give rise to them? Can we, for example, take the reaction of surprise to be sufficient evidence for the existence of unusualness? Clearly, the answer to this question has extremely important implications for the assessment of creativity. The second question is whether the aesthetic responses are unique to the viewer of the creative product or whether they also appear in the creator himself. Obviously the creator also judges his own product, yet his judgment need not and clearly does not always agree with the verdict of an "external" judge. Before questions such as these can be examined, however, it is necessary to return to the criteria of creativeness and to ask what else needs to be added to the three that have already been suggested.

The Coalescence of Meaning. The properties of unusualness, appropriateness, and transformation in varying combinations characterize a large proportion of those things we are willing to call creative. These dimensions are applicable to products stemming from very divergent sources, from the scientist and philosopher as well as from the craftsman and artist. Yet there is another important quality that does not seem to be covered by these criteria. This quality, which appears in some of the most highly creative products, serves as our fourth criterion, *condensation.*

As was mentioned previously, novelty wears out quickly. The history of fad and fashion is, in essence, an elaborate documentation of the short life and relativity of unusualness. In striking contrast, however, to the ephemeral quality of the novel object is the endurance of the greatest creative achievements of man. These we continually seek to re-examine and re-experience. Although the criteria of appropriateness and transformation may partially explain this endurance, something additional seems to be involved.

Products that warrant close and repeated examination are those that do not divulge their total meaning on first viewing. These products offer something new each time we experience them, whether they are great works of art or highly developed scientific theories. They have about them an intensity and a concentration of meaning requiring continued contemplation.

Because confusion and disorder also compel the viewer's attention (as he tries to make sense out of what he sees), it is necessary to distinguish between condensation and chaotic complexity. The chief difference would seem to involve the unity and coherence of meaning derived from condensation as compared with the unrelated and irrelevant meanings derived from disorder. An assortment of debris gathered in a junkyard and the ordered arrangement of the same material by an artist serves to illustrate the distinction being made here. Any meaning derived from the random assortment of junk is fortuitous and is obtained either from a chance association between the elements or from irrelevant associations that the material might stimulate in the viewer. By contrast, the ordered arrangement, if it is worthy of artistic notice, contains more meaning than can be understood at first glance. The color and shape of the objects, their texture, their spatial location, and their original function all combine to enhance their aesthetic appeal.

In the highest forms of creative condensation the polar concepts of simplicity and complexity are unified. That which at first glance appears simple turns out on closer inspection to possess only *apparent* simplicity. Conversely, that which at first appears complex is found to embody a hidden simplicity that binds together the many complex elements. Some of the more successful poems of Robert Frost and some of the paintings of Klee and Miro illustrate well the use of the simple to represent the complex. The reverse situation, in which initial complexity cloaks a hidden simplicity, occurs frequently in musical works, where repeated listening is often required before the major themes and their variations become apparent.

The condensation achieved by a creative product summarizes essences, and the summary may be expanded and interpreted in a multiplicity of ways—intellectually or affectively, in terms of image or idea. It may be interpreted differently by different viewers or by the same viewer on different occasions. This multiplicity of interpretation and the extensiveness of the expansions generated by the condensation are an indication of its summary power, and an appraisal of *summary power* provides an important judgmental standard for the evaluation of creative condensation.

Parenthetically, it might be noted that the latter two response criteria of transformation and condensation are closely related to the two main mechanisms of the dream work in psychoanalytic theory.[10] Thus, the present formulation includes elements that, from a psychoanalytic point of view, illustrate the role of primary process in creative activity.[11]

Before leaving this discussion of condensation, two additional points need to be mentioned. The first deals with the increased ambiguity and complexity of the criteria of creativeness as we go from unusualness to condensation; the second deals with their developmental interdependence. At this point the meaning of unusualness appears to be more clearly demarcated than the meaning of condensation, and this is partly because condensation is just a more complex concept than unusualness. Indeed, each of the four criteria, in the order presented here, seems to be more complex than the one before it. As it is used here, the term complex could be partially translated as meaning "obscure and complicated," but we wish to stress a more derivative connotation, namely, "difficult to judge." We recognize that difficulty in judgment is a consequence of complexity rather than its meaning, but such a distinction is unimportant in the present context. The important point is that judgments of condensation and transformation will be more difficult to make than judgments of unusualness and appropriateness; there will be more differences in viewpoint, and agreement will be more difficult to reach even within schools of thought. This implies that judges will have to know more, or do more, or take more time when judging the criteria of transformation and condensation than they will when applying the other two criteria. In this judgmental sense, condensation and transformation are more complex than unusualness and appropriateness.

In addition to this progression in complexity, the four criterion response properties of creativeness are also ordered with respect to developmental interdependence. Each of the four criteria, from unusualness to condensation, is applied in turn conjointly with the previous ones, so that in this sense each is dependent on the ones that precede it. This sequential requirement is only partial, however, in the interdependence of transformation and condensation. The transformations of a creative product must be appropriate and unusual; the condensation must also be appropriate and unusual, but it may not always represent a transformation. If we accept unusualness and appropriateness as necessary properties for a product to be considered creative, then the hierarchical ordering of transformation and condensation provides an additional basis, along with degrees of variation within each of the response dimensions, for distinguishing levels of creative attainment within the class of creative products.

Having added a fourth response property, condensation, we return to a consideration of aesthetic responses to examine the possible effect of this new criterion upon the viewer. So far our hypothetical viewer has been surprised by unusualness, satisfied by appropriateness, and stimulated by transforming qualities of creative products. The question now is how will he react when he confronts a product of high condensation, one that exists on many levels of meaning. The definition of the criterion itself almost contains a description of the experiencing viewer. A condensed product is an object worthy of pondering; it should be examined slowly, carefully, and repeatedly. In a word, the viewer is called upon to *savor* a condensation. The surprise, the satisfaction, and the stimulation that characterize responses to other aspects of creativeness are present as well in the response to a condensation, but there is an important difference. In the reaction to a condensation these other responses are enduring and intensified. Surprise occurs not only on the first encounter, but also on subsequent ones as new and unusual aspects of the product are discovered; satisfaction deepens with repeated exposure as the appropriateness of each element in the product is more fully revealed; stimulation is enriched as each new reaction to the product builds on those that have preceded it. It is this continued freshness of the product and of the viewer's response to it that makes it an object worthy of savoring.

Sometimes, of course, a viewer returns to a creative product not to experience a new expansion of the condensed essence, but to savor an old familiar satisfaction, to return to the scene of past joys. But this type of savoring is likely to be quite transient, since the initial delight would tend to pale with simple repetition and the appreciation of new expansions and nuances in the meantime would make it difficult to recapture the old experience with its original innocence.

With the addition of condensation to the list of response properties and of savoring to the list of aesthetic reactions, we complete our discussion of creative products and appreciative responses (see Table 2 for an outline of the development thus far). One further point needs to be made explicit, however: just as criterion response properties are relative to judgmental standards, so are aesthetic

TABLE 2

Response Properties	Judgmental Standards	Aesthetic Responses
unusualness	norms	surprise
appropriateness	context	satisfaction
transformation	constraints	stimulation
condensation	summary power	savoring

responses. The degree and character of surprise depends upon the norms of expectation in much the same manner as unusualness does. Similarly, satisfaction is relative to the context, stimulation to the nature and strength of the constraints, and savoring to summary power.

Personal Qualities and Cognitive Styles

Among psychologists, creativity has frequently been thought of as a single dimension or at least as a unified cluster of traits, resembling—and to some extent overlapping—general intellectual ability. Some researchers, particularly factor analysts such as Guilford, have isolated a set of cognitive factors related to different aspects of intellectual production, but the relation of these factors to creative production is less well delineated. Other investigators have argued that creative behavior depends as much on personality as on cognitive power, and they have accrued evidence to show that the highly creative person is more impulsive, makes greater use of fantasy processes, is more tolerant of ambiguity, and so forth, than is his less creative peer.

At the level of everyday experience it is recognized that creative expression of the highest quality tends to come from people who limit their efforts to a single mode of expression. The great scientist is generally not also the great poet, the great painter is not also the great dancer, and even the great composer is not also the great conductor. Moreover, in the eye of the public, personality characteristics tend to be associated with a *medium* of expression rather than with the level of expression or any other features of creative production. Thus, in terms of personality characteristics, the outstanding poet looks more like the incompetent poet than he does like the outstanding scientist, who, in turn, looks more like his less competent colleagues than he does like the superb composer. Both the professional view and the public view, therefore, acknowledge that the maker of creative products looks different from his fellow men, but there is little agreement on the form this difference takes. Is it chiefly cognitive or does it involve personality components as well? Is the difference linked to a mode of expression entailing, as it were, a way of life, or is it more closely related to stylistic qualities of the products themselves? Each view of the creative process implies a position about the nature of the creator, which in turn helps to determine the types of variables emphasized in the assessment of creativity.

Within the present context there is a set of personal qualities that may be considered to match, so to speak, the response properties used as criteria of creativeness. The present view is not meant to imply that trait names should be used as labels in characterizing people. The appropriateness of that practice depends on such matters as the dominance of the trait in question, its distribution in the population, and so on. Rather, we wish to suggest a relation between personal qualities and properties of the creative response.

The question of whether personal qualities are necessary for the production is still another matter. Do personal qualities "cause" the appearance of the creative criteria? Might an infrequent or appropriate response occur by chance, or must it always occur as the result of a particular human condition? Again, the view taken here does not prejudge the answer to the causal question, although it does imply that the consistent production of creative responses cannot occur by chance and that the "cause" of such a phenomenon entails psychological as well as social and environmental influences.

In the present view the person who consistently produces infrequent or unusual responses is thought of as being highly *original*. The relativity of the judgments of unusualness also affects the judgment of personal originality. Persons whose responses look quite unusual when judged against one standard and who would, therefore, be thought of as original, might lose the halo of originality when the judgmental norms are changed. The personal quality of originality is an attainment, in the sense that it is inferred from the repeated production of unusual responses. In addition, there are several personal qualities that are predisposing to originality, that increase the likelihood of unusual responses but do not guarantee them. These predisposing characteristics include intellectual abilities, cognitive styles, motives, and values. For example, ideational fluency, impulse expression, and cognitive styles of tolerance of unreality, tolerance of inconsistency, and the like would appear to be likely candidates for predisposing the individual toward originality.[12]

The production of an appropriate response would seem to be accomplished most easily by a person who is highly *sensitive* to the demands of his environment and to the subtleties of the material with which he is working. His sensitivity may result from a conscious *analysis* of the relations between elements, but it need not. There is some evidence, at least in some fields, that the most sensitive people cannot articulate their awareness with any degree of precision. Their sensitivity is *intuitive;* the person who behaves intuitively is sensitive to cues he cannot identify verbally. Either an analytic attitude or an intuitive attitude or both in combination could serve as predisposing cognitive styles for sensitivity.

Transformation involves transcending traditional boundaries and limitations. Personal qualities that seem to contribute to the production of transformations are of two sorts, cognitive and noncognitive. Relevant cognitive qualities are those that deal with the stability and fluidity of conceptual systems, intellectual categories, and the like. The production of transformations reflects *flexibility* and calls for qualities not unlike those involved in breaking a mental set. In perceptual terms this type of intellectual fluidity would be reflected in the ability to perceive objects in their own right—independent of their symbolic representation, their stereotyped function, or their relatedness to the immediate needs of the viewer. This kind of perceptual freedom has been given the label "allocentric perception" by Schachtel.[13] At the cognitive and ideological level, this flexibility has been called "open-mindedness" by Rokeach.[14]

The noncognitive qualities that contribute to the production of a transformation include a playful attitude toward reality and a willingness to expose (even to flaunt) ideas, attitudes, and objects that violate tradition. An attitude of playfulness, a desire to toy with reality is important because most transformations seem to come as a discovery on the heels of many trials. In that sense transformations involve an element of "luck," but it is the kind of luck that cannot occur without the predisposing attitudes that lead to experimentation and intellectual play. No single adjective adequately summarizes the personal qualities that contribute to the production of transformations. The word that comes closest to describing the cognitive qualities without doing violence to the noncognitive qualities is the adjective *flexible*.

Just as a condensation may often contain a paradoxical union of simplicity and complexity, so does the production of the condensation call for a fusing of contradictory personal qualities. There is first the coalescence of personal and universal concerns, with the strangely paradoxical result of losing in self-awareness while gaining in total awareness. Although the product may bear the marks of its maker, his personal needs and interests have been consumed, as it were, by the more abstract relevance of the product itself. Second, there is the intimate interplay, even fusion, of thought and feeling that contributes to a condensation. Even the most "logical" production—such as an elegant mathematical solution to a problem—demands an openness to thoughts and feelings that are only dimly perceived and that may not be easily stated. Third, there is an alternate blending of working styles, a cyclic pattern of patience and passion, of reflection and spontaneity, a continual shifting from total acceptance of one's ideas and actions to a critical rejection of them. In a very useful discussion of the creative process, Erich Fromm distinguishes between two phases of productive behavior.[15] According to Fromm, the first phase is essentially feminine in quality. It is the birth-giving phase, the moment of conception. Following this, a more masculine phase occurs during which the creator must hone and polish his work to ready it for social judgment. In this second phase irrelevancies and superfluities are eliminated, the uniqueness of the work is more sharply defined, and its content is more effectively expressed. The central theme underlying the production of a condensation involves, then, the unification of things that are normally thought of as separate—producer and product, personal and universal concerns, cognitive and affective processes, masculine and feminine styles of work.

The complexity of condensations and the personal qualities from which they emerge make it difficult to employ a single adjective to describe the person who is most apt to produce condensations. Yet, in the interests of symmetry and in order to provide a mnemonic device for summarizing the conceptual scheme presented here, we searched for a word that would come close to capturing the sense of our description. In our opinion, the word that does the most justice to what has been said about the producer of condensations is *poetic*. Webster's *New World Dictionary* describes a poem, and thus indirectly a poet, as "expressing facts, ideas, or emotions in a style more concentrated, imaginative, and powerful than that of ordinary speech." The terms "concentrated," "imaginative," and "powerful" are relevant here and apply of course to many products that would not be commonly thought of as poems. It is this more global referent of "poetic" that we imply when we use the word to characterize people who create effective condensations. The categories are summarized in Table 3.

TABLE 3

Predisposing Cognitive Styles	Personal Qualities	Response Properties	Judgmental Standards	Aesthetic Responses
tolerances of incongruity, of inconsistency, etc.	original	unusualness	norms	surprise
analytic and intuitive	sensitive	appropriate-ness	context	satisfaction
openminded	flexible	transforma-tion	constraints	stimulation
reflective and spontaneous	poetic	condensation	summary power	savoring

The creative person, his product, and the world's response to it combine to form the drama of human invention. The transaction among these three elements is intimate and our understanding of any one enhances our understanding of the other two. But to examine these elements singly is not enough. Though at present far from it, social science must work toward a conceptualization that serves to unify the psychological, aesthetic, and social aspects of this phenomenon. It is not enough, of course, to offer pious hopes for a future ecumenical council whose job it will be to unify these divergent views of the creative process. Two kinds of preparatory work are necessary before such a grand design is sought. First, we must add greater detail to early attempts at unification—such as the one presented here. The present scheme, at best, is an incomplete outline that must be elaborated more fully if its potential contribution is to be realized. Second, we must initiate empirical studies that will give weight to these efforts at theory, thus preventing them from deteriorating into mere word games.

In the final analysis, however, it is well to remember that theories of creativity are themselves creative products. As such, they must abide by the same laws as those they are designed to unearth. A realization of this fact should temper our zeal in advocating any single prescription for how best to proceed. The day on which we are certain about how to construct a theory of creativity will also be the day on which we are certain about how to construct a poem.

REFERENCES

1. S. E. Golann, "Psychological Study of Creativity," *Psychological Bulletin,* Vol. 60 (1963), p. 560.

2. G. Santayana, *The Sense of Beauty* (New York, 1896), p. 16.

3. J. P. Guilford, "Creative Abilities in the Arts," *Psychological Review,* Vol. 64 (1957), p. 116.

4. S. A. Mednick, "The Associative Basis of the Creative Process," *Psychological Review,* Vol. 69 (1962), pp. 220-232.

5. J. S. Bruner, "What Social Scientists Say about Having an Idea," *Printers' Ink Magazine,* Vol. 260 (1957), pp. 48-52.

6. J. Dickey, *The New York Times Book Review* (December 22, 1963), p. 4.

7. J. S. Bruner, *op. cit.*

8. J. S. Bruner, "The Conditions of Creativity," in H. E. Gruber, G. Terrell and M. Wertheimer (eds.), *Contemporary Approaches to Creative Thinking* (New York, 1962).

9. *Ibid.,* p. 3.

10. S. Freud, *The Interpretation of Dreams* (New York, 1955).

11. F. Pine, "Thematic Drive Content and Creativity," *Journal of Personality,* Vol. 27 (1959), pp. 136-151; and E. S. Tauber and M. R. Green, *Prelogical Experience* (New York, 1951).

12. F. Barron, "The Disposition Toward Originality," *Journal of Abnormal and Social Psychology,* Vol. 51 (1955), pp. 478-485; and F. Barron, *Creativity and Psychological Health* (Princeton, N. J., 1963).

13. E. G. Schachtel, *Metamorphosis* (New York, 1959).

14. M. Rokeach, *The Open and Closed Mind* (New York, 1960).

15. E. Fromm, "The Creative Attitude," in H. Anderson (ed.), *Creativity and its Cultivation* (East Lansing, Mich., 1963).

DONALD W. MACKINNON

The Study of Creative Persons:
A Method and Some Results

THE PSYCHOLOGIST who undertakes to study highly creative persons in hopes of discovering what it is that makes them stand out from the mass faces in an especially vivid form the problem which confronts every student of human behavior and character. His task is to decide what the nature of his enterprise is—whether a humanistic study or a science, and if a science, what kind of science?

No American psychologist has faced this problem, this dilemma, quite so directly and unflinchingly as has Gordon W. Allport who has repeatedly reminded us that "The outstanding characteristic of man is his individuality," while at the same time citing the age-old dictum that the individual, the single case, is not the concern of science: "Scientia non est Individuorum."[1]

Three quite different solutions have been proposed for the problem thus raised. In the one camp are those who accept the fact and the maxim and consequently assert that individuality cannot be an object of scientific study. They have had no clearer spokesman than Max Meyer, the American psychologist who was a forerunner of Watsonian behaviorism, who wrote that "A description of one individual without reference to others may be a piece of literature, a biography, a novel. But science? No."[2]

In the second camp are those who have insisted that if science as usually practiced is not able to deal with the fact of individuality, then a new science adequate to the task must be created. Here one finds the German philosopher, Wilhelm Dilthey,[3] and his pupil, the psychologist and educator Eduard Spranger,[4] who urged a dichotomizing of psychology into, on the one hand, a descriptive psychology that would be adequate for the understanding of the individual case, and on the other hand, an analytical psychology that would be capable of explaining the generality.

In this camp one also finds the German philosopher, Windelband,[5] who brought the conflict between *description* and *analysis* and between *understanding* and *explanation* into even sharper focus, urging the recognition of two opposed types of science: the *nomothetic* vs. the *idiographic*. The natural sciences that seek to establish causal laws of the greatest generality he designated as nomothetic. The social and cultural disciplines that use the methods of history in their investigation of unique events, he proposed should be called idiographic. Having distinguished nomothetic and idiographic methods, he insisted that the latter had fully as much right as the former to be called "scientific." The methods of history, he argued, have the same scientific dignity as the methods of the physical sciences. Writing in 1894, he pointed out that psychology had been trying to become, like the physical sciences, nomothetic, but that there was equal reason for it to develop into an idiographic science which, like history, biography, and literature, would attempt to understand particular and unique events. Such an idiographic psychology would have as its object of study human individuality.

In the third camp have been those psychologists who have sought to reconcile the opposed points of view, arguing that the distinction between individuality and general lawfulness has been drawn too sharply. Here one finds Allport who, though he has emphasized the individual, has always urged that attention be given also to general laws, especially as they may be established within the individual; and Lewin[6] who, though constantly emphasizing general lawfulness, was always concerned to point out how one proceeds from the individual case to the general law and from the general law to the individual case. The scope of a psychology that truly reconciles these opposites—what Allport has called "a broadened psychology"—has been nowhere better epitomized than in Kluckhohn and Murray's delineation of the province of the study of man.

"Everyone," they point out, "is in certain respects (a) like all other men, (b) like some other men, and (c) like no other man."[7] In the investigations here reported, we cannot claim to have studied the creative person in all of these respects, but I would assert that the method of research which we have employed is sufficiently complex and varied to permit our consideration of each person as an individual in his own right as well as in comparison with all others whom we have studied.

The method is that of personality assessment, and it is as suitable for idiographic studies as for nomothetic researches. It is, however, not so much one method as it is a multiplicity of methods, and techniques, and procedures so designed and chosen as to yield the fullest possible picture of those persons who are chosen for assessment. It involves an intensive study of individuals singly and in interaction with others. Our Institute, a remodeled fraternity house, serves as the assessment center where the persons to be studied are brought together (usually ten at a time) for several days (most often a three-day weekend). There they participate in problem-solving experiments and in specially contrived social situations of a stressful character, the so-called situational tests, which call for their best behavior in a variety of socially defined roles. They are given tests and questionnaires which permit them to manifest many facets of their personalities and to express their opinions, attitudes, interests, and values. They also experience tests that are designed to reveal what they do not know about themselves or are unwilling or unable to tell us; and, of course, each of them participates in an intensive psychiatric interview so designed as to elicit the significant events of the life history and to reveal the structure of the present personality.

An assessment program yields for each participant a multiplicity —literally hundreds—of measures, scores, ratings, and recorded impressions all of which can be intercorrelated to reveal what goes with what in the life histories and in the structured personalities of the assessees, and each of which can, in turn, be correlated with independently obtained best estimates of our subjects' professional creativity. There is no method which yields so full and detailed a picture of a person as does assessment, and for that reason it is the method we have employed in our attempts to analyze and to understand the creative person.

The very richness of our data forces me to decide whether, in this report, I shall concentrate upon the idiographic, describing in the fullest possible detail the biography and individuality of some one highly creative person or give greater attention to the nomothetic, reporting what we have found to be most generally true of creative persons. Since I have decided upon the latter, I would caution that no one person will quite match the picture that I shall draw. There are as many paths along which persons travel toward the full development and expression of their creative potential as there are creative people. There is no single mold into which all who are creative fit.

Indeed, we began our researches with the assumption that there are different kinds of creativity: artistic creativity, scientific creativity, and creativity that requires that the practitioner of it be at one and the same time both artist and scientist; and in our studies we have sampled all three domains: novelists, poets, and essayists as representative of artistic creativity; research scientists, engineers, and inventors who represent scientific creativity; and as examples of creativity that is at once artistic and scientific we have chosen to work with mathematicians and architects. Picking our samples in this manner makes it possible to say something about the characteristics of creative persons across several fields of endeavor and also to delineate the ways in which creative persons in one field are different from creative persons in other areas.

Had we, in these several fields, assessed only those who are recognized for their high degree of creativeness we would not be able to say what it is that distinguishes creative persons from their less creative colleagues. In order to make sure that the traits that characterize the highly creative persons in a given profession are somehow related to their creativity it is necessary to demonstrate that these same traits do not also characterize the less creative members of the profession. Thus it was that we chose for study in each group individuals who, in the opinion of experts in those fields, ranged from highly creative to relatively uncreative.

It was necessary, however, that we offer the experts in each field a definition of creativity which was acceptable to them and which would guide them in making their nominations. In our study of architects, for example, our definition was this: "Originality of thinking and freshness of approach to architectural problems; constructive ingenuity; ability to set aside established conventions and procedures when appropriate; a flair for devising effective and original fulfillments of the major demands of architecture: technology (firmness), visual form (delight), planning (commodity), and human awareness and social purpose."[8]

There is much more that could be said about method and research design in the study of creativity, but instead I turn to the substantive findings of our investigations.

Let us look first at the creative person in his professional role and then as an individual. To obtain the former picture each subject was asked to sort fifty statements describing talents, skills, interests, values, work habits, and points of view which anyone in his profession might have. The task for each person was to sort these statements into five categories ranging from those most characteristic to those least characteristic of him. Intercorrelating these self-descriptions and factor analyzing the resulting matrix of intercorrelations, Gough,[9] in his study of creativity in industrial research scientists, extracted eight "person-factors," or, if you will, eight types of scientific researchers. He labeled and briefly described the eight types in this manner:

Type 1. The Zealot

This man is dedicated to research activity; he sees himself as a driving, indefatigable researcher, with exceptional mathematical skills and a lively sense of curiosity. He is seen by others as tolerant, serious-minded, and conscientious, but as not getting along easily with others and as not being able to "fit in" readily with others.

Type 2. The Initiator

This man reacts quickly to research problems, and begins at once to generate ideas; he is stimulating to others and gives freely of his own time; he sees himself as being relatively free of doctrinaire bias—methodological or substantive—and as being a good "team" man. Observers describe him as ambitious, well-organized, industrious, a good leader, and efficient. They also characterize him as being relatively free of manifest anxiety, worry, and nervousness.

Type 3. The Diagnostician

This man sees himself as a good evaluator, able to diagnose strong and weak points in a program quickly and accurately, and as having a knack for improvising quick solutions in research trouble spots. He does not have strong methodological preferences and biases, and tends not to be harsh or disparaging toward others' mistakes and errors. Observers see him as forceful and self-assured in manner, and as unselfish and free from self-seeking and narcissistic striving.

Type 4. The Scholar

This man is blessed with an exceptional memory, and with an eye for detail and order. However, he is not a research perfectionist nor an endless seeker for ultimates. He does not hesitate to ask help when blocked in his work, and feels that he can adapt his own thinking to that of others. He is well-informed in his field, and is not given to bluffing. Observers describe him as conscientious and thorough, and as very dependable, but as lacking confidence and decisiveness of judgment.

Type 5. The Artificer

This man gives freely of his own time, and enjoys talking shop with other researchers. He is aware of his own limitations and does not attempt what he cannot do. He sees himself as having a special facility for taking inchoate or poorly formed ideas of others and fashioning them into workable and significant programs. Observers see him as honest and direct, getting along well with others, and as usually observant and perceptive and responsive to nuances and subtleties in others' behavior.

Type 6. The Aesthetician

This man favors analytical over other modes of thinking, and prefers research problems which lend themselves to elegant and formal solutions. His interests are far-ranging, and he tends to become impatient if progress is slow or if emphasis must be put upon orderliness and systematic detail. His own view of experience is primarily an aesthetic one. Observers see him as clever and spontaneous, but as undependable and immature, somewhat lacking in patience and industry and indifferent about duties and obligations.

Type 7. The Methodologist

This man is vitally interested in methodological issues, and in problems of mathematical analysis and conceptualization. He is open about his own research plans and enjoys talking about them with others. He has little competitive spirit and tends to take a tolerant view of research differences between himself and others. Observers characterize him as a considerate, charitable person, free from undue ambition; at the same time they report a certain moodiness and an occasional tendency toward complicated and difficult behavior.

Type 8. The Independent

This man eschews "team" efforts, and dislikes and avoids administrative details connected with research work. He is not a driving, energetic research man, although he does have a lively sense of intellectual curiosity. He prefers to think in reference to physical and structural models rather than in analytical and mathematical ways. Observers describe him as active and robust in manner and hardheaded and forthright in judgment. He appears relatively free from worry and self-doubt, but inclined to behave impolitely or abruptly.

This vivid demonstration of stylistic variations among scientific researchers in industry should remind us that stylistic differences will be found in all fields of work, if only we look for them. Nor can we forget that, in addition to these types of style characteristic of sub-groups of workers, each individual has his own unique and idiosyncratic stylistic traits.

It is of some interest, in passing, to note that there is a relationship between a research scientist's stylistic type and his superiors' and his peers' evaluation of his creativeness and general competence as an industrial researcher.

When the types are ranked according to their mean score on this criterion the following ordering is obtained: (1) Methodologist, (2) Initiator, (3) Zealot, (4) Artificer, (5) Diagnostician, (6) Aesthetician, (7) Independent, and (8) Scholar.

In view of the description of these types and the fact that these individuals were working as researchers in industrial organizations, the order in which they are ranked for creativeness and general competence is about as one would expect—the methodologist and the initiator being more valued and seen as contributing more than the aesthetician, the independent, and the scholar. One cannot but wonder, however, whether the rank order might not have been reversed if these scientists had been working in an academic research setting and had the criterion been collected there. Would not, perhaps, the scholar, the independent, and the aesthetician then be most highly valued? Of course, we do not know, but the very fact that the question is raised in our minds should be a reminder that the criterion of creativeness is as bound to the situation in which creative behavior occurs as is the behavior itself.

Turning now to the images which our subjects have of themselves as persons rather than as professionals, it is abundantly clear that highly creative persons are inclined to think well of themselves. When asked to check on a list of 300 adjectives those which they thought were self-descriptive, 98 per cent of highly creative architects say they are imaginative; then with decreasing frequency but in no instance with less than 80 per cent checking the adjectives, they describe themselves as active (92 per cent); honest, idealistic, inventive (90 per cent); artistic, civilized, conscientious, intelligent (88 per cent); reasonable (85 per cent); adaptable, determined, fair-minded, independent, individualistic, progressive (82 per cent); and appreciative, capable, cooperative, enthusiastic, friendly, healthy, industrious, interests wide, and serious (80 per cent). Creative architects do, indeed, think well of themselves, but with some justification, for it is clear that we, the assessment staff, see them very much as they see themselves. Indeed we check for them even more favorable adjectives than they check for themselves.

Yet there is a paradox to be noted here, for creative architects also check more unfavorable adjectives as self-descriptive than do their less creative peers. Actually it appears that the creative architects have such a good opinion of themselves, are basically so self-confident and self-accepting that they feel free to describe themselves frankly, critically, and in unusual ways.

In general, it is clear that highly creative persons have self-images quite different from those of less creative persons. For example, highly creative architects more often describe themselves as inventive, determined, independent, individualistic, enthusiastic, and industrious. In striking contrast, architects who are relatively uncreative more often than their highly creative colleagues describe themselves as responsible, sincere, reliable, dependable, clear thinking, tolerant, and understanding. In short, where creative architects more often stress their inventiveness, independence, and individuality, their enthusiasm, determination, and industry, less creative members of the profession are impressed by their virtue and good character and by their rationality and sympathetic concern for others.

One finds in these contrasting emphases in self-description a hint of one of the most salient characteristics of the creative person, namely, his courage. It is not the physical courage of the type that is rewarded by the Congressional Medal of Honor or the Carnegie Medal, though a highly creative person may have courage of this kind too. It is rather personal courage, courage of the mind which I would not hesitate to call spiritual courage, that is so central a trait of the person who in his creativeness stands aside from the social collectivity and often in conflict with it.

The courage of the creative person manifests itself in many forms and in many different behaviors.

It is the courage to be oneself in the fullest sense, to grow in great measure into the person one is capable of becoming, developing one's abilities and actualizing one's self. Since the creative person is not preoccupied with the impression he makes on others, and is not overly concerned with their opinion of him, he is freer than most to be himself. To say that he is relatively free from conventional restraints and inhibitions might seem to suggest that he is to some degree socially irresponsible. He may at times appear to be so, and in some instances he doubtless is if judged by the conventional standards of society, since his behavior is dictated more by his own set of values, and by ethical standards that may not be precisely those of others around him.

Creative persons are not conformists in the realm of greatest importance to them, the area of their creative striving, but on the other hand they are not deliberate nonconformists, either. Instead, they are genuinely independent. They are often, in fact, quite conventional in matters and in actions that are not central to their areas of creative endeavor. It is in their creative striving that their independence of thought and action are revealed. Indeed, it is characteristic of the highly creative person that he is strongly motivated to achieve in situations in which independence in thought and action are called for, but much less inclined to strive for achievement in situations where conforming behavior is expected or required.

In his perceptions both of the outer world and of his inner life the courage of the creative person is again clearly to be seen. It manifests itself in his perceptual openness to experience of the inner life as well as of the outer environment and culture. One of the most important dimensions along which persons differ is that of the open-closed mind. The open-minded person is keenly perceptive, the closed-minded individual strongly judgmental. Though it is an over-simplification to state it so bluntly it is nonetheless true that whenever a person uses his mind for any purpose he performs either an act of perception (he becomes aware of something) or an act of judgment (he comes to a conclusion about something). And most persons are inclined to show a rather consistent preference for and greater pleasure in one or the other of these; preferring either to perceive or to judge.

One who emphasizes and prefers an attitude of judging will lead a life that is controlled, carefully planned, and orderly, and when the preference for judging is habitual and strong he becomes judgmental and in the extreme prone to prejudging. He is then the prejudiced person.

On the other hand, a preference for the perceptive attitude results in a life that is more open to experience both from within and from without, and characterized by flexibility and spontaneity.

Several of our tests, as one would expect, reveal the creative person to be perceptive and open to experience.

On the several scales of a test designed to measure tendencies toward the major psychiatric disturbances such as depression, hysteria, paranoia, schizophrenia, and the like, our creative subjects earn mean or average scores which range from five to ten points above the general population's standard score of fifty. It must be noted, however, that elevated scores on these scales do not have the same meaning for the personality functioning of persons who, like our subjects, are getting along reasonably well in their lives and professional careers, that they have for hospitalized patients. For our creative subjects the higher scores on the clinical dimensions are actually less suggestive of psychopathology than of good intellect, richness and complexity of personality, and a general lack of defensiveness—in other words, the courage to be fully open to experience and especially to experience of one's inner life. We must also note, though, that there is in the profiles of many of our creative subjects rather clear evidence of psychopathology, but also evidence of adequate control mechanisms.

On a series of tests designed to measure the relative strength of the masculine and feminine components of personality, there is a clear tendency for creative men to score higher on femininity than their less creative colleagues. The meaning of these scores could easily be misinterpreted. They are more indicative of breadth of cultural and intellectual interests than of sexual deviation. They suggest that the more creative a man is the more he reveals an openness to his own feelings and emotions, a sensitive intellect and understanding self-awareness, and wide-ranging interests including many which in the American culture are thought of as feminine.

If, as the Swiss psychologist, C. G. Jung,[10] has most strongly argued, and if, as most psychologists believe, man is psychologically bisexual, carrying within himself both masculine and feminine traits and interests and identifications, then it would appear that the more creative male, without denying or suppressing his own masculinity, gives more expression to the feminine side of his nature, than do his less creative peers. In the absence of homosexual interests and behavior, his higher scores on femininity are indicative of a more effective reconciliation of his masculine and feminine traits. As Jung would phrase it, creative males are not so completely identified with their masculine *persona* roles as to blind themselves to or to deny expression to the more feminine traits of the *anima*. In other words, they more than their less creative colleagues have more fully actualized the opposed potentialities of their nature.

The perceptiveness of the creative person and his openness to richness and complexity of experience is also strikingly revealed in his perceptual preference for the complex and asymmetrical, rejecting or disliking that which is symmetrical and simple. All creative groups we have studied have shown this preference, and in general the more creative a person the stronger it is. If one considers for a moment the meaning of this preference, it is clear that creative persons are especially disposed to admit complexity and even disorder into their perceptions without being made anxious by the resulting chaos. It is not so much that they like disorder per se, but that they prefer the richness of the disordered to the stark barrenness of the simple. They appear to be challenged by disordered multiplicity which arouses a strong need which in them is serviced by a superior capacity to achieve the most difficult and far-reaching ordering of the richness they are willing to experience.

The traits of the creative person which I have so far reviewed suggest that in controlling his impulses, his images, and his ideas the creative individual eschews the ego-defensive mechanisms of repression and suppression. Much of experience which other less courageous persons would repress or deny is accepted by the creative person. But in accepting so much of his own experience, which for him as for anyone else may be disturbing, he must, one would think, experience more anxiety than his more restricted and constricted peers. Evidence that such is precisely his fate is provided in a comparison of the scores of more and less creative persons on a measure of felt and experienced anxiety. The more creative earn higher scores.

It is not, however, that the creative person is extremely impulsive and uncontrolled. It is rather that he has consciously to assume responsibility for the control and expression of impulses and images which in the neurotically inhibited person are beyond conscious control and expression because they are not admitted into experience. Being unconscious they are controlled in the more inhibited person, not by the conscious ego, but by the unconscious superego working through the mechanisms of repression and denial. Our more creative subjects not only experience more anxiety, they also have stronger egos.

We may now inquire into the cognitive style of the creative person. In his openness to experience, which is so marked, is he inclined to focus upon his immediate sensory experience, savoring what is, or does he immediately perceive the deeper meanings and possibilities inherent in things and situations and ideas which he experiences? In other words, in his perceptions is he a sense-perceptive, concentrating primarily on the sensory attributes of his experience and centering his attention upon the existing facts as they are given, or is he an intuitive-perceptive, ever alert to links and bridges between what is present and that which is not yet thought of? Does he focus habitually upon what is or upon what may be?

On a test designed to measure these two cognitive orientations —a preference for sense-perception vs. a preference for intuitive-perception—90 per cent or more of each of the creative groups we have studied have shown a preference for intuition, in contrast to the general population among whom only 25 per cent score as intuitives. It is not that this finding is surprising; one would not expect creative persons to be stimulus- and object-bound but instead ever alert to the as-yet-not-realized. It is rather the magnitude of the preference for intuitive perception that is so striking among highly creative persons.

Closely related to the creative person's preference for intuition are his preferred interests and his emphasized values.

On an inventory of interests which measures the similarity of a person's expressed interests with the known interests of individuals successful in a number of occupations and professions, all of our creative subjects have shown, with only slight variation from group to group, interests similar to those of the psychologist, author-journalist, lawyer, architect, artist, and musician, and interests unlike those of the purchasing agent, office man, banker, farmer, carpenter, veterinarian, and interestingly enough, too, policeman and mortician. Leaving aside any consideration of the specific interests thus revealed we may focus our attention on the inferences that may be drawn from this pattern of scores which suggest that creative persons are relatively uninterested in small details, or in facts for their own sake, and more concerned with their meanings and implications, possessed of considerable cognitive flexibility, verbally skillful, interested in communicating with others and accurate in so doing, intellectually curious, and relatively disinterested in policing either their own impulses and images or those of others.

On the Study of Values, a test designed to measure in the individual the relative strength of the six values of men as these values have been conceptualized and described by Eduard Spranger,[11] namely, the theoretical, economic, aesthetic, social, political, and religious values, all of our creative groups have as their highest values the theoretical and the aesthetic.

For creative research scientists the theoretical value is the highest, closely followed by the aesthetic. For creative architects the highest value is the aesthetic, with the theoretical value almost as high. For creative mathematicians the two values are both high and approximately equally strong.

It is of some interest, further to note, that despite the success with which as entrepreneurs creative architects carry out their architectural practice, the economic is their lowest value. Indeed, in a representative sample of 124 architects, the theoretical value correlates with the rated creativity of the architects $+.18$, the aesthetic value $+.35$, and the economic value $-.48$.

So far no reference has been made to the level of intelligence of the creative person.

In recent years, Guilford's work on the structure of intellect[12] and especially his identification, by means of factor analysis, of several dimensions of creative thinking, viz., adaptive flexibility, originality, sensitivity to problems, etc., has led to a widespread hope and expectation that his tests of creative ability would provide us with reliable means for the identification of creative persons. So far, however, this hope has not been realized.

In an intensive study of research scientists in the Air Force[13] Guilford's tests of creativity failed to predict the criterion and in our own studies these same tests have likewise shown essentially zero correlation with the criterion. In view of such negative findings the use of Guilford's battery of creativity tests for the identification of creative persons would be, to say the least, questionable.

It is not that the tests of this sort fail to tap the kind of psychological processes that are involved in creative thought, requiring, as they do, that the subject think of unusual uses for common objects or the consequences of unusual events. It is rather that they fail to reveal the extent to which a person faced with a real life problem is likely to come up with solutions that are novel and adaptive and which he will be motivated to apply in all of their ramifications.

If superior performance on such high level aptitude tests as those developed by Guilford expressly for the measurement of creative thinking do not predict creativity in the real world, as opposed to the factor analytic world, one may well wonder what, if any, is the relationship between tests of general intelligence and creativity.

With the exception of mathematicians, among whom there is a low positive correlation between intelligence (as measured by the

Terman Concept Mastery Test) and the level of their creativeness, we have found in our creative groups essentially no relationship between intelligence so measured and creativity. And this, I would point out, is not due to a narrow restriction in the range of their intelligence scores. As an example, creative architects earn a mean score of 113 on the Concept Mastery Test with individual scores ranging widely from 39 to 179 (these are not IQ's, but arbitrary test scores), yet their scores on this measure of intelligence correlate —.08 with their creativity as rated by architectural experts. Among research scientists the correlation is —.07. Despite this finding I question if anyone would doubt that over the whole range of intelligence and creativity there is a positive relationship between the two variables; there were no feeble-minded subjects in any of our groups nominated for their outstanding creativeness. The proper interpretation of our findings is, I believe, that above a certain required minimum level of intelligence, which varies from field to field and in some instances may be surprisingly low, being more intelligent does not guarantee a corresponding increase in creativeness. It simply is not true that the more intelligent person is necessarily the more creative one.

I do not wish to imply that the quantity and quality of intellective processes are irrelevant to creative performance. Obviously, they are of the greatest importance; but alone and in the absence of other traits and dispositions they will not make for creativity, nor will mere intelligence identify creative potential or predict creative performance. What appears from our researches to be more important in determining the creativeness of an individual are the structure of his personality, his enduring interests, values, and motives, his cognitive style, and his whole-hearted commitment to the creative enterprise.

There has emerged from our studies clear evidence of a close relationship between what a person thinks and does and the image he has of himself. Again, illustrating from our study of architects, I am struck by the accuracy of their self-perceptions and by the remarkable consistency with which they conform in their thought and in their behavior to the type of person they see themselves as being.

The creative architect thinks of himself as creative, and his image of what a creative architect is, as well as his image of what a creative architect should be, exert a far-ranging influence upon what he thinks and what he does in practice.

Above all else he thinks of himself as imaginative; unquestionably committed to creative endeavor; unceasingly striving for creative solutions to the difficult problems he repeatedly sets for himself; satisfied only with solutions that are original and that meet his own high standards of architectural excellence; aesthetically sensitive; an independent spirit free from crippling restraints and impoverishing inhibitions; spontaneous; forthright, and self-accepting. He has a sense of destiny about his career as an architect.

The picture which the relatively uncreative architect holds of himself and conveys to others is in striking contrast. Where the creative architect is most impressed by his imagination and inventiveness, the less creative architect sees himself as most saliently conscientious, responsible, and sincere. In his professional role he prides himself on his ability to get along with others and to accept and work over their ideas and concepts. He thinks of himself as most importantly a team man; and it is clear that both as an architect and as a person he is strongly oriented to others, emotionally dependent upon them, and overly accepting of the values and judgments of his profession and of society.

The pictures thus revealed of the more and the less creative person are not limited to architects. In all the groups we have studied we have found that self-image and ego-ideal are of crucial importance in determining the level of creativeness with which a person lives his life and practices his profession, and the differences between more and less creative architects are essentially the same as the differences between the more and less creative members of all the groups we have assessed.

REFERENCES

1. Gordon W. Allport, *Personality: A Psychological Interpretation* (New York, 1937), p. 3.

2. Max F. Meyer, "Review of Gustav Kafka (ed.), Handbuch der Vergleichenden Psychologie," *Psychological Bulletin*, Vol. 23, No. 5 (May 1926), p. 271.

3. Wilhelm Dilthey, "Ideen über eine beschreibende Psychologie," (1894), *Gesammelte Schriften*, Vol. 5 (Stuttgart, 1957), pp. 139-240.

4. Eduard Spranger, *Types of Men*, trans. Paul J. W. Pigors (Halle [Saale], Germany, 1928).

5. W. Windelband, *Geschichte und Naturwissenschaft* (Strassburg, 1894).

6. Kurt Lewin, *A Dynamic Theory of Personality* (New York, 1935).

7. Clyde Kluckhohn and Henry A. Murray, *Personality in Nature, Society, and Culture* (New York, 1948), p. 35.

8. Donald W. MacKinnon, "Genus architectus creator varietas Americanus," *Journal of the AIA*, Vol. 34, No. 3 (September 1960), pp. 31-32.

9. Harrison G. Gough and Donald G. Woodworth, "Stylistic Variations Among Professional Research Scientists," *Journal of Psychology*, Vol. 49, First Half (January 1960), pp. 87-98.

10. Carl G. Jung, *Two Essays on Analytical Psychology* (New York, 1956).

11. Spranger, *op. cit.*

12. J. P. Guilford, "Three Faces of Intellect," *American Psychologist*, Vol. 14, No. 8 (August 1959), pp. 469-79.

13. C. W. Taylor, W. R. Smith, B. Ghiselin, and R. Ellison, *Explorations in Measurement and Prediction of Contributions of One Sample of Scientists.* Technical Report ASD-TE-61-96. Lackland Air Force Base, Personnel Laboratory, AF Systems Command, 1961.

MICHAEL A. WALLACH

Creativity and the Expression of Possibilities[*]

IN THE GROWING amount of lip service that is paid in our culture to "creativity" there is divulged, I think, an awareness that something about human endeavor and human nature that was heretofore a background phenomenon now has emerged for explicit consideration. Only because modern man has become, if you will, sufficiently self-conscious about how he functions psychologically and socially—as reflected in the growth of the social sciences over the last few generations—has this awareness of which I speak become increasingly prominent. Such emphasis upon the social sciences seems to betoken a basic shift from absolutism to relativism in the definition of human institutions and modes of conduct—a realization that, no matter what range of characteristics may constitute invariants of human nature, man nevertheless is considerably more plastic or fluid, more open to possibilities in how he thinks and how he behaves, than could ever have been believed even as recently as fifty years ago.

The shift that I have just mentioned seems to be related to a quite general rethinking that has taken place in recent decades concerning the nature of mathematics, science, and the arts—in other words, much of man's distinctively human endeavors. I should like to describe, first of all, my view of this conceptual change concerning mathematical, scientific, and aesthetic affairs. Then I want to suggest what this change seems to imply concerning the psychology of human thinking, and to review some relevant evidence on children's thinking in particular. After considering certain major characteristics of how thinking proceeds, finally, I want to

[*] A version of this paper was presented as an Invited Address sponsored by the Division of Educational Psychology at the annual meeting of the American Psychological Association, New York City, September, 1966.

turn to a very practical social issue on which I feel the earlier discussion has a direct bearing: namely, the advent of instruction by teaching machines and computerized devices.

Mathematical, Scientific, and Aesthetic Activity

It was not until the last few generations that clear status became awarded to a fundamentally arbitrary, conjectural, or constructivist element in the range of human activities comprised by mathematics, science, and aesthetics. Let us look first at an example in a branch of mathematics—geometry. Out of a concern for trying to understand the nature of physical space, Euclid set forth a number of concepts relating to space—such as "straight line" and "point"—and a number of propositions that specified particular relationships among these concepts. The propositions were called postulates, and from these postulates other information —described as theorems that followed from the postulates—could be deduced.

What did Euclid think he was doing when he devised his geometry? He believed that he was setting forth postulates that were obviously—that is, intuitively—true as descriptions of the nature of physical space, and then obtaining new information about space by determining what those postulates implied by way of theorems. The theorems were considered to convey new information because they could generate surprise in the person making the deductions—even though, in principle, the theorems were contained by the postulates in the sense of following by logical deduction from the postulates alone. Deduction of the theorems thus was appropriately construed as an advancement of knowledge, since only an omniscient genius would be blessed with the power to see at a glance all the theorems that the postulates implied. What Euclid —and many geometers after him—seemed to confuse, however, was that the canon of correctness determining whether a theorem had been appropriately inferred from given postulates had nothing to do with whether the theorem or the postulates were true as statements about the nature of physical space. There were, in other words, two kinds of truth and falsity involved here, not just one. There was the question of whether the logical operations for deriving theorems from postulates had been correctly performed —whether translation rules had been correctly applied; and there was the question of whether the postulates and theorems provided correct descriptions of what space was like.

For a long time nobody was particularly concerned with the second kind of truth and falsity when considering geometry. Euclid and other geometers simply believed that learning about space only involved making sure that the path from postulates to theorems had been correctly traversed. Who could question whether the postulates were correct? They were presumed to follow intuitively from the nature of space. Concealed from view, therefore, was a crucially important psychological process which Euclid had performed. The invention of the postulate system itself had involved the construction of a set of possibilities: in other words, it was in fact an invention and not just a discovery of how the world was constituted. There was an element of arbitrariness involved—a choice of some postulates rather than others.

In order to reveal the setting up of postulates in geometry as in some degree an act of conjecture, a proposal, the history of geometry had to wait for the invention of other self-consistent sets of postulates that could be entertained as alternative possibilities to the set devised by Euclid. The mathematician as a generator or producer of possible sets of assumptions then came to be recognized as a new role to be placed alongside that of the mathematician as a translator who traces the steps of a logical derivation. In regard to their nature as geometries, or kinds of mathematical systems, there is, of course, nothing to choose between Euclid's geometry or one or another system of non-Euclidean geometry. Thus, for example, one mathematician, Riemann, developed a system of geometry involving the postulate that straight lines always meet somewhere. Contrast this with Euclid's assumption that for any given straight line there can be drawn through any point not on that first straight line a second line that is parallel to the first. Riemann would assume, rather, that no parallel can ever be drawn to a straight line through a point not on that straight line. As long as Riemann's set of postulates is consistent within itself, then it is as valid a geometry as that offered by Euclid. The two geometers have invented or created equally self-consistent postulate sets. Theorems inferred from one set will be no better or worse than —only different from—theorems inferred from the other set.[1]

Mathematics is a game, therefore, involving the generation of conceptual possibilities—one or another postulate system—and the tracing out of their logical implications. What about science? Here the other kind of truth and falsity mentioned previously comes into consideration. When a scientist forms a theory, he sets up definitions of concepts and states propositions stipulating how these concepts are related—thus far, his behavior resembles that of the mathematician. However, the theorems that the scientist infers from these propositions or assumptions constitute predictions—hypotheses— about observable characteristics of the environment. Not only, then, is the scientist interested in being correct regarding how he goes about inferring predictions from his initial postulates, but he also would like these predictions to be ratified by experience. To the extent that they are confirmed in this way, he can feel more confident about the assumptions—the theory—from which he started.

The matter may be illustrated by returning now to the Euclidean and Riemannian forms of geometry and considering what is necessary in order to transmute them from systems of mathematics into scientific theories. The postulates must be given physical interpretations—that is, the concepts and the rules for relating them must be coordinated to operations that can be performed on the environment. By proceeding in this manner, Euclidean and Riemannian geometry can become alternative possible scientific theories about what space is like. If, for example, one proceeds to give the concept of "straight line" the physical interpretation of "light ray," experiments involving astronomical distances can be performed which demonstrate that Riemann's postulates actually offer a better description of the nature of extensive ranges of space than do those of Euclid. Since light rays follow a curved path in the sun's gravitational field, Euclid's postulate that a parallel can be drawn to a straight line through any point not on that straight line does not provide as good a fit to reality as Riemann's postulate that the lines in question must meet somewhere.[2]

The proposed concepts and the proposed relationships interconnecting them that constitute a scientific theory thus are subject in principle to criteria of evaluation that are lacking in the case of a system of mathematics. As in the case of the mathematician, however, two rather different forms of psychological activity can be found in the scientist's mode of conduct: he must invent or generate his theory, and he must trace his way along the deductive path that will lead him from the starting points provided by his postulates to the proving ground provided by his experimental predictions. It was a relatively recent realization on the part of philosophers of science (e.g., Hempel) that there remains a goodly degree of arbitrariness in the scientist's choice of postulates, in that the only major constraint operating upon him consists of whether the predictions he can deduce for test receive confirmation.[3] To be sure, there are questions of consistency among the postulates chosen and questions of parsimony, but these apply to the mathematician as well. Since the proof of the pudding only is in the eating, the scientist is free to seek his theoretical postulates wherever his fancy may lead him. He may, as a physicist, for example, seek to comprehend—i.e., make confirmable predictions about—electrical phenomena by drawing his postulates from the ways in which water behaves in pipes. He can juxtapose elements of his experience, make use of analogical and metaphorical think ing, in as free-wheeling a manner as he wishes.

Often, in fact, important advances in the ability of a branch of science to predict phenomena of interest to it have been found to depend upon the generating of new postulate systems through such processes as what one scientist—Einstein—has referred to as "associative play" and "combinatory play."[4] In this respect, science as well as mathematics would seem to have its game-like properties. An attitude that betokens the playful entertaining of possibilities —the setting of a wide latitude of acceptance limits regarding how the individual will permit himself to think about a subject—may be present in practitioners who are at the cutting edge of each of these domains of knowledge.

We have drawn, then, a distinction between two psychological phases in the work of either a mathematician or a scientist—the generation of conceptual possibilities and the rational deduction of what these possibilities imply within some logical structure. In making this distinction we have emphasized the growing realization that has occurred in recent examinations of the nature of mathematics and science to the effect that the first of these phases— generation or invention of possibilities—involves the constructing of combinations and juxtapositions of concepts in ways that smack of the arbitrary and that suggest a considerable emphasis upon tolerance for conjecture—conjecture as to what may be aesthetically pleasing in mathematics, conjecture as to what may be predictively useful in science. Postulates, then, whether mathematical or scientific, are not given in nature—not discovered—but rather are built by recourse to the exploration of combinatorial or associational possibilities. Since it is human beings who devise the postulates, the latter will, of course, relate to what people have experienced of nature, but in no way that automatically or intuitively confers truth status upon the postulates. Rather, in mathematics, criteria of truth and falsity do not apply to postulates at all, while in science, criteria of truth and falsity apply to the hypotheses derived from the postulates—and as we saw in the case of Riemann, predictions that turn out to be confirmed by experience can often be found to derive from postulates which, if anything, would be declared false on intuitive grounds. Strange, counter-intuitive scientific theories can lead to confirmable predictions.

Let us turn now to man's aesthetic activities. The human being as an artist or composer or writer seems to function very much as does the human being who devises systems of mathematics. Just as the invention of alternative systems of mathematics in recent years —non-Euclidean geometries, non-Aristotelean logics—has pointed to an arbitrary, constructivist element in the establishing of postulate sets, so also the growing awareness in recent years of the multiplicity of human cultures and the increasingly rapid dissemination of new art forms has led to the realization that a comparable element of the arbitrary and the conjectural underlies aesthetics. For such a realization to come about, it probably was necessary that Western European man be dethroned from the position of assumed eminence over the rest of the world's cultures and over earlier civilizations that, until recently, was awarded him by those who provided his philosophy and his chronicles of history and society. It is this dethroning, in fact, that may have contributed heavily to the sudden spurt we have witnessed in the timetable by which aesthetic forms succeed one another.

Until about the last hundred years or so, it was relatively easy for a person who was reared in the Western European cultural tradition to assume that there were some clear paths of progress for the evolution of artistic forms. True, there had been setbacks in the pursuit of these lines of development, as when the classical world was destroyed by hordes of barbarian invaders, but the paths themselves nevertheless remained evident. Just as Euclid could believe his postulates to be intuitively true, so the assumptions underlying musical composition or painting, for example, could be thought of as basically correct in the sense of being attuned to the universal conditions that would maximize aesthetic pleasure. Change there was, to be sure, but only of limited kinds: assumptions were clarified and polished as time went on, and those who worked in the arts became more expert at deriving consequences from these assumptions—carrying out aesthetic projects that were stylistically consistent with what the assumptions called for, i.e., were "good exemplars" of the given aesthetic style. But the basic assumptions themselves were not questioned.

Consider an example first with regard to painting, and then we shall turn to one regarding music. Assuming that painting should be representational—i.e., that art should be, as he put it, ". . . the sole imitator of all visible works of nature"—da Vinci[5] tried to clarify and make explicit the postulates required for achieving maximum veridicality in one's painting. In his detailed writings about, for instance, perspective and light, he tried to set down propositions which, if followed, would yield paintings that looked as real as possible. A particular painting, then, was a derivation from these postulates, and can be judged for the degree of its consistency with the rules that da Vinci claimed to be following. Few artists, of course, wrote down what they viewed as their aesthetic postulates in the manner that da Vinci did, and so for most artists it is more difficult to determine how consistent a given art product is with the canons that provide the artist with his starting point. In principle, however, this exercise can be carried out in most cases, since one can—often with considerable accuracy—infer the postulates that guided the work of a given artist from a knowledge of when and where he lived, with whom he studied, and what art he admired. Although the criteria for judging consistency and inconsistency of a painting with the artist's postulates are necessarily going to be ambiguous in some degree, the situation otherwise is not unlike that of determining whether a given mathematical theorem is consistent with—and hence derived correctly from—a given set of mathematical postulates. And, of course, da Vinci made the same mistake that we ascribed to Euclid: namely, believing that the postulates were intuitively valid—or at most, in need of minor modifications that would bring them into line with what would make for maximum veridicality in one's paintings. Da Vinci once again, then, believed himself to be discovering rather than inventing and constructing.

It is evident at this point in time, however, that the postulates used by da Vinci and by others painting in similar ways can be questioned as such. Representational veridicality need not be a goal of painting. Other sets of postulates that have nothing to do with that goal, but rather with, for example, what are viewed as aesthetically permissible combinations of abstract line forms, may be erected in place of da Vinci's postulates. As there are non-Aristotelean systems of logic and non-Euclidean geometries, so also there are traditions of visual art that take their departures from a variety of stylistic starting points.

The same conclusion is evident when we consider the composition of music. For a long time it was believed in the Western world that certain principles concerning admissible harmonic combinations and certain rules of counterpoint provided an intuitively appropriate aesthetic basis for writing music. A fundamental set of postulates emerged, in other words, that was presumed to provide the starting point from which all musical composition should set forth. With respect to harmonic postulates, for example, it was assumed that the musical interval of the third constituted the basic building block in terms of which chords should be constructed—that chords built in terms of thirds generated maximum aesthetic pleasure. To be avoided, or at best to be introduced by surrounding it with various kinds of harmonic apologies, was the interval of the fourth, which was considered—again presumably on intuitive grounds—to be displeasing to the ear.[6]

The intuitive basis of such a decision is hard to accept, however, when one considers that the reverse set of harmonic assumptions regarding the use of thirds and fourths can be found exemplified in the music of India, where the fourth is considered a pleasing musical interval while the third is not.[7] So also, recent developments in Western music have included the emergence of new styles that involve different postulates of composition than those embodied in the traditional music of the West. For instance, as in the case of Indian music, the work of Schoenberg, a Western composer, also emphasizes fourths rather than thirds as a basic interval. Schoenberg reached his decision to emphasize fourths by wishing to give equal status to all twelve of the tones that lie within an octave, in contrast to the convention in classical Western music of emphasizing three tones, each of which is separated from the next by an interval of a third. He found that if one traversed the keyboard in fourths one would touch the twelve different tones contained by an octave and then return to the point of origin, without having touched any tone more than once. Such an outcome led Schoenberg to conclude that the fourth hence would be the proper interval on which he should center his attention.[8]

The typical citizen of India with musical experience will, of course, find the music of his country more pleasing than music in the classical tradition of Western Europe. So too, Europeans who listen to enough of the music of Schoenberg and other twelve-tone composers will often come to find music of that kind pleasing—once they have, by exposure to it, become sufficiently familiar with the particular premises of its composition. Alternative sets of harmonic and melodic postulates can be fashioned, then, and music written which is stylistically consistent with one or another set. As in the case of visual art, one can in principle expect to be able to discriminate better from less good embodiments of a particular compositional style, once one can define with sufficient clarity the stylistic postulates that a given composer believes himself to be following. Particular compositions are, in this sense, "theorems" that derive from a set of postulates as to how music should be written, and one can determine how consistent a given composition is with the rules by which its composer wishes to work. But just as there is nothing to choose between alternative geometries as systems, so also one cannot adjudicate between classical harmony and the harmonic rules used in, say, twelve-tone music. There is no "rational" or intuitively self-evident ground for claiming that one or the other system of musical assumptions is aesthetically superior. Rather, they are different, and each can form the basis for a composer's work.

As was shown to be the case for mathematics and for science, then, so also when it comes to man's aesthetic activities there seem to be two distinguishable kinds of psychological processes that take place: the construction of a set of premises—on at least partly arbitrary grounds—as to what are to be the ground rules; and then the exploration of the consequences implied by these rules. Just as recent thinking in mathematics and science has come to call attention to the multitudinous bases upon which postulate sets or theories can be erected, so also recent aesthetic criticism has come to emphasize the importance of the artist as empowered not only to trace through the implications of a given set of aesthetic assumptions—to work within a given style—but also to invent and try out different sets of possible assumptions.

Thus, for instance, we find the critic Susan Sontag advising much the same kind of thing in art to which Einstein called attention in physics—the need for engaging in associative play and combinatory play regarding the putting together of conceptual elements in order to generate new possible starting points.[9] By juxtaposing, by putting into association, elements that have not previously been viewed as related, new possibilities emerge on which aesthetic, mathematical, or scientific traditions can be founded. Sontag is particularly interested in forms of art which emphasize the artist's role as a provider of new possibilities, new juxtapositions of elements from experience. In cubism, for example, parts of familiar objects are placed in new associations and connections with one another. In surrealism, a familiar object will be placed in a context with which it was not heretofore joined. As a result the object is rendered strange, as it were, and filled with new evocative power. In "pop" art, a similar evocation of the strange by the familiar is achieved by juxtaposing an everyday object such as a can of soup with an environment—the museum— that carries connotations from an entirely different domain of experience. So, too, the music of a composer such as John Cage will involve the use of a piano that has been systematically rebuilt so as to provide a different repertoire of available tonal qualities. And a play by Jean Genet will involve an experiment with the unfamiliar juxtaposition of having black people impersonate white people.

No doubt Sontag may fall prone to an excessive celebration of the unique for its own sake, but the fact remains that she is representative of a new wave of awareness in the arts that aesthetic assumptions are in large measure constructed by man rather than given in nature, and hence are fair game for experimentation. The discipline of working systematically within a particular set of assumptions in order to explore their implications is, of course, important, as well. But some excess in Sontag's direction seems quite excusable at this point since one is describing a realization that has come about only over the last few generations of man's long aesthetic history. It has become evident, then, that the artist can appropriately devote effort to the building of new ways of combining and relating aesthetic materials; he need not only restrict himself to working with systems that already exist.

On the Psychology of Human Thinking

In mathematics, in science, and in art, we have found evidence for two phases of human endeavor—the setting up of conceptual possibilities and the analysis of what these possibilities imply. We have noted that the first phase, that of constructing assumptions, has been masked from view until relatively recently in human history by the belief that the process at issue was not in fact one of invention or conjecture but rather one of intuitive apprehension or analysis concerning how nature is ordered. Man's thinking in all of the areas that we have described hence seems to be characterized, on the one hand, by the generation or production of ideational possibilities, and, on the other, by taking a particular set of such possibilities—with its system of logic as to what else the set implies—and examining deductively the set's implications. We may call the first of these processes the *expression of possibilities;* the second, the *analysis of implications.* I would like to suggest that the two processes involve very different attitudes toward error.

The analysis of implications refers to the kind of activity that is traditionally associated with tests of intellective ability and of academic achievement in our society. Called for on such tests is the close separation of what is "right" from what is "wrong" in terms of some given set of premises which the respondent must have within his grasp in order to proceed effectively. In the case of ability tests, the premises or postulates are sufficiently general that they are presumed to be familiar to everybody—as when the respondent's degree of clarity of understanding of the words in his language is tested; or the premises are supplied with the test —as when the conditions of some problem are set forth and the respondent is asked to solve it. In each of these situations, the psychological issue is presumed to consist in how well the child can manipulate some givens—how precisely his verbal behavior will reflect, for example, the rules for word usage in his culture, or how incisively he can reason about what the solution to a problem must be in light of the data that have been presented. Tests of academic achievement, on the other hand, presumably require the child not only to demonstrate the ability to make correct inferences, but also to show that he has mastered the premises in one or another area of knowledge—such as the particular vocabulary needed for describing the history of America in the eighteenth century or the particular symbols used for presenting numerical problems in algebraic form.

In point of fact, however, the distinction between ability and achievement, or between intelligence tests and tests of academic accomplishment, is difficult to maintain in practice. Those children who score high on ability indicators also tend to score high on academic achievement indicators as well. Furthermore, children scoring high regarding measures of verbal ability also tend to score high on measures of quantitative ability, and children who score high regarding one area of potential academic accomplishment represented in their school curriculum also tend to score high when it comes to other academic achievement areas that form part of their curriculum.[10] There is, then, some single dimension of relative proficiency in terms of which children are ordered by all of these instruments, whether the tests are described as measures of one or another kind of intelligence or as indices of one or another type of school achievement.

Since the degree of specificity of the experience needed for dealing successfully with the test materials varies over a considerable range and yet children tend to exhibit a consistent level of proficiency on all of these types of tests, the intensity of a child's relative exposure to the sorts of materials that form the concern of these tests doesn't seem to constitute the determining factor in his performance. Rather, what seems to be at issue is the child's skill in using analytic systems correctly—in carrying out translations and transformations of information in ways that conform to the logical requirements that are prescribed in his culture and that are assumed or stipulated on the tests. In order to know how to transform and how to translate, one must be able to retain the rules of the system and have a sharp sense of discrimination for what is and what isn't permissible in the light of those rules. It is apparently the case—on the basis of the evidence—that the capacity to analyze implications correctly represents a very generic type of thinking skill that transfers with alacrity from one substantive domain to another. This is the kind of ability to which the notion of "general intelligence" seems to refer, and it is what we have found to be at issue in the work of a mathematician, a scientist, or an artist as he seeks to move toward some product or goal that is consistent with a set of starting assumptions—whether these assumptions be mathematical postulates, a scientific theory, or rules of harmony.

In the exercise of intelligence, the individual as he works in any area of content must be highly sensitive to error. Analysis of implications requires that a true course be maintained with respect to one's premises, however vague and unverbalized these may be. For a mathematician or scientist, the postulates from which one works will be quite explicit indeed: they can be written down in a list. But for a cubist painter, or for a child or adult demonstrating his knowledge of the principles of grammar by distinguishing correct from incorrect examples of speech, the assumptions may be difficult to render explicit and yet the person will be described by knowledgeable others as using the assumptions correctly. What of the kind of thinking, on the other hand, that is involved in the expression or generating of possibilities? When a person constructs a set of assumptions, when he entertains a conjecture as to particular concepts that may go together, when he juxtaposes elements of his experience that neither he nor anyone else had previously placed in association, what can we expect to be the attitude that the person maintains toward error? In this latter case, it seems to me, a very different attitude toward error can be expected: tolerance instead of severity.

An attitude of relaxed contemplation of possibilities can be found in many introspective accounts concerning moments of personal creativity or inventiveness, as these accounts have been culled from interview and diary material provided by artists, mathematicians, and scientists.[11] One can point to a sense of playful experimentation in which the danger of error has relatively little significance. Recall Einstein's references to "associative play" and "combinatory play." It is as if judgment becomes suspended in some degree, and leeway is provided for the entertaining of unusual concatenations of ideas and images. To suggest that there is relatively little attention paid to the possibility of error in this kind of thinking is to say that the person doing the thinking does not view error as a source of disgrace, as a way to lose face. A permissiveness with respect to error that can never be tolerated when one is engaged in the analysis of implications, therefore, may well take on importance if one is seeking to express or generate possibilities.

While our society has paid considerable attention to evaluating how proficient a person is at analyzing implications, much less concern was paid until very recently to the question of a person's capacity for generating unusual ideas and regrouping elements of experience in fresh ways. I would speculate that the reason for this neglect stems from the historical situation described earlier with respect to mathematics, science, and the arts, where the prevailing assumption was for a very long time that analysis of "what is there" —intuitive apprehension of some order of givens—provides the appropriate starting points for work in each of these domains. If that were the case, then something on the order of general intelligence would be the only kind of attribute that would require measurement. Our reading of the recent history of these human activities, on the other hand, has suggested a different perspective.

A question that immediately arises, however, is whether this different perspective is operationally distinguishable from the one that formerly prevailed. If not, then the psychological utility of distinguishing between analysis of implications and expression of possibilities in man's thinking would be doubtful, even though the distinction could be defended on epistemological grounds. To put the operational issue directly, we need to inquire whether the individuals who possess greater intelligence—i.e., the persons who are better able to analyze implications—are the same as the individuals who possess greater ability to conjure up conceptual possibilities. At first blush it looks as if these persons should indeed be one and the same. After all, isn't an inventive or creative scientist going to be more intelligent than one who is less inventive or less creative? On the other hand, if different attitudes toward error are involved in analyzing implications and in expressing possibilities, then the psychological picture might be more complex.

The answer seems to be that if you test for the ability to express conceptual possibilities under conditions that threaten the individual with penalties for error, proficiency at constructing possibilities will tend to be found only in the case of the persons who also are skilled at analyzing implications. However, if you test for the ability to express conceptual possibilities under conditions that maximize freedom and permissiveness with respect to error—so that the chance of making a mistake does not constitute a threat—then proficiency at constructing possibilities turns out to be quite independent of the ability to analyze implications.[12] Under these latter conditions, some persons who are skilled at analyzing implications turn out to be skilled at expressing conceptual possibilities as well, but others who are skilled at analyzing implications are found to be poor at generating conceptual possibilities. So too, while some persons who are poor at analyzing implications also are poor at expressing conceptual possibilities, others who are poor at analyzing implications turn out to be highly skilled at producing conceptual possibilities. There is, in short, no relationship between the two kinds of thinking skills, when the ability to generate conceptual possibilities is assessed in a way that frees the person from the fear of making mistakes.

We have proposed, in turn, that a permissive attitude toward error is more conducive to the type of thinking that is concerned with generating possibilities than is a severe or punitive attitude toward error. The ability to construct possibilities thus is found to be independent of the ability to analyze implications precisely under those circumstances that should be propitious to the former's display.

The type of evidence on which the preceding statements rest includes the following. In some of our recent research, the generating of conceptual possibilities was assessed in fifth-grade children with various kinds of materials. For example, an object would be named, such as a shoe or a newspaper, and the child would be asked to mention as many uses as possible that he could think of for the object. These requests took place in a play context, with the child encouraged to take as much time in responding as he wished. Fear of error thus was minimized. Under such circumstances, the number of conceptual possibilities that the child generates, and the number that he presents which are unusual in the sense of being his personal possession rather than being ones which other children think of as well, are found to be quite independent of how "bright" or "dull" the child is in terms of general intelligence indicators.[13] On the other hand, comparable work by other investigators has involved the use of similar procedures which were administered, however, under circumstances that emphasized a test-like context and hence implied that error was to be penalized. The generating of conceptual possibilities in the latter type of setting, where there is no permissive attitude toward error, tends to co-vary with level of general intelligence.[14]

In sum, then, we find that the ability to analyze implications, with its requirement of alertness and sensitivity to the possibility of error, tells us nothing about a child's ability to suggest unusual and plentiful conceptual possibilities in situations where no penalty for error is present. A child is just as likely to be skilled at one of these types of thinking and poor at the other as he is to be skilled at both or poor at both. If analysis of implications requires sensitivity regarding possible errors while the expression of conceptual possibilities requires permissiveness regarding possible errors, what can we say by way of characterizing the individuals who are proficient with respect to both abilities, proficient at one but not the other, and proficient at neither?

Something like the following characterizations would seem to apply. The child who displays high levels of both abilities must be capable of shifting with flexibility from an attitude of error tolerance to an attitude of error rejection, as a function of what he is working on. By contrast, a child with strong ability to analyze implications and low ability to entertain conceptual possibilities must be rigidly locked in an attitude of error rejection—the chance of error is not to be tolerated. For the child who is unable to analyze implications skillfully but nevertheless shows a high ability to generate conceptual possibilities, on the other hand, the opposite kind of inflexibility appears to prevail—namely, a pervasive attitude of error tolerance which the child is unable or unwilling to modulate. The child who is low in regard to both abilities, finally, gives no evidence of possessing specific attitudes of error tolerance or of error rejection; there is relatively little behavior to suggest selective permissiveness or selective minimization of the possibility of error.

In terms of pedagogy, I feel that the clearest educational challenge exists in the case of the children who are relatively able to analyze implications but relatively unable to generate conceptual possibilities. There is little doubt that, as educational environments become richer and teachers become equipped with a wider variety of technical aids, general improvements can take place in the level of analytic skills possessed by children who are initially poor at analysis of implications. The gradual rise in scores on intellective-ability tests that we have witnessed over recent years testifies to this kind of pedagogical effect. It is an effect, however, that amounts to cultivating "more of the same," since we have found that sensitivity to what is correct and incorrect in terms of given rule systems already constitutes the very core of what qualifies in our society as educability and as educational achievement. The educational message that gets communicated to those children who are capable of analyzing implications but poor at producing conceptual possibilities, on the other hand, represents in my estimation a serious deception. These children are informed that as far as the society is concerned, they are doing fine educationally. Yet, they cannot adopt the kind of tolerance toward error that may lie at the root of much significant innovation in mathematics, science, and the arts. The challenge for education, then, is to do something different for these children—something that may have the effect of freeing them from an inflexibly maintained attitude of avoidance toward error. It would seem that they need to learn that circumstances exist under which it is an acceptable practice to withhold one's judgment about correctness or incorrectness—to live with the chance of making a mistake.

Before considering the educational situation further, however, we should ask whether there is any independent evidence to suggest that the kind of children whom we have described as pervasively oriented toward error rejection do in fact behave that way. Thus far, we have inferred this orientation from the conjunction in their case of high analytic skills coupled with low ability to suggest conceptual possibilities. Is there direct evidence to support this interpretation? Several studies in our recent research do, in fact, provide such support.[15] For example, the children in question are found to be particularly unlikely to entertain the possibility of describing schematic drawings of people in affective terms that could be considered bizarre—but nevertheless might possess some validity. So also, these children turn out to be particularly unlikely to engage in kinds of classroom behaviors that appear disruptive to an independent observer, and they are relatively hesitant about speaking out in the course of classroom discussions. While others seek out these children as friends, furthermore, the children in question are themselves relatively reticent to express friendship strivings toward others. At least one characteristic of the children under consideration which these strands of evidence seem to have in common is an attitude of avoiding activities that may incur error—that may turn out to have been a mistake. It is as if the risk of making mistakes in one's judgment—in social matters as well as in cognitive matters—is not to be chanced.

In the case of children who are skilled at the analysis of implications but poor at the expressing of conceptual possibilities, then, we have persons who may be barred from performing innovative roles in the society by virtue of their overly severe attitude toward error, but yet who are told by the educational system that nothing is lacking in their performance. As far as the schools are concerned, these children are very intelligent and show high scholastic achievement: their performances on tests of intellective ability and on tests of academic accomplishment are unimpeachable. The educational arrangements that presently exist, therefore, are letting these children down. Does it appear that any help for them will be forthcoming in the educational system of the future?

The Hardware Revolution in American Education

The future looks very bleak to me for these children. The new wave in American education at the elementary and high school levels will from all indications consist of an emphasis upon instruction by teaching machines and by computers. What is such instruction like and what kind of thinking does it aid?

By and large, the major characteristic that distinguishes automated forms of instruction from ordinary books is the immediacy and specificity of feedback that can be provided to the child concerning the correctness or incorrectness of answers that he offers. The hallmark of the technique is the provision to the child of a "responsive environment," to take a term that derives from the name of a company that manufactures one of the new kinds of computerized teaching machines: that is, an environment that offers immediate evaluative criteria to the child for judging the answers that he provides to questions, and that by its evaluation guides the child's behavior toward the making of more and more correct responses and fewer and fewer incorrect ones.

Consider how this principle of immediate and specific feedback works at each of two levels of hardware complexity. In some of the simpler teaching machine devices of the kind originated by B. F. Skinner, a question appears in the machine's window when the student turns a knob. The student writes his answer to the question and then turns the knob again so that his written answer slides up under a transparent cover and thus cannot be altered. The correct answer then immediately moves into the student's view, letting him know thereby whether his own answer was right or wrong. In some of the more complex devices, such as those developed by O. K. Moore, Richard Kobler, and others, the child may sit at a typewriter keyboard and hear a request over a loudspeaker from a tape recording that asks him to spell a particular word. If the student types a correct letter, the letter appears on a screen in front of him; if he types an erroneous letter, on the other hand, it does not appear on the screen and the recorded voice informs him that the letter is wrong and he should try again. Persistent error at a letter may finally lead to the machine's presenting the word spelled correctly on the screen, followed by a request from the loudspeaker that the child now try again. In another device, the child sees a question on a television screen and chooses what he believes to be the correct answer by pointing a flashlight at one of the multiple-choice alternatives that appear on the screen. A voice then informs the child whether the answer he selected was right or wrong.[16]

There is little doubt that automated instructional devices will gain increasing influence as a means of pedagogy, and this for two reasons. First, the use of instrumentation is highly consonant with the dominant American value pattern, deriving as this pattern does from the extensive homage paid by our society to physics and engineering. Hardware—electronic if possible, mechanical if not—

tends per se to be taken as a sign of progress. Second, various industries in this country are developing a sizeable financial stake in the propagation of automated instruction, and are not likely to treat these investments lightly. Thus, a number of electronics and computer firms have obtained connections with firms concerned with the preparation of educational materials.

It seems to me that the impact of automated instruction will be to provide an all-the-greater emphasis upon the kind of thinking defined by what we have called the ability to analyze implications. As we have seen, the cardinal virtue possessed by automated instruction over ordinary reading matter is the provision of immediate and specific evaluative feedback to the child. Automated devices thus can be expected to be particularly suited to the teaching of rule systems—systems for translating or transforming cognitive elements —and indeed it is in this kind of area that their major successes have been achieved.[17] A teaching machine offers an efficient means of instructing a child in how to spell, or in how to read, or in how to work arithmetic problems, or in how to learn vocabulary. These are kinds of tasks that involve orienting the child as to what constitute correct and incorrect inferences within a prescribed set of givens, such as number rules, spelling rules, or grammar rules. At least one source of the considerable power possessed by automated instruction for the kinds of tasks in question is that the child can be encouraged to apply the rules correctly without having to go through attempts to teach him explicit verbal forms of these rules. It is the case, after all, that knowing explicit overt statements of rules can often be a very different matter from knowing how to work correctly with rules, and much of education has concentrated upon the former while taking its goal as the latter.

What worries me, however, is that the socio-cultural support behind automated instructional devices will inevitably lead to increased emphasis in the schools on whatever it is that can best be taught through the use of these devices. And this means, of course, a further emphasis upon that which already is central: the kinds of skills represented by intellective-ability tests and by indicators of how well the child has mastered academic content domains. Automated instructional devices, even more than intelligence tests themselves, will convey to the child the message that the world is made up of analytic systems and that the child's task is to master these systems. Immediate and focused feedback as to correctness and error signifies all the more dramatically to the child that right answers are the primary virtue in school: that one should conduct oneself so as to achieve correct answers as quickly and consistently as possible.

Clearly, this is not the kind of pedagogical orientation that will stimulate an entertaining of conceptual possibilities that are deviant and far-fetched and hence well may be wrong. A tolerant attitude toward the possibility of error—a withholding of evaluative judgment in order to generate novel analogical or metaphorical connections between ideas that have not previously been juxtaposed—this is not the kind of thinking to which automated instructional devices lend themselves. Children who are skilled at analysis of implications but poor at generating conceptual possibilities, therefore, are likely to become, if anything, all the more set in their overly severe attitude toward error with the advent of automated instruction. And, if anything, the awarding of increasing ideological prominence in educational circles to automated instructional devices suggests that it will become increasingly difficult in general to win educational recognition for the importance of developing times and places wherein evaluation is withheld and the trying out of possibilities encouraged.

While some proponents of automated instruction try to argue otherwise—that the use of such devices will free the teacher for pursuit of other educational goals[18]—I strongly doubt that such will be the outcome. Given the overwhelming commitment of our society to science and technology as a prime value, and given a growing industrial commitment to the propagation of automated instruction as the way in which education should be carried out, I find it hard to conceive of non-automated instruction in any role other than that of second-class citizen. The teachers will not be on the top of the pyramid, freed from disagreeable chores by labor-saving machines. Rather, on the top of the pyramid will be the educational engineers who fashion devices and programs for automated instruction, and the educational administrators who route the students through these devices and programs.

Viewed in this perspective, it turns out, ironically enough, that automated instructional devices, for all their modern hardware, may well constitute an anachronism. By underplaying the side of human thinking that involves conjecture and invention—a side that, as we have seen, has come increasingly into focus as performing a central role in man's mathematical, scientific, and aesthetic activities—automated instructional devices may lead educational practice back to a one-sided, overly rationalistic view of how thinking proceeds.

REFERENCES

1. For readings relevant to these points, see, for example, Carl G. Hempel, "On the Nature of Mathematical Truth," in Herbert Feigl and Wilfrid Sellars (eds.), *Readings in Philosophical Analysis* (New York, 1949), pp. 222-237; Jean Nicod, "Geometry in the Perceived World," in Philip P. Wiener (ed.), *Readings in Philosophy of Science* (New York, 1953), pp. 19-26; William K. Clifford, "On the Bending of Space," in P. P. Wiener (ed.), *op. cit.*, pp. 52-59; and C. G. Hempel, "Geometry and Empirical Science," in P. P. Wiener (ed.), *op. cit.*, pp. 40-51.

2. W. K. Clifford, *op. cit.;* C. G. Hempel, "Geometry and Empirical Science," *op. cit.*

3. C. G. Hempel, *Fundamentals of Concept Formation in Empirical Science* (Chicago, 1952).

4. Brewster Ghiselin (ed.), *The Creative Process* (New York, 1955), p. 43.

5. Elizabeth G. Holt (ed.), *A Documentary History of Art,* Vol. 1 (New York, 1957), p. 284.

6. Donald F. Tovey, *The Forms of Music* (New York, 1957).

7. Arnold Bake, "The Music of India," in Egon Wellesz (ed.), *Ancient and Oriental Music* (London, 1957), pp. 195-227.

8. Arnold Schoenberg, *Structural Functions of Harmony* (New York, 1954); and A. Schoenberg, *Style and Idea* (New York, 1950).

9. Susan Sontag, *Against Interpretation* (New York, 1966).

10. See, for example, Michael A. Wallach and Nathan Kogan, *Modes of Thinking in Young Children* (New York, 1965).

11. See, for example, B. Ghiselin (ed.), *op. cit.*

12. See the results reported in M. A. Wallach and N. Kogan, *op. cit.*, in conjunction with their analysis of earlier studies by others.

13. *Ibid.*

14. See, for example, Jacob W. Getzels and Philip W. Jackson, *Creativity and Intelligence* (New York, 1962); and Victor B. Cline, James M. Richards, Jr., and Walter E. Needham, "Creativity Tests and Achievement in High School Science," *Journal of Applied Psychology*, Vol. 47, No. 3 (June 1963), pp. 184-189.

15. M. A. Wallach and N. Kogan, *op. cit.*

16. For some general discussions of the points under consideration, see, for example, Edward B. Fry, *Teaching Machines and Programmed Instruction* (New York, 1963); P. Kenneth Komoski, "Programmed Instruction and its Place in Education," in Morris Philipson (ed.), *Automation: Implications for the Future* (New York, 1962), pp. 415-427; Simon Ramo, "A New Technique of Education," in M. Philipson (ed.), *op. cit.*, pp. 428-442; Omar K. Moore, "Autotelic Responsive Environments and Exceptional Children," in Jerome Hellmuth (ed.), *The Special Child in Century 21* (Seattle, 1964), pp. 87-138; John McCarthy, "Time-Sharing Computer Systems," in Martin Greenberger (ed.), *Computers and the World of the Future* (Cambridge, Mass., 1964), pp. 220-248; Patrick Suppes, "Plug-In Instruction," *Saturday Review*, Vol. 49, No. 30 (July 23, 1966), pp. 25-30; and Don D. Bushnell, "For Each Student a Teacher," *Saturday Review, op. cit.*, p. 31.

17. See, for example, O. K. Moore, *op. cit.*

18. See, for example, P. K. Komoski, *op. cit.*

LOREN EISELEY

Darwin, Coleridge, and the Theory of Unconscious Creation

TWO GREAT geniuses of the nineteenth century, two men from widely distinct social worlds, yet of strangely similar cast of intelligence, have, by the vicissitudes of fortune, become posthumously involved in a stormy controversy among twentieth-century biologists. One was the poet, Samuel Taylor Coleridge, opium addict, creator of *The Rime of the Ancient Mariner* and the weird moonlit fragment *Christabel*. "For over a century," writes the critic Max Schulz, "the tradition has been that they [Coleridge's poems] defy analysis because the best of them are enchanted records of unearthly realms peopled by Mongol warriors, old navigators, albatrosses, and Lamia witchwomen. . . ."[1] Students of the subject have been until recently loth to perceive the conscious craftsman behind the dreamer. The tendency has been to accept "the sacred river," the sunless sea of dream as the primary source of Coleridge's inspiration. Out of these misty depths, according to entranced critics, were drawn in poetic ecstasy fragments of travelers' tales transmuted forever in the subconscious mind of the poet. The public appeal of this romantic interpretation of great poetry is tremendous. It flatters our imagination and our conception of the mysterious life of the literary artist.

The other man, Charles Darwin, the equally noted discoverer of natural selection, has at first glance a different and scientific appearance. Yet his mind, too, was stuffed with the multitudinous lore of both incredibly wide reading and personal oceanic experience. He openly proclaimed himself a millionaire of odd and curious little facts. There floated in his vast memory the tortoises and lizards of islands under tropic suns. He had dug for fossil bones in Patagonia, and climbed Andean peaks in solitude. Navigators and albatrosses were part also of his experience. He, like Coleridge, had read insatiably.

But in his case the public imagination was, and is still, caught by the symbol of a great voyage, the voyage of the *Beagle*. After Darwin's book, *The Origin of Species*, was published in 1859 he wrote to the Reverend Baden Powell, "If I have taken anything from you, I assure you it has been unconsciously."[2] This was in response to a letter in which Powell had reproved Darwin for not referring to one of his works. Thus the legend of the unconscious, the role of the "sacred river," was destined to leave the realm of poetry and enter the field of science. The floating fragments from Darwin's sacred river need no longer be assigned place, name, or priority. They had become the property of genius, they had entered the dark domain of demonic creation. As it is in literature, where historic footnotes are not demanded of the poet, so now it was about to become in science. Charles Darwin was to be elevated beyond giving an account of even partial priority as that rule applied to other men.

Darwin's own excuse of the "unconscious" has been increasingly used in recent years by defenders of the great biologist in considering the problem of Darwin's meager attention to his predecessors. If Darwin "unconsciously" borrowed material without acknowledgment, some scholars imply that no blame can be attributed to him. Rather, they frown upon those historians of science who persist in probing beneath the insights of genius in order to seek the sources of their inspiration. Yet we must still ask, was the one man who should know where he got the idea of his famous theory unconscious of where he got it? Or did he consciously draw a veil over one predecessor in particular, rationalizing, perhaps, as he is known to have done on one occasion, when he implied that the man who successfully convinces the public of a new idea deserves all the credit which may accrue to him.[3]

The theory of the "unconscious" has been emphasized by Darwinian defenders particularly following the publication in 1959, in the *Proceedings of the American Philosophical Society*, of an article which explored the possible role played by Edward Blyth, a young British naturalist, in the formulation of the theory of natural selection.[4]

We now know that Blyth stated the basic tenets of the theory of natural selection in two articles in *The Magazine of Natural History* in the years 1835 and 1837.[5] We know also that Darwin footnoted Blyth copiously in his books on many subjects, but never on natural selection, although it is clear from the nature of his reading and interior evidence from his notebooks and early essays, as well as one letter, that he was familiar with the magazine containing these important articles. The recent publication of *Darwin's Notebooks on Transmutation of Species,*[6] in 1960, showed clearly that Darwin was aware of Blyth's writings on natural selection. In the *Second Notebook,*[7] never intended for publication, reference is made to the article of 1837 in which Blyth writes, after having earlier in 1835 described the conservative effects of natural selection: "May not, then, a large proportion of what are considered species have descended from a common parentage?"[8]

Several who are unwilling to credit Blyth with influencing Darwin refuse to quote this line of 1837—the very year that Darwin conceived of the role of natural selection in evolution. Sir Gavin de Beer, who edited the Notebooks, footnotes Blyth's article as mentioned by Darwin in the *Second Notebook,* but fails to point out its obvious import. In a brief discussion of Blyth in the Introduction to the *First Notebook* he at first remarks that Darwin probably owed nothing to Blyth so far as the construction of his theory is concerned.[9] He confesses, however, in the same paragraph, that "there is nothing improbable in his [Darwin's] having copied some from Blyth." He then cautiously concedes that "Darwin (and others) may have been wrong in thinking that he owed him [Blyth] or them nothing on this score." Four years later, in 1964, in his biography of Darwin, de Beer has again retreated from a direct confrontation of the full nature of Blyth's speculations when he says that although Blyth "had been playing with the very tools that Darwin so successfully used, it is difficult to see that Darwin was indebted to him, for his conclusions were the exact negation of what Darwin was trying to prove."[10] Concerning this statement it is of interest to note that George Wald, writing on "Innovation in Biology," in the *Scientific American,* remarks that "all great ideas come in pairs, the one the negation of the other, and both containing elements of truth."[11] Edward Blyth, as we have seen, in a moment of insight glimpsed momentarily both faces of Natural Selection. It was enough to give an astute mind like Darwin's the clue that he was seeking. Today it is well recognized that this principle is composed of both creative and conservative aspects. In nature, natural selection maintains the species as well as promoting slow and tested change at the same time.

Theodosius Dobzhansky, who uses the "unconscious" theory to explain Darwin's failure to acknowledge his predecessors, accepts the fact that "the fundamental premises of the theory of natural selection are contained in Blyth's essays,"[12] but maintains that Darwin might have been mistaken about the sources of some of his ideas, and his thinking process might not have been wholly free of subconscious components.[13] Dobzhansky's theory of the "subconscious components" as the probable cause of Darwin's omission of credit to Edward Blyth should be considered carefully because it gives us an opportunity to explore one interpretation of the creative processes of genius.[14]

"Is the origin of every idea which crosses our minds always clear to us?"[15] Dobzhansky asks. Nobody, he contends, has a perfect memory and is always aware of his thinking processes.

Probably everyone is familiar with the feeling that an idea which arises in one's mind, or a phrase which emerges from one's pen, have been met with somewhere, but one cannot recall just where or when. This feeling is sometimes justified but perhaps more often illusory. Might not even Darwin have been mistaken about the sources of some of his ideas?[16]

It is the mystery of the creative process in the mind of genius which the discovery of Edward Blyth forces us to face, argues Dobzhansky. In Darwin's defense, Dobzhansky cites John Livingston Lowes' well-known study of Coleridge, *The Road to Xanadu*. Dobzhansky feels, as did Lowes, that "it is not illegitimate to compare the creative processes of a poet, Coleridge, with those of a scientist, Darwin."[17] Since the creative work of a poet and of a scientist are not fundamentally different,[18] Dobzhansky maintains that Darwin had little more awareness of the soil in which his theories grew than did Coleridge of the sources of his poetry. Unfortunately for Dobzhansky's reliance upon Lowes' interpretation of Coleridge, however, later critics no longer see the great romantic poet as purely an inspired somnambulist. In the first volume of Kathleen Coburn's edition of Coleridge's notebooks, says Schulz, "the notations of ideas and images for future poems recorded in them reveal a mind knowing where it is going and moving purposefully toward that goal."[19]

Could Darwin have been unaware of the fact that he had read and utilized the articles written by Edward Blyth on the subject which he was later to claim completely as his own discovery? Lowes has written:

The "deep well of unconscious cerebration" underlies your consciousness and mine, but in the case of genius its waters are possessed of a peculiar potency. Images and impressions converge and blend even in the sleepy drench of our forgetful pools. But the inscrutable energy of genius which we call creative owes its secret virtue at least in part to the enhanced and almost incredible facility with which in the wonder-working depths of the unconscious the fragments which sink incessantly below the surface fuse and assimilate and coalesce. The depths are peopled to start out with (and this is fundamental) by conscious intellectual activity, keyed, it may be, as in Coleridge's intense and exigent reading, to the highest pitch. Moreover (and this crucially important consideration will occupy us in due time), it is again conscious energy, now of another and loftier type, which later drags the deeps for their submerged treasure, and moulds the bewildering chaos into unity. But interposed between consciousness and consciousness is the well. And therein resides the peculiar significance of such a phantasmagoria as lies before us in the [Coleridge's] Note Book, the seemingly meaningless jumble of which we have tried to grasp.[20]

In striking contrast to this view, however, Werner W. Beyer, another Coleridge authority, emphasizes the role of the conscious and deliberate in the creative process. Writing in *The Enchanted Forest*, which the author says begins where *The Road to Xanadu* ended, Beyer states that Lowes' stress upon the importance of the unconscious "has given such wide currency to the concept of unconscious metamorphosis that its conscious counterpart has threatened to be ignored."[21] Beyer presents interesting evidence of Coleridge's use in his poetry of a crucial source until now undetected. This deals with the part C. M. Wieland's tale *Oberon*, translated by Coleridge around November 20, 1797, seems to have played in the genesis of *The Wanderings of Cain*, *The Rime of the Ancient Mariner*, *Christabel*, and *Kubla Khan*. Beyer has no doubt that Coleridge was aware of Wieland's poetry as a source of his own, since Coleridge translated the tale, and wrote this fact in a letter to Joseph Cottle.[22] Lowes, himself, in a letter of November 24, 1939, wrote to Beyer concerning this newly produced evidence:

Why, in view of the fact that on p. 243 of *The Road to Xanadu* I referred to S.T.C.'s flat statement that he was translating *Oberon*, I didn't go farther, I can't, to save my soul, imagine![23]

It was *conscious* judgment, Beyer insists, that led Coleridge to his discoveries of the potentialities of *Oberon*. More than Lowes suspected,

. . . conscious and unconscious appear to have collaborated and interpenetrated in the genesis of the fabulous ballad [*Rime*]. *As others have thought, the deliberate, purposive, and volitional appear to have played a far greater role in the complex process of discovering and envisioning, assimulating and transforming the multifarious stuff for its fabric and form.* . . . Oberon *makes it clear, I think, that the genesis of the* Ancient Mariner, *which it generously abetted, was not so largely a product of the subconscious as Lowes assumed.*[24] (Italics mine, L. E.)

Beyer also cites another Coleridge authority, R. C. Bald, who,

> . . . after a study of the later notebooks [of Coleridge], similarly stressed what Lowes had seemed to minimize; the *conscious* element in the creative process, the deliberateness of Coleridge's reading, for purposes of poetry, and the recency of some of it which therefore could not have been long submerged in the subconscious. . . .[25]

Since it has been noted that the creative processes of a poet (Coleridge) may be compared to the creative processes of a scientist (Darwin), it is impossible not to see the parallel between these two geniuses in their working processes. *Oberon*, Beyer remarks, appears to have provided a scenario that Coleridge found

> . . . adaptable, kindling, and of high "symbolic potential." . . . It seems to have provided many materials, too, but, more important, to have served as a flexible form or matrix to help organize the richly diverse ingredients drawn from innumerable other sources and experience previously unrelated. And the conscious guidance it evidently afforded appears to put a somewhat different complexion on the story of the genesis of the great ballad, and at the same time to shed new light on various obscure passages.[26]

Coleridge once made the remark that men are caterpillars, very few of whom succeed in successfully transmuting themselves into butterflies. To introduce a bit of modern knowledge, one might observe that the caterpillar possesses glands in its head which at the proper moment assist him to make that beautiful transformation. In the case of men, even brilliant men, some outside incident, some catalytic agent concealed in the environment, may be the initiator of the transformation we call "creativity" or "genius." The man must be receptive, his mind afloat perhaps with the random forms which contain an unevolved future. It is then that the hidden key to the locked secret must be found. Otherwise the potential inspiration may drift past unrecognized into oblivion.

As *Oberon* was such a stimulus, a scenario for Coleridge's great poems, Blyth's articles on natural selection were conceivably Darwin's scenario, containing as they did the full series of stepping stones over which, as I have elsewhere pointed out, Darwin passed on his way into the new world of organic novelty. Lowes remarked as much of Coleridge:

> [In 1797] . . . a vast concourse of images was hovering in the background of Coleridge's brain, waiting for the formative conception which should strike through their confusion, and marshal them into clarity and order.[27]

In October or November, says Beyer, "the young poet-in-waiting discovered *Oberon,* and speedily began translating its teeming kaleidoscopic scenes—scenes which were *as if made for that service.*"[28] (Beyer's italics.) Coleridge may be compared to the young scientist Darwin, home from his voyage, freshly impressed with new lands and unknown creatures. Darwin suspected the reality of life's transformations, but he remained without a satisfactory mechanism to show how organisms were actually adapted to fit diverse environments.

Darwin wrote in his *Autobiography,* "Nor did I ever intermit collecting facts bearing on the origin of species; and I could sometimes do this when I could do nothing else from illness."[29] Then, said Darwin, he read by chance the work of Thomas Malthus in October 1838, and claimed to see in Malthus' work the key to natural selection in the animal world. It is, however, genuinely possible to conceive that it was the work of Blyth which Darwin, the scientist-in-waiting, read. Here was material which was, in the words of Beyer spoken in reference to Coleridge, "as if made for that service."

In the case of Coleridge, there exists a written admission that he was translating Wieland's *Oberon.* In the case of Charles Darwin, although he at no time mentioned Edward Blyth's ideas on natural selection,[30] interior evidence such as I produced in 1959 and which also appears in Darwin's *Second Notebook on Transmutation of Species* shows that he was fully aware of the papers which contained these ideas.

Fortunately Dr. Gerald Henderson of Brooklyn College has kindly allowed me to utilize additional evidence from his own recent unpublished investigations at the Cambridge University Library. Darwin's personal volume of *The Magazine of Natural History* of 1837 reveals annotations on Blyth's paper in Darwin's own hand. Moreover, a set of Darwin's page reminders which include Blyth's paper has been pinned to the inside of the back page. I will not encroach further upon Dr. Henderson's researches except to reiterate that Darwin knew and studied the 1837 paper he was never to mention in print. The volume at Cambridge is a presentation copy given to Darwin by Edward Charlesworth, its then editor.

Coleridge himself said: "Though [my mind] perceives the *difference* of things, yet [it] is eternally pursuing the likenesses, or, rather, that which is common [between them]."[31] The following lines were written concerning Coleridge. They could also have been written about Charles Darwin:

We have to do, in a word, with one of the most extraordinary memories of which there is record, stored with the spoils of an omnivorous reading, and endowed into the bargain with an almost uncanny power of association.[32]

J. B. Beer adds:

. . . from sources so widely separated in space and time, Coleridge had often elicited an image or a phrase which was infinitely richer than the sum of its source.[33]

Coleridge, far from defending the bathos of unconscious discovery, remarked with surprising practicality even in the midst of a commentary on sleep: "O then what visions have I had, what dreams —the Bark, the Sea . . . Stuff of Sleep & Dreams, *& yet my Reason at the Rudder.*"[34] (Italics mine, L. E.) He lists sensations, items of interest in his notebooks, just as does Darwin, but this is the stuff of poetry, not poetry itself, just as Darwin's associations of ideas and lists of sources are the stuff of science but not the completed act of reason.

As Professor Schulz has indicated, Coleridge was not engaged in séance writing. Neither, we might add, was Darwin. In his *Biographia Literaria* Coleridge remarks of poetic endeavor that much may be gleaned from travels, books, natural history, and that all may be acquired as part of the writer's trade but that these cannot substitute for the ear of genius. He does not forget Lamb's dictum that "the true poet dreams being awake."[35] The artist dominates his subject.

Similarly it was from no "sunless sea" of memoryless dream that Darwin drew his own illumination. It was more like being led across the stepping stones of a brook into an enchanted land from which the first intruder, Edward Blyth, had leaped safely back to "reality." Darwin, by contrast, a genius like Coleridge with "Reason at the Rudder," grasped immediately that he had come upon the long sought magic which would bring order amongst all his idle facts and relate them in a rational pattern. He saw a vision for which he was prepared, but which he might never have glimpsed save for his perusal of Edward Blyth. The weary world traveler had had to come all the way back to London to find his secret in an unread magazine.

The widespread popularity of the "unconscious" theory concerning Charles Darwin can readily be explained by the fact that a cult of hero worship has developed about the great biologist, such as frequently happens to a prominent innovator in any field.[36] Darlington, the British geneticist, has commented ironically: "Among scientists there is a natural feeling that one of the greatest of our figures should not be dissected, at least by one of us."[37] In the face of evidence that Darwin made unacknowledged use of material from Blyth, the theory of the unconscious is the easiest, most polite way of evading the exploration of a delicate subject. Numerous naturalists who would never treat contemporaries so gently under similar circumstances are eager to make a "sleep walker" of a scientist whose letters and notes are models of persistent conscious inquiry upon a great range of subject matter.

George Gaylord Simpson, referring to Darwin's statement in his autobiography that he "never happened to come across a single one [naturalist] who seemed to doubt about the permanence of species,"[38] and Darwin's belief that he owed no debt to his predecessors, said: "These are extraordinary statements. They cannot be literally true, yet Darwin cannot be consciously lying, and he may therefore be judged unconsciously misleading, naive, forgetful, or all three."[39]

Nora Barlow has also used the "unconscious" theory to explain her grandfather's denial that the subject of evolution was in the air. Doubtless Darwin's isolation at Down kept him from being aware of opinions from workers in other fields than his own, said Lady Barlow, "so that he unconsciously overlooked indications that belief in the permanence of species was waning."[40] Nevertheless some of the very journals he consulted contained references to the evolutionary hypothesis.

As opposed to the theory of the unconscious, it strikes one that Darwin was, in general, a keenly alert, conscious thinker, and he was so characterized by his associate, Thomas Huxley.[41] It is strange that in Darwin's *The Descent of Man* and *Variation of Animals and Plants Under Domestication*[42] all factual material drawn from Blyth was carefully listed but the two papers of Blyth concerning natural selection should be quietly ignored. It is difficult to accept this as mere coincidence. In *Variation* a footnote refers to the same volume of *The Magazine of Natural History* of 1835 in which Blyth's first paper on natural selection appeared.[43] Also a footnote in *Variation* states: "Mr. Blyth has freely communicated to me his stores of knowledge on this and all other related subjects,"[44] a somewhat cryptic and unenlightening statement. There is no possibility of doubt that Darwin used and studied *The Magazine of Natural History* in which Blyth's papers appeared.

Another odd circumstance has recently been brought to light by Gavin de Beer, even though he has refrained from any comment as to its potential significance. I refer to the recent disclosure that a number of pages are missing from Darwin's *First Notebook on Transmutation of Species*. The great importance of the *First Notebook* in tracing Darwin's early thought has been stressed by de Beer.[45] Yet fifty pages are missing from this *Notebook,* in which Darwin wrote on the first page: "All useful pages cut out. Dec. 7/1856/. (and again looked through April 21, 1873)."[46] Nothing was said about destroying the notes. As his son, Francis Darwin, pointed out in reminiscences of his father, Charles Darwin "felt the value of his notes, and had a horror of their destruction by fire. I remember, when some alarm of fire had happened, his begging me to be especially careful, adding very earnestly, that the rest of his life would be miserable if his notes and books were to be destroyed."[47]

De Beer, who reported in 1960 on these missing pages, said they had been searched for unsuccessfully in the Cambridge University Library, at Down House and the Royal College of Surgeons, and in the British Museum of Natural History. "The nature of their contents can only be surmised after a close study of the two hundred and thirty pages that remain," de Beer remarked, "and an estimate can be made of what is missing from the information and the argument."[48] Although there are some pages missing from the other *Notebooks,* it is those from the *First Notebook* that would seem to have the most bearing upon the origin of Darwin's theory, since it was begun in July 1837, before the date when he said he received his inspiration from Malthus. To reiterate my own words, I believe it significant that "Darwin opened his first notebook on the 'species question' in 1837. In January of that year Edward Blyth ventured the beginning of a second paper in which there is comment upon the principle of natural selection."[49] This comment, as we have seen, goes considerably beyond Blyth's first statement of 1835. It introduces, if briefly, the possibility of organic change. The name and work of Edward Blyth are not noted in the existing portion of the *First Notebook,* although they do appear in the *Second.*

"The idea of natural selection, so far as can be seen from the extant portions of the *Notebooks,* seems to have occurred to Darwin as a combination of the effects on him of the facts of variation, adaptation, and extinction,"[50] observed de Beer. Actually the missing fifty pages could have contained a great deal of information extending to Blyth's own views on these subjects. De Beer has avoided the suggestion that this fragmentary document may have contained more detailed references to Blyth's works. Since these pages compose the first part of the diary, their disappearance, taken with other evidence, cannot fail to hint of a genuinely "missing link" in the story of Natural Selection.

Much has been made by some of Darwin's defenders of his poor memory, though others have maintained it was prodigious. Huxley, who certainly knew him well, contended that Darwin had "a great memory."[51] Darwin himself remarked of his memory, that it "suffices to make me cautious by vaguely telling me that I have observed or read something opposed to the conclusion which I am drawing, or on the other hand in favour of it; *and after a time I can generally recollect where to search for my authority.*"[52] (Italics mine, L. E.)

It is also true, however, that Darwin did not have to depend upon memory, as he was a remarkably methodical man in his work. In discussing his work habits he mentioned the fact that since in several of his books he had used extensively facts observed by others, he kept

from thirty to forty large portfolios, in cabinets with labelled shelves, into which I can at once put a detached reference or memorandum. I have bought many books, and at their ends I make an index of all the facts that concern my work; or, if the book is not my own, write out a separate abstract, and of such abstracts I have a large drawer full. Before beginning on any subject I look to all the short indexes and make a general and classified index, and by taking the one or more proper portfolios I have all the information collected during my life ready for use.[53]

One of Darwin's own statements, to which I have previously referred, strikes one as remarkably illuminating. In regard to an incidental matter of priority upon another biological matter which had occupied his attention briefly, he wrote in his autobiography: "It is clear that I failed to impress my readers; and he who succeeds in doing so deserves, in my opinion, all the credit."[54]

This statement is curiously revelatory to the perceptive student of character. There is involved in it a strange indifference to historical priority by a man in actuality highly sensitive on this score so far as his own great generalization was concerned. Was Charles Darwin engaged in psychologically justifying a philosophy which permitted him to dismiss forerunners from whom he had drawn inspiration— men like his friend, "poor Blyth,"[55] who "failed to impress" and therefore deserved no recognition from the world? One is forced to reflect upon this possibility, which has even been seized upon and brought forward by later writers as a justification of Darwin's attitude toward his predecessors.

There will always be an ineluctable mystery concerning the origin of the theory of Natural Selection, just as there will always be a shadowy web surrounding the real Charles Darwin, a web unseen but as real as the black cape in which we see him enveloped in a photograph taken of him on the verandah at Down at the age of seventy-two. One of Darwin's most ardent supporters, George Gaylord Simpson, states with perceptive acuteness:

The mystery persists. The man is not really explained, his inner adventures are not fully revealed in his own autobiography, in the family biography by Francis Darwin, or in the many other biographical sketches and books. There will always be something hidden, as there is in every life. . . .[56]

It seems to be an inescapable conclusion that the mystery lies concealed in the remarkable similarity between Coleridge, the "library cormorant," as he chose to describe himself, and Darwin, a similar cormorant observer of nature and of nature recorded in books. Each man had his catalyzer and both were reticent enough that it has taken over a century to find the catalyzer.

REFERENCES

1. Max Schulz, *The Poetic Voices of Coleridge* (Detroit, Mich., 1963), p. 5.

2. Gavin de Beer (ed.), "Some Unpublished Letters of Charles Darwin," *Notes and Records of the Royal Society of London*, Vol. 14, No. 1 (June 1959), p. 53.

3. Nora Barlow (ed.), *The Autobiography of Charles Darwin, 1809-1882* (London, 1958), p. 125.

4. Loren Eiseley, "Charles Darwin, Edward Blyth, and the Theory of Natural Selection," *Proceedings of the American Philosophical Society*, Vol. 103, No. 1 (February 1959), pp. 94-158.

5. Edward Blyth, "An Attempt to classify the 'Varieties' of Animals, with Observations on the marked Seasonal and other Changes which naturally take place in various British Species, and which do not constitute Varieties," *The Magazine of Natural History*, Vol. 8 (1835), pp. 40-53: Art. IV. "On the Psychological Distinctions between Man and all other Animals; and the consequent Diversity of Human Influence over the inferior Ranks of Creation, from any mutual and reciprocal Influence exercised among the Latter," *ibid.*, Vol. 1 (n.s.) (1837), pp. 1-9: Art. I; pp. 77-85: Art. IV; pp. 131-141: Art. VI.

6. De Beer (ed.), "Darwin's Notebooks on Transmutation of Species," *Bulletin of the British Museum (Natural History)*, Historical Series, Vol. 2, Nos. 2-5 (1960).

7. *Ibid., Second Notebook,* Part II, Vol. 2, No. 3, p. 106.

8. Blyth, "On Psychological Distinctions," etc. (1837), p. 147: Art. VI.°

9. De Beer, Introduction to *First Notebook,* Part I, Vol. 2, No. 2, p. 36.

10. De Beer, *Charles Darwin: Evolution by Natural Selection* (New York, 1964), p. 102.

11. George Wald, "Innovation in Biology," *Scientific American,* Vol. 199, No. 3 (September 1958), p. 100.

12. Theodosius Dobzhansky, "Blyth, Darwin, and Natural Selection," *The American Naturalist,* Vol. 93, No. 870 (May-June 1959), p. 204.

13. *Ibid.,* p. 205.

14. When Dr. Dobzhansky proposed his theory in *The American Naturalist* he very graciously asked me if I would care to make a response. At the time, travel and administrative duties prevented me from accepting Dr. Dobzhansky's invitation. The present article exploring this subject was really stimulated by his generosity, and I am very glad to acknowledge this fact.

15. Dobzhansky, p. 205.

16. *Ibid.*

17. *Ibid.,* p. 206.

18. There is a failure here, however, to distinguish between creativity in the arts and sciences and its traditional modes of expression. The poet is not called upon to footnote or to give the history of his ideas. The scientist by tradition honors and cites the significance of his precursors.

19. Schulz, p. 7.

20. John Livingston Lowes, *The Road to Xanadu* (Boston, 1927), pp. 59-60.

21. Werner W. Beyer, *The Enchanted Forest* (New York, 1963), p. 113.

22. *Ibid.,* p. 49.

23. *Ibid.,* p. 47.

24. *Ibid.,* p. 113.

25. *Ibid.,* p. 66, citing R. C. Bald, "Coleridge and *The Ancient Mariner,*" *Nineteenth-century Studies* (Ithaca, N. Y., 1940).

26. *Ibid.,* p. 75.

27. Lowes, p. 228.

28. Beyer, p. 186.

° All references to articles by Edward Blyth in this paper will refer to page numbers as reprinted in *Proceedings of The American Philosophical Society,* Vol. 103, No. 1 (February 1959).

29. Barlow, *Autobiography*, p. 99.

30. He was able, however, to refer to everything else about Blyth's work in detail.

31. S. T. Coleridge, *Anima Poetae*, ed. by E. H. Coleridge (London, 1895), pp. 87-88.

32. Lowes, p. 43.

33. J. B. Beer, *Coleridge the Visionary* (New York: Collier Books, 1962), p. 185.

34. S. T. Coleridge, Notebook XVI, 6–13 December 1803.

35. Schulz, p. 104, citing Lamb.

36. A parallel is seen in the case of Coleridge. A suggestion of plagiarism made by De Quincey concerning his friend Coleridge brought several critical replies. De Quincey, says John Metcalf, was accused of "bad taste, not to say treachery." One Coleridge enthusiast even declared that "One might as well . . . accuse the bee of theft for gathering treasures from many flowers." Sara Coleridge, while admitting her father's plagiarism, pleaded that "if he took, he gave." (See John Metcalf, *De Quincey: A Portrait* [New York, 1963], p. 115.)

37. C. D. Darlington, *Darwin's Place in History* (Oxford, 1959), p. 57.

38. Barlow, *Autobiography*, p. 124.

39. George Gaylord Simpson, review of *The Autobiography of Charles Darwin, 1809-1882*, ed. by Nora Barlow, *Scientific American*, Vol. 199, No. 2 (August 1958), p. 119.

40. Barlow, *Autobiography*, p. 153.

41. Leonard Huxley (ed.), *Life and Letters of Thomas Henry Huxley* (2 vols.; New York, 1902), Vol. II, p. 42.

42. Material for *Variation* was drawn from Darwin's original "big book" of the *Origin*.

43. Charles Darwin, *Variation of Animals and Plants Under Domestication*, 1st authorized American edition (2 vols.; New York, 1868), Vol. I, pp. 335-336, n. 8.

44. *Ibid.*, Vol. I, p. 164, n. 1.

45. De Beer, Introduction to *First Notebook*, p. 26.

46. De Beer, *First Notebook*, p. 41.

47. Francis Darwin (ed.), *The Life and Letters of Charles Darwin* (2 vols.; New York, 1959), Vol. I, p. 129.

48. De Beer, Introduction, *First Notebook*, p. 26.

49. Eiseley, p. 99.

50. De Beer, Introduction to *Third Notebook*, Part III, Vol. II, No. 4, p. 126.

51. Huxley, Vol. II, p. 42.

52. Darwin, *Life and Letters*, Vol. I, p. 82.

53. *Ibid.*, p. 80.

54. Barlow, *Autobiography*, p. 125.

55. Darwin, *Life and Letters*, Vol. II, p. 109.

56. Simpson, p. 122.

A version of this article appeared originally in *The Library Chronicle*, published by the University of Pennsylvania, Philadelphia, Vol. XXXI, No. 1 (Winter 1965).

E. PAUL TORRANCE

Scientific Views of Creativity and Factors Affecting its Growth

Definitions of Creativity

IF CREATIVITY and its growth are to be viewed scientifically, creativity must be defined in a way that permits objective observation and measurement and is compatible with common and historical usage. At the time I began a program of research concerned with factors affecting creative growth, I was unable to find such a definition for which there was any sort of consensus.

Some definitions are formulated in terms of a product (invention and discovery, for example); others, in terms of a process, a kind of person, or a set of conditions. The production of something new (to the individual or to the culture) is included in almost all of these definitions. Some writers have defined creativity as being different from conformity and as requiring non-habitual rather than habitual behavior. Some specify that creative contributions must be true, generalizable, and surprising in view of what existed at the time of the discovery. Some scholars insist that the term "creative" be reserved for very rare and particularized kinds of ability, while others apply the term to a general creative ability possessed to some degree by all essentially healthy individuals. Others have suggested that we think in terms of different levels of creativity, ranging from simple expressive creativity, where skills and the quality of the product are unimportant, as in the spontaneous drawings of children, to a kind of creativity that is manifested in an entirely new principle or assumption around which completely new developments flourish.

On the basis of an analysis of the diverse ways of defining creativity and what I consider the requirements of a definition for keeping a program of research on factors affecting creative growth in context, I defined creativity as the process of becoming sensitive to problems, deficiencies, gaps in knowledge, missing elements, disharmonies, and so on; identifying the difficulty; searching for solutions, making guesses, or formulating hypotheses about the deficiencies; testing and retesting these hypotheses and possibly modifying and retesting them; and finally communicating the results. This definition describes a natural human process. Strong human needs are involved at each stage. If we sense some incompleteness or disharmony, tension is aroused. We are uncomfortable and want to relieve the tension. Since habitual ways of behaving are inadequate, we begin trying to avoid the commonplace and obvious (but incorrect) solutions by investigating, diagnosing, manipulating, and making guesses or estimates. Until the guesses or hypotheses have been tested, modified, and retested, we are still uncomfortable. The tension is unrelieved, however, until we tell somebody of our discovery.

There are many other reasons for favoring this definition. It enables us to begin defining operationally the kinds of abilities, mental functioning, and personality characteristics that facilitate or inhibit the process. It provides an approach for specifying the kinds of products that result from the process, the kinds of persons who can engage most successfully in the process, and the conditions that facilitate the process. The definition also seems to be in harmony with historical usage and equally applicable in scientific, literary, dramatic, and interpersonal creativity. Some scholars, however, disagree with my definition, and I shall review a few of their objections.

Ausubel[1] objects to the definition on the grounds that it does not distinguish between creativity as a highly particularized and substantive capacity and as a generalized constellation of intellectual abilities, personality variables, and problem-solving traits. He states that he does not deny the existence of general creative abilities but that such abilities do not constitute the essence of creativity. When one tries to spell out the abilities involved in the creative process as I have defined it, he obtains what Ausubel refers to as "a generalized constellation of intellectual abilities, personality variables, and problem-solving traits." This does not mean that this constellation constitutes the essence of even the process as I have defined it. A high degree of these abilities (usually designated as fluency, flexibility, originality, and ability to sense deficiencies, elaborate, and redefine) does not guarantee that the possessor will behave in a highly creative manner. A high level of these abilities, however, increases a person's chances of behaving creatively, and I believe that the validation studies to be summarized later support this contention.

There is considerable historical precedent for referring to creative abilities and tendencies as "a constellation of general abilities, personality variables, and problem-solving traits," rather than as a particularized and substantive capacity. Numerous scholars of the past have referred to creativity as a constellation of generalized abilities that may be manifested in particular ways depending upon interests, sensory deficiencies or acuities, and opportunity. For example, Burnham in 1892 pointed out that since Kant's *Critique of Pure Reason* it has been customary to distinguish between reproductive imagination and creative productive imagination. There was a recognition that the mental abilities involved in remembering and reproducing information are different from those brought into play in recombining original impressions to produce new wholes. It is especially interesting that Burnham[2] saw creative imagination as limited by reproductive imagination but as varying in degree rather than in kind. It was the reproductive imagination or memory that is particularized, according to him. He also maintained that "all children, unless they be idiots, have productive or creative imagination in some measure."

There are also objections[3] that I have no right to use the term "creative" outside such fields as art, music, and writing. Kreuter and Kreuter charge that the orientation of my work has clearly been toward the recognition and development of scientific creativity and that even my definition shows this concern. My research associates have included artists, musicians, creative writers, philosophers, theologians, psychologists, sociologists, and anthropologists, and we have contributed to the professional literature in these and other fields. In our experimental work, we have actually included more activities related to art, creative writing, creative dance, and creative music than to science. Whenever I have talked with creative artists and writers about what happens to them when they are engaged in the creative process and how they guide the creative behavior of their students, the definition I have given seems to fit their creativity as well as it does that of the creative scientist.

Scientific investigators during the early part of this century generally championed the concept of a non-particularized, content-free mental creativity. Spearman, for example, asserted that "the power of the human mind to create new content—by transferring relations and thereby generating new correlates—extends its sphere not only to representation of ideas, but also to fully sensuous presentations, such as are given in ordinary seeing, hearing, touching, and the like, of every one of us."[4]

Simpson[5] advanced similar arguments in connection with his test of creative imagination. He defined creative ability as the initiative that one manifests by his power to break away from the usual sequence of thought. He believed that we should be concerned with identifying the searching, combining, synthetic type of mind and argued, as I have, that we should add tests of creative thinking ability to traditional tests of intelligence. He pointed out that intelligence tests call for reproductive kinds of abilities and do not evaluate what he termed "a vital creative energy." Noting that his test deals primarily with a visual imagery stimulus to creative action, Simpson conceded that some people would probably respond more creatively to an auditory stimulus. He argued, however, that in his test one gets an image of some object that he wishes to draw, but that the whole thinking process is involved in forming this image or association of neurograms. He held that visual imagery usually expands into scraps of kinesthesias, auditory imagery, and personal, organic, or verbal references.

Another objection to my definition of creativity is that it does not distinguish between creativity or creative problem-solving and other types of problem-solving. Some have maintained that it equates creativity with all thinking. It is one of the limitations of a brief verbal definition that there must be implicit distinctions and that only a few distinctions can be made explicit. Certainly implicit in my definition are the distinctions usually made by other scholars between creative thinking and problem-solving. Generally, creative thinking has been treated as one special kind of problem-solving. Newell, Shaw, and Simon state that problem-solving may be called creative "to the extent that one or more of the following conditions are satisfied:

1. The product of the thinking has novelty and value (either for the thinker or for his culture).

2. The thinking is unconventional, in a sense that it requires modification or rejection of previously accepted ideas.

3. The thinking requires high motivation and persistence, taking place either over a considerable span of time (continuously or intermittently) or at high intensity.

4. The problem as initially posed was vague and undefined, so that part of the task was to formulate the problem itself."[6]

Identifying Creative Ability or Potential

If one accepts the definition of creativity that I have offered, it becomes possible to recognize creative behavior, creative thinking abilities, and creative potential both through test and non-test procedures. How it is done will depend in large degree upon the reasons for wanting to recognize creativity, who is attempting to do so, and what professional resources are available. From the standpoint of the teacher and counselor, it would seem important to recognize those kinds of potential that make a difference in the way persons should be taught and guided. A major reason for my interest in developing measures of the creative thinking abilities is that I believe that such instruments can provide one useful basis for making instruction different for different students. Since abilities constitute, at least to some extent, the basis of needs and motivations, knowledge about a person's creative thinking abilities frequently provides clues about differential preferences for ways of learning.

The history of the development of tests of creative thinking, creative imagination, originality, and the like is a long and interesting one.[7] Although there has been a variety of promising developments extending over at least the past seventy-five years, there has been so little sustained interest and support for them that there is not yet on the market a standardized battery of tests of creative thinking. During the past few years, Guilford[8] has begun to make available through commercial channels some of his tests of divergent thinking, but it is not yet certain how low on the educational ladder these can be extended. Drawing upon Guilford's work for clues concerning task dimensions and scoring criteria, my associates and I believe that we are approaching a point where we can make available for experimental use alternate batteries of tests for use from kindergarten through graduate school.

These tests represent one rather sharp departure from the factor-type tests developed by Guilford and his associates. We made deliberate attempts to construct test tasks that would be models of the creative process, each involving different kinds of thinking and each contributing something unique to the batteries under development. Test tasks are thus fairly complex and have features that make use of what we know about the nature of the creative thinking processes, the qualities of creative products, and creative personalities.

Even a minimal description of the test tasks in these batteries, their objectives, and the results accruing from their use would require many times the space allotted to this paper. A brief description of some of the test tasks, their administration, and scoring, however, should show how the tests are related to the definition already offered and to the factors that affect creative growth.

One of the clearest and most straightforward models is found in the Ask-and-Guess Test of which there are several forms. In all forms, subjects are shown a picture (Mother Goose prints for children and certain professional groups, pictures similar to those used in the Thematic Apperception Test for nurses, a picture of boys starting a small business for salesmen, and so forth) and given the following series of instructions:

The next three tasks will give you a chance to see how good you are at asking questions to find out things that you do not know and in making guesses about possible causes and consequences of events. Look at the picture. What is happening? What can you tell for sure? What do you need to know to understand what is happening, what caused it to happen, and what will be the result?

Young children are asked to dictate their responses to an adult and older children and adults are asked to write theirs. In the written version, the following instructions are given for the first of the three tasks:

On this page, write out all of the questions you can think of about the picture on the page before this one. Ask all of the questions you would need to know for sure what is happening. Do not ask questions that can be answered just by looking at the drawing.

After five minutes, subjects are given the following instructions for the second task (Guessing Causes):

In the spaces below, list as many possible causes as you can of the action shown in the picture. You may use things that might have happened just before the event in the picture or something that happened a long time ago that made the event happen. Make as many guesses as you can. Do not be afraid to guess.

After another five minutes, the following instructions are given for the third task (Guessing Consequences):

In the spaces below, list as many possibilities as you can of what might happen as a result of what is taking place in the picture. You may use things that might happen right afterwards or things that might happen as a result long afterwards in the future. Make as many guesses as you can. Do not be afraid to guess.

The first task is designed to reveal the subject's ability to sense what he cannot find out from looking at the picture and to ask questions that will enable him to fill in the gaps in his knowledge. The second and third tasks are designed to reveal the subject's ability to formulate hypotheses concerning cause and effect. The number of relevant responses produced by a subject yields one measure of ideational fluency. The number of shifts in thinking or number of different categories of questions, causes, or consequences gives one measure of flexibility. The statistical infrequency of these questions, causes, or consequences or the extent to which the response represents a mental leap or departure from the obvious and commonplace gives one measure of originality. The detail and specificity incorporated into the questions and hypotheses provide one measure of ability to elaborate.

In another task, subjects are asked to produce unusual or provocative questions about common objects such as tin cans, cardboard boxes, or ice. Subjects are encouraged to ask questions that lead to a variety of different answers and that might arouse interest and curiosity in others concerning the object.

The Product Improvement Task calls for the production of clever, interesting, and unusual ways of changing a toy stuffed animal (for example, a toy dog, monkey, elephant, or kangaroo) so that 'it will be more interesting for children to play with. The Unusual Uses Test calls for interesting and unusual uses of common objects such as tin cans, cardboard boxes, and books. The Just Suppose Test presents the subject with an improbable situation and asks him to "just suppose" that the situation happened and to think of all of the things that might occur as a result. The improbable situations include such things as:

> Just suppose when it was raining all the rain drops stood still in the air and wouldn't move—and they were solid.
> Just suppose someone got caught in a big soap bubble and couldn't get out.

Each "Just Suppose" is accompanied by an interesting drawing depicting the improbable situation.

The Imaginative Stories Test calls for writing imaginative stories about animals and people having some divergent characteristic. Subjects are asked to select from one of a set of ten titles such as:

> The Flying Monkey.
> The Lion That Won't Roar.
> The Man Who Cries.
> The Woman Who Can But Won't Talk.

The Sounds and Images Test asks the subject to produce imaginative and original images suggested by each of a series of four sound effects, ranging from a familiar and well-organized sound effect to one consisting of six rather strange and relatively unrelated sounds. The four-sound series is presented three times, and each time the subject is asked to stretch his imagination further.

Each of the tasks is based on a rationale developed from some research finding concerning the nature of the creative process, the creative personality, or the conditions necessary for creative achievement. The tasks are designed to involve as many different aspects of verbal creative functioning as possible. Most of the tasks are evaluated for fluency (number of different relevant ideas), flexibility (number of shifts in thinking or different categories of response), originality (number of statistically infrequent responses that show creative intellectual energy), and elaboration (number of different ideas used in working out the details of an idea).

Although a variety of figural test tasks have been developed, the standardized batteries consist of three tasks, each designed to tap a somewhat different aspect of creative functioning. The Picture Construction Test is accompanied by the following instructions:

At the bottom of this page is a piece of colored paper in the form of a curved shape. Think of a picture or an object in which this form would be an important part. Then lift up the piece of colored paper and stick it wherever you want it on the next page, just like you would a postage stamp. Then add lines with pencil or crayon to make your picture.

Try to think of a picture that no one else will think of. Keep adding new ideas to your first idea to make it tell as interesting and as exciting a story as you can.

When you have completed your picture, think up a name or title for it and write it at the bottom of the page in the space provided. Make your title as clever and unusual as possible. Use it to help tell your story.

This, as well as the other two figural tasks, can be administered at all educational levels from kindergarten to graduate school and to various occupational groups. It is a task to which kindergarteners can respond in groups and one which provides sufficient encouragement to regression to be useful with graduate students and other adults. In each battery a different shape (such as a tear drop or jelly bean) is used as the stimulus object.

The stimulus material for the Figure Completion Test consists of ten incomplete figures and is accompanied by the following instructions:

By adding lines to figures on this and the next page, you can sketch some interesting objects or pictures. Again, try to think of some picture or object that no one else will think of. Try to make it tell as complete and as interesting a story as you can by adding to and building up your first idea. Make up a title for each of your drawings and write it at the bottom of each block next to the number of the figure.

The Repeated Closed Figures Test consists of two pages of closed figures (circles, squares, triangles, and so on). The instructions for the Circles version of this test are as follows:

In ten minutes see how many objects or pictures you can make from the circles below and on the next page. The circles should be the main part of whatever you make. With pencil or crayon add lines to the circles to complete your picture. You can place marks inside the circles, on the circles, and outside the circles—wherever you want to in order to make your picture. Try to think of things that no one else will think of. Make as many different pictures or objects as you can and put as many ideas as you can in each one. Make them tell as complete and as interesting a story as you can. Add names or titles in the spaces provided.

This triad of test tasks in a sense represents three different aspects of creativity or three different creative tendencies. The Incomplete Figures task calls into play the tendency toward structuring and integrating. The incomplete figures create tension in the beholder who must control this tension long enough to make the mental leap necessary to get away from the obvious and commonplace. Failure to delay gratification usually results in the premature closure of the incomplete figures and an obvious or commonplace response. The invitation to "make the drawing tell a story" is designed to motivate elaboration and the further filling in of gaps. The Circles Test, as well as other closed figures tasks, brings into play the tendency toward disruption of structure in order to create something new. The repetition of a single stimulus requires an ability to return to the same stimulus again and again and perceive it in a different way. The Picture Construction Test sets in motion the tendency toward finding a purpose for something that has no definite purpose and to elaborate it in such a way that the purpose is achieved. Discoveries and their applications may take place in two major ways: (1) there may be deliberate attempts to discover a creative solution to a problem or (2) some discovery may occur and the discoverer sets out to see what problems the discovery will solve. Theoretically, the Picture Construction Test symbolizes the latter.

These tasks tend to discriminate between the good elaborators and the productive original thinkers. Some subjects produce a large number of very original ideas but fail to elaborate any of them very well; some produce very few ideas of any kind but make them very elaborate or "fancy"; still others produce a large number of very commonplace ideas with little elaboration.

Thus, it is seen that we have tried deliberately to base the test stimuli, the test tasks, instructions, and scoring procedures on the best that we know from research about creativity. The same test tasks, in most instances, have been administered at all educational levels. This has made it possible to determine whether or not children and young people identified as "creative" behave in ways similar to the ways in which eminent creative people of the past behaved when they were children and young people. It also enables us to determine whether or not adults identified today as relatively creative on the basis of outside criteria behave in ways that can be called "creative" on the basis of test scores. In general, the evidence has been rather positive in spite of the complexities introduced by problems of motivation, unfavorable conditions, and the difficulties of conducting well-controlled studies. Much of this evidence has been summarized in *Guiding Creative Talent* and in *Rewarding Creative Behavior*.[9] Only the briefest review is possible here.

In observational studies,[10] we found that children scoring high on tests of creative thinking initiated a larger number of ideas, produced more original ideas, and gave more explanations of the workings of unfamiliar science toys than did their less creative peers when placed in five-person groups. When matched for intelligence, sex, race, and teacher, the most creative children in forty-six classrooms from grades one through six more frequently than their controls had reputations for having wild and fantastic ideas, produced drawings and other products judged to be original, and produced work characterized by humor, playfulness, relative lack of rigidity, and relaxation. Weisberg and Springer[11] studied a sample of gifted (high IQ) fourth-grade pupils. In comparison with those who made the lower test scores those who made the higher scores were rated significantly higher on strength of self-image, ease of early recall of life experiences, humor, availability of Oedipal anxiety, and even ego development. On the Rorschach Ink Blots, they showed a tendency toward unconventional responses, unreal percepts, and fanciful and imaginative treatment of the blots. Their performance was described as being both more sensitive and more independent than that of their less creative peers. Among sixth-grade children, Fleming and Weintraub[12] found significant negative relationships between the measures of originality, fluency, and flexibility and measures of rigidity. Yamamoto[13] found correlations of around .50 between creativity test scores and a composite measure of originality based on creative writings.

Studies with adults have also been encouraging. In my own graduate classes, I have found rather consistently that those who achieve high scores on the tests of creative thinking develop original ideas in the content area of the course and make more creative applications of knowledge than do their less creative peers. Hansen and I found that the more creative business education teachers asked more provocative questions, more self-involving questions, and more divergent ones than their less creative peers. Hansen found a number of other significant differences between her high and low creative teachers, showing that the more creative teachers, as identified by the tests, behaved more creatively in the classroom as judged by detailed classroom observations. Blockhus[14] found that the students of the more creative business education teachers showed more growth in originality during a semester than did the pupils of the less creative ones. Sommers[15] found that students carefully identified by college industrial arts instructors as creative scored significantly higher on the tests of creative thinking than did their less creative peers. Wallace[16] found that saleswomen ranking in the upper third on sales in a large department store scored significantly higher on tests of creative thinking than did their peers ranking in the lower third. He also found that the more creative women had tended to gravitate to those departments judged by personnel managers as requiring more creativity. Wallace[17] also found that measures of originality and fluency differentiated the several echelons of personnel in a large national sales organization. The measures of flexibility and elaboration failed to differentiate the highest echelon of sales executives from the lower groups but differentiated within the various lower levels.

Some studies have shown that the measures described herein are positively related to various kinds of school achievement, while others have shown that such measures are unrelated or negatively related to measures of school achievement. A careful examination of these studies suggests that methods of assessing school achievement and methods of instruction may both be important factors in creative growth.

Bentley[18] found the following set of correlation coefficients for four different measures of achievement in a graduate class of 110 students in educational psychology and a composite measure of creative thinking ability based on a battery of the Minnesota tests and the Miller Analogies Test, an instrument commonly used in graduate school admission procedures:

Achievement Measure	Creativity	Miller's
Recognition (multiple-choice test)	.03	.47
Memory (completion and short-answer test)	.11	.41
Productive Thinking (creative applications)	.53	.37
Evaluation and Judgment (decision making)	.38	.27

If one examines closely the research concerning the interaction between different kinds of abilities and different methods of instruction, an interesting picture unfolds.[19] When knowledge is obtained by authority, a measure of mental age or intelligence is a better predictor of achievement than measures of originality, fluency, and the like. When knowledge is obtained in creative ways, for example by discovery or experimentation, the measures of originality, fluency, and the like seem to be better predictors than scores on intelligence tests. More will be said about these studies in the final section of this paper.

Checklists of activities done on one's own, checklists of creative achievements, biographical or life experience inventories, an inventory of personal-social motivations, a personality checklist, and a variety of other non-aptitude measures also promise to be useful. Other investigators[20] have reported promising results from such well-known instruments as Strong's Vocational Interest Blank, the Allport-Vernon-Lindzey Study of Values, the Myers-Briggs Type Indicator, the California Psychological Inventory, the Barron-Welsh Art Scale, the Thematic Apperception Test, and biographical inventories.

Educators need not be dependent upon tests for identifying creative potential among students, even though tests may make them aware of potentialities that would otherwise be missed. Non-test indicators may be obtained both in regular classroom activities and by creating classroom situations especially designed to evoke creative behavior. A great variety of suggestions concerning these non-test indicators has been offered by Taylor,[21] Torrance,[22] and others. One cannot identify even outstanding jumping ability if he depends solely upon observations of how high individuals just happen to jump in ordinary activities. In order to identify persons of outstanding jumping ability, one must create situations that motivate and/or require jumping. The analogy seems appropriate regarding the identification of creative talent.

Factors Affecting Creative Growth

Many complain that we do not yet know enough about the factors affecting creative growth. In my opinion, we have known enough about these factors since the time of Socrates and Plato to do a far better job of creative education than is commonly done. Socrates knew that it was important to ask provocative questions and to encourage natural ways of learning. He knew that it was not enough to ask questions that call only for the reproduction of what has been learned. He knew that thinking is a skill that is developed through practice and that it is important to ask questions that require the learner to do something with what he learns—to evaluate it, produce new ideas from it, and recombine it in new ways. Plato knew that "what is honored in a country will be cultivated there." He knew that it was important for educators to be aware of the potentialities of students and that potentialities are rarely discovered under a discipline that is excessively harsh and coercive. He said, "Do not train boys to learning by force or harshness; but direct them to it by what amuses their minds, so that you may be the better able to discover with accuracy the peculiar bent of the genius of each."

Some readers may wonder why I have chosen to place so much emphasis on the identification of creative potentiality and the measurement of what I have called the creative thinking abilities. Scientific studies of factors that affect creative growth require measurement, and the rationale of the test tasks, test task instructions, and methods of assessing or scoring test responses helps to elaborate my definition of creativity and provides a wealth of clues concerning the factors that assess creative growth. More important, however, is the conviction that a teacher must usually recognize creative potentiality in a child or young person before he is willing to permit him to learn in a non-habitual or creative way. On one occasion, I asked a class of two hundred students, including many experienced teachers, to describe some instance in which they had permitted or encouraged a student to learn in a creative way and had then observed that the experience made an important difference in the achievement and behavior of the student. Eighty-two per cent of them were able to recall such an incident, and a content analysis of their responses showed that in eighty-six per cent of the incidents the recognition of a creative potentiality was crucial to the teacher's willingness to permit or encourage such activity.

Although there are certainly many gaps in knowledge concerning the factors that affect creative growth, there is a great variety of research findings that give useful guidance. It would be impossible here even to list these findings. I have collected about thirty related studies conducted by my associates and me in *Rewarding Creative Behavior: Experiments in Classroom Creativity.* These studies help to delineate the roles in creative growth of such factors as ways of rewarding creative behavior (for example, by being respectful of unusual and provocative questions and of unusual ideas), creative motivations or attitudes of the teacher, creative activities and opportunities for practicing skills in creative thinking, differential rewards for boys and girls, differential rewards for originality, competition, unevaluated practice, creative rather than critical peer-evaluated practice, evaluative discussions about creative productions, peer pressures in homogeneous and heterogeneous groups, trouble-shooting evaluation, and helping children and young people value their own ideas. Attention is also given to differences in the ways different cultures encourage and discourage characteristics associated with the creative personality.

I am asked frequently if these and other recent studies advance us any further in the direction of a more creative kind of education than did Progressive Education. Some observers even assert that there is no difference between what I have called creative ways of learning and Progressive Education. Progressive Education aroused so much controversy and still engenders such strong negative reactions that the label of Progressive Education is still used to condemn almost all educational innovations. If one examines what we have learned during the ten years since the dissolution of the Progressive Education Association in 1955, it should become evident that it is possible for us to advance beyond the major precepts of Progressive Education and to come closer to achieving the American dream of a kind of education that will give every child a chance to grow and to achieve his potentialities.

It is an oversimplification but it may be said that Progressive Education rested its case on the following six precepts:

1. Individual differences among children must be recognized.
2. We learn best by doing and by having a vital interest in what we are doing.

3. Education is a continuous reconstruction of living experience that goes beyond the four walls of the classroom.
4. The classroom should be a laboratory for democracy.
5. Social goals, as well as intellectual goals, are important.
6. A child must be taught to think critically rather than to accept blindly.[23]

On the basis of what we have learned during recent years about the human mind and its functioning, mental abilities and their development, and the interaction of mental abilities and ways of learning and teaching, all of these precepts seem valid as far as they go, but they do not go far enough. Let us take, for example, the precept that "individual differences among children must be recognized." This precept cannot be of great help unless we know *what* individual differences are important in individualizing instruction and *what* individual differences in mental functioning, motivation, and personality are brought into play in various ways of learning. What we have learned during the past ten years has enabled us to remove some of the uncertainty experienced by educational researchers of the 1920's and 1930's.

We need no longer be puzzled by McConnell's finding in 1934 that mental age as measured by an intelligence test is more highly related to achievement in second-grade arithmetic when taught by authoritative identification than when taught by the methods of discovery advocated by many Progressive Educators. Hutchinson in 1963 in a study involving learning in junior-high-school social studies also found that, under traditional authoritarian teaching, there is a statistically significant positive correlation between mental age and achievement but not between measures of creative thinking and achievement. In experimental conditions offering considerable opportunities for learning in creative ways the reverse was true. In another 1963 study involving fifth-grade children using programed instruction in language arts, Gotkin and Massa found significant negative relationships between measures of creative thinking and achievement. A year earlier, Stolurow had found higher positive correlations between measures of originality and achievement than between mental age and achievement with programed materials in mathematics and statistics. The difference was that Gotkin and Massa used programed materials that permitted only tiny mental leaps and gave little opportunity for making, identifying, and correcting errors, while Stolurow's programed materials emphasized a trouble-shooting or hypothesizing approach that builds specific but multiple associations to a stimulus.

In 1964 MacDonald and Raths found that highly creative children are more productive on frustrating tasks than are less creative children. Furthermore, they enjoy such tasks more than their less creative peers do. The least creative children are less productive in open tasks, and the most creative ones react less favorably to closed tasks. Thus, pupils of varying levels of creative thinking ability react differently to different kinds of curriculum tasks and are possibly best taught by varying procedures.

To me, by far the most exciting insight that has come from our research is that different kinds of children learn best when given opportunities to learn in ways best suited to their motivations and abilities. Whenever teachers change their ways of teaching in significant ways, a different group of learners become the stars or high achievers. This advance has far-reaching implications for educating a larger number of people to a higher level and for achieving a higher level of dignity and mental health in our society.

Regarding the second precept that "we learn best by doing and by having a vital interest in what we are doing," we recognize now that people do not learn automatically by doing no matter how interested they are. This type of learning requires sensitive and alert guidance and direction. Children must be taught the skills of inquiry and research—the spirit and skills of historiography, the concepts and skills of descriptive and experimental research. Curiosity and creative needs are strong enough and universal enough to make creative ways of learning useful for all individuals, but creative ways of learning should not be an exclusive way of learning for all children nor for any single child, even though he may prefer learning in creative ways and learn little when we insist that he learn exclusively by authority.

I see no real quarrel with the third precept that "education is a continuous reconstruction of living experience and goes beyond the four walls of the classroom." From an understanding of the creative process, we recognize that one thing must be permitted to lead to another. To accept such a precept requires a great deal of courage on the part of the teacher. Both teachers and pupils have to learn to think in terms of possible consequences of this "continuous reconstruction of living experiences beyond the four walls of the classroom." The same threats to security arise when schools accept the fourth and fifth precepts that the classroom should be a laboratory for democracy and that social goals, as well as intellectual goals, are important.

From the accumulated experiences of many teachers, it seems clear that when these precepts are accepted, learning becomes alive, much creative behavior occurs, and there is cooperation with parents and action by them. It is also clear that the acceptance of these precepts can be very threatening to the security of the teacher and calls not only for courage but for skills in group dynamics, creative problem-solving, and strategies for coping with change and stress. We have now accumulated enough knowledge about these areas to make these precepts more meaningful than they were in the heyday of Progressive Education.

We are also beginning to understand the inadequacies of the sixth precept that "a child must be taught to think critically rather than to accept blindly." We know now that it is not enough to be able to criticize the ideas of others. It is necessary that students be able to produce ideas of their own, to be critical of their own ideas, and to use tests that keep them from deceiving themselves. Furthermore, we have learned that in the production of ideas it is sometimes necessary to suspend judgment temporarily to avoid undue interruptions in our thinking. After ideas have accumulated, it is then necessary to formulate criteria for judging these ideas and making decisions. If knowledge is to be used constructively in solving problems creatively, the learner must have a constructive, though not altogether uncritical, attitude toward information. He must be willing to entertain and test the possibility that the information may be true and useful. In two different experiments,[24] I found that students who assumed a constructive rather than a critical attitude toward available information were able to produce a larger number of creative solutions and more original ones.

We have made enough advances in educational thinking to make a more creative kind of education possible. The major questions facing us now are: "Will we choose to use these advances in knowledge and thinking and will we choose in time?" I believe we have reached a stage in history when we must make such a choice. In the past, we have been able to survive with static goals and concepts. Change is occurring so rapidly that we cannot survive if we insist on thinking and living in static terms. We must accept the creative challenge.

REFERENCES

1. D. P. Ausubel, *The Psychology of Meaningful Verbal Learning* (New York, 1963).

2. W. H. Burnham, "Individual Differences in the Imagination of Children," *Pedagogical Seminary*, Vol. 2 (1892), pp. 204-225.

3. See, for example, K. Kreuter and Gretchen Kreuter, "The Useful Genius: Intelligence, Creativity, and American Values," *Saturday Review* (October 17, 1964), pp. 64-67; and R. J. Mueller, "Can the Public School Foster Creativity?" *ibid.* (December 19, 1964), pp. 48-49, 64.

4. C. Spearman, *Creative Mind* (London, 1930), p. 140.

5. R. M. Simpson, "Creative Imagination," *American Journal of Psychology*, Vol. 33 (1922), pp. 234-243.

6. A. Newell, J. C. Shaw, and H. A. Simon, "The Processes of Creative Thinking," in H. E. Gruber, G. Terrell, and M. Wertheimer (eds.), *Contemporary Approaches to Creative Thinking* (New York, 1962), pp. 65-66.

7. E. P. Torrance, *Guiding Creative Talent* (Englewood Cliffs, N. J., 1962); and *Rewarding Creative Behavior: Experiments in Classroom Creativity* (Englewood Cliffs, N. J., 1965).

8. J. P. Guilford, *Personality* (New York, 1959).

9. E. P. Torrance, *Guiding Creative Talent, op. cit.;* and *Rewarding Creative Behavior, op. cit.*

10. E. P. Torrance, *Rewarding Creative Behavior, ibid.*

11. P. S. Weisberg and Kayla J. Springer, "Environmental Factors in Creative Function," *Archives in General Psychiatry*, Vol. 5 (1961), pp. 554-564.

12. E. S. Fleming and S. Weintraub, "Attitudinal Rigidity as a Measure of Creativity in Gifted Children," *Journal of Educational Psychology*, Vol. 53 (1962), pp. 81-85.

13. K. Yamamoto, "Creative Writing and School Achievement," *School and Society*, Vol. 91 (October 19, 1963), pp. 307-308.

14. Wanda A. Blockhus, "Creativity and Money Management Understandings," Doctoral dissertation, University of Minnesota, 1961.

15. W. S. Sommers, "The Influence of Selected Teaching Methods on the Development of Creative Thinking," Doctoral dissertation, University of Minnesota, 1963.

16. H. R. Wallace, "Creative Thinking: A Factor in Sales Productivity," *Vocational Guidance Quarterly*, Vol. 9 (1961), pp. 223-226.

17. H. R. Wallace, "Creative Thinking: A Factor in the Performance of Industrial Salesmen," Doctoral dissertation, University of Minnesota, 1964.

18. J. C. Bentley, "The Creative Thinking Abilities and Different Kinds of Achievement," M.A. research paper, University of Minnesota, 1961.

19. See, for example, T. R. McConnell, "Discovery vs. Authoritative Identification in the Learning of Children," *University of Iowa Studies in Education,* Vol. 9, No. 5 (1934), pp. 13-62; L. M. Stolurow, "Social Impact of Programmed Instruction: Aptitudes and Abilities Revisited," Paper presented at the American Psychological Association Annual Convention, St. Louis, Mo., September 2, 1962; L. G. Gotkin and N. Massa, *Programmed Instruction and the Academically Gifted: The Effects of Creativity and Teacher Behavior on Programmed Instruction with Young Learners* (New York, 1963); W. L. Hutchinson, "Creative and Productive Thinking in the Classroom," Doctoral dissertation, University of Utah, 1963; and J. B. MacDonald and J. D. Raths, "Should We Group by Creative Abilities?" *Elementary School Journal,* Vol. 65 (1964), pp. 137-142.

20. D. W. MacKinnon (ed.), *The Creative Person* (Berkeley, Calif., 1961); and C. W. Taylor and J. Holland, "Predictors of Creative Performance," in C. W. Taylor (ed.), *Creativity: Progress and Potential* (New York, 1964), pp. 15-48.

21. C. W. Taylor, "Developing Creative Characteristics," *The Instructor,* Vol. 73, No. 9 (May 1964), pp. 5, 99-100.

22. E. P. Torrance, "Non-Test Ways of Identifying the Creatively Gifted," *Gifted Child Quarterly,* Vol. 6 (1962), pp. 71-75; and *Gifted Children in the Classroom* (New York, 1965).

23. C. Atkinson and E. T. Maleska, *The Story of Education* (New York, 1962), p. 78.

24. E. Paul Torrance, *Rewarding Creative Behavior, op. cit.*

JEROME B. WIESNER

Education for Creativity in the Sciences

THE RAPID expansion of scientific and technical fields, and the spiraling rate of change within them, has created many puzzling, vexsome problems for the society at large and the technical community in particular. The profusion of fresh concepts and theories, new materials and novel devices has resulted in rapidly changing products and production techniques and larger technical systems characterized by greater and greater complexity.

An obvious consequence of these trends is the accelerated technical obsolescence of the material basis of our society leading to rapid replacement of machines in industry and appliances in the home. Another consequence is the obsolescence of much of the specialized training of the manpower that sustains the system. For example, although it was possible to train an engineer twenty-five years ago on the assumption that his skills would be useful for most, if not all, of his professional life, such an approach to engineering education is altogether unrealistic today. Ten years is perhaps the longest time a typical research or design engineer can expect to be effective today without a continuing education or a major effort to refurbish and update both his basic and his specialized professional skills. So it is not surprising that the demand in some of the main technical fields for the most recent graduates of the better engineering schools exceeds the demand for experienced men with, unavoidably, more dated academic training.

The emphasis on technical innovation has drawn attention to the fact that a very small number of the working scientists and engineers are responsible for most of the new ideas. Workers with developed creative gifts are in very short supply and great demand.

These facts suggest not only the need to review what is now being taught, with the aim of enhancing the creative ability of students and of developing skills which might remain productive longer, but also the importance of considering what the educational system can contribute to the periodic academic updating of the specialists it has already produced. We should explore what techniques can best be applied to educating for creative productivity in science and engineering.

Perhaps it is best to begin by describing how I am defining the terms "productivity" and "creativity." Although these words are frequently used synonymously, it is possible to recognize a useful distinction between them. The term "creativity" is principally used to mean activity resulting in contributions that have novelty and value in the intellectual sphere of human experience, including the sciences, as well as literature, music, and the visual arts. In all such contexts, "creativity" universally implies a departure from, and advance beyond, what is conventionally attainable. However, there is an important characteristic of creative contributions in science that is not significantly present in creative contributions in many other fields, namely, quantitatively definable logical relationships to pre-existing scientific knowledge. Thus, although the emotional and intuitive appeal of a new idea or concept, or its esthetic richness, may make it "creative" in a philosophic or artistic sense, normally it must also meet the criterion of being logically relatable, in quantitative terms, to the body of science in order to be considered scientifically "productive." An idea must clearly follow from what is already known if it is to result in an enrichment of available scientific knowledge or of associated technologies.

This distinction is of more than purely semantic interest because of our concern with both "education" and "creativity/productivity." Clearly an element of rigorous, logical discipline must be characteristic, at some point, of the creative efforts of a productive scientific worker, and such discipline may be altogether absent from behavior generally called "creative" in non-scientific fields. Accordingly, by the phrase "productivity in the sciences" I mean to encompass the sum of intellectual activities which contribute to the expansion of scientific and technological knowledge. Thus, "creativity" is a more general term than "productivity," and when "creativity" or "creative" is used in connection with science and technology, it is to be assumed that productivity is also involved.

Now, what kinds of creative activity does society expect from scientists and engineers? For our purpose it is sufficient to group these activities into the following three categories: (1) *scientific research,* concerned specifically with the problem of increasing our understanding of nature; (2) *applied scientific and technological research,* concerned with the development of new tools, techniques, and tool-technique combinations for the solution of particular problems involving practical (rather than purely philosophical) objectives; (3) *engineering design,* primarily concerned with esthetic, materially efficient, and/or economic adaptation of available technology to particular social purposes. The common creative element in these activities might be described as that imaginative insight which, by effectively increasing what is already known, makes available to mankind a somewhat different, broader, and better understood body of experience.

However, if a direct connection between an individual's capacity to undertake creative activity and the educational process to which he has been subjected is to be usefully established, we should fix our attention on scientific research, because the characteristics of such research, and its successful practitioners, have been perhaps more carefully studied than those of other creative activities.

Research creativity is best delineated by a review of the characteristics of eminently successful, that is, extraordinarily creative, scientists. Most of them (as indicated in the pioneering studies of Anne Roe) have the following factors in common: a childhood environment in which knowledge and intellectual effort were so highly valued for themselves that an addiction to reading and study was firmly established at an early age; an unusual degree of independence which, among other things, led them to discover early that they could satisfy their curiosity by personal efforts; an early dependence on personal resources, and on the necessity to think for oneself; an intense drive that generated concentrated, persistent, time-ignoring efforts in their studies and work; a secondary-school training that tended to emphasize science rather than the humanities; and high, but not necessarily remarkably high, intelligence.

In addition to these more or less personal attributes of creative scientific workers, there are some plausible and reasonably well accepted psychological descriptions of the creative aspects of the research process itself.°

Successful conduct of research is associated more with particular mental attitudes and habits than with specialized techniques or procedures, although the latter may be present in certain phases of the

° My version of these descriptions and some of my conclusions have been most influenced by the works of Roe, MacKinnon, and Mooney.

work. Certainly, creative persons develop styles of their own which are characteristic of their mode of working. Such attitudes and habits permit relatively unrestrained observation of phenomena and a persistent, uninhibited pursuit of logical consequences in spite of recurring need to revise or reject prior convictions.

The specifically creative phases of the research process appear to be relatively loose, informal, and personal, and have very little in common with the highly structured, logical, and formal public descriptions of the results. It seems clear that it is this private, relatively unstructured, and perhaps only partly conscious process that results in the creation of new ideas and insights.

Thus, although analogy and metaphor are techniques definitely proscribed for formal reasoning, they may turn out to be dominant in the intuitive, sometimes illogical and initially random process of scanning and searching for new connections and clues. To be creatively efficient such scanning and searching might well need an uninhibited, habitually exercised capability to consider, and explore, ideas in direct contradiction to accepted facts; and, obviously, the larger the universe of relevant data, the greater the efficiency of the process.

Now let us assume that this description of the creative process and that of the characteristics of outstandingly creative scientists are both valid. From the point of view of our general interest in increasing productivity in the sciences, the important question then becomes: What kind of educational methodology would tend to maximize both the number of individuals who are scientifically productive and their personal scientific productivity? Since the descriptions we have provided above do not, by any means, have the status of scientific facts, inferring an appropriate educational process from them is clearly a highly speculative undertaking. However, a more solid scientific basis for discussion of this subject does not appear to be available now. Accordingly, we shall go ahead, keeping in mind, however, that the scientific texture of our conclusions is likely to be rather soft.

The essential problem is that of devising an educational process which will allow the development of easy competence in rigorous methods of reasoning; the amassing of the large collections of facts and theories that constitute current knowledge; and the inculcation of habits for efficient use of available ideas and facts, without the simultaneous establishment of inhibitions and intellectual rigidities that limit the free and imaginative use in research (or in other work) of all the skill and knowledge that have been acquired.

Fifty years ago Alfred North Whitehead remarked that "the key fact in education, and the reason for most of its difficulties" is that "necessary technical excellence can be acquired only by training which is apt to damage those energies of mind which should direct the technical skills." The student with an enormous fund of knowledge, polished techniques, and a total lack of creative ability is an all-too-frequent product of our system. We can take a somewhat more positive approach to the problem: we seek not only to provide training without damaging youthful drive and imagination, but to go beyond that and teach the youthful mind how it might use all of its resources for creative intellectual pursuits in a more effective manner. The only time-tested formula for carrying out this process is that of associating the prospective scientist with a person who has demonstrated both this creative ability and the capacity to transfer his spirit to youngsters.

Focusing attention, for the moment, on the needs of individuals rather than society as a whole, we can specify the main characteristics of an educational process designed to enhance productivity in the sciences.

The basic habit of maintaining a skeptical, actively critical point of view toward all knowledge and opinion must be ingrained. Such habits will minimize the development of unconscious inhibitions against consideration of the widest possible spectrum of possibilities in approaching a problem of interest.

There must be encouragement and stimulation of imaginative and unconventional interpretations of experience in general; this is particularly true in problem-solving activities. It is important, especially in childhood and early youth, that novel ideas and unconventional patterns of action should be more widely tolerated, not critized too soon and too often.

Since logically interrelated bodies of factual material can be more efficiently scanned and searched, the accumulation of facts during training should emphasize principles, laws, and structural relationships.

We must explicitly encourage the development of habits and skills in looking for, and using, analogies, similes, and metaphors to juxtapose, readily, facts and ideas that might not at first appear to be interrelated. Early in this development we should foster a clear understanding of the special character and usefulness of the private, informal process of conducting a search for new ideas and insights;

and of the distinction between it and the equally necessary but more elaborate and rigorous machinery needed for verification of results, and their systematic development for incorporation into the accepted body of knowledge.

We should help the maturing individual develop a personal "style," suited to his personality, abilities, and complement of knowledge, for approaching problems, research or other, in his special fields of interest. This "style" should reflect the particular mix of mental work habits he has developed to define a problem and to go from it to a spectrum of possible solutions. In a more fundamental sense it would also reflect the habitual pattern of resolving the apparent contradiction between the individual's private, imaginative, playful approach to research and the more formal and rigid reasoning process he would employ to establish and extend the results of that research so that it became "productive" as well as "creative."

Although the above "prescription" has been formulated for the educational needs of future research scientists, all that has been said is equally applicable to engineers whose careers will be devoted to enlarging the boundaries of applied science and technology. As Gordon S. Brown, Dean of the School of Engineering at M.I.T., has pointed out, such engineers "are composers rather than arrangers. Their work is predominantly intellectual, and it depends on a profound knowledge of science. They may work as scientists, but their knack of seeing the useful rather than searching for the unknown characterizes them as engineers."

Whether we refer to the research scientist or the research engineer, it is obvious that he will be professionally productive only if his knowledge of relevant subject matter extends to the frontiers of his own fields of activity. In general, this means that his studies must be pursued through the doctoral level. And, just as the purpose of the curriculum followed by the future scientist will be to saturate him with an essentially instinctive understanding and appreciation of the fundamental scientific disciplines, so must this be the case with the research engineer. He must be able to think quantitatively and to formulate his problem in terms of conceptual or mathematical models as a matter of second nature. No other set of skills can insure to the same degree that his work will be productive, and that his training will not rapidly become obsolete.

Let us assume that the above set of specific proposals defines reasonably well the requirements of an effective educational program for productivity in science. What then?

If we were dealing with a technical problem involving the application of the physical sciences, having agreed on a series of reasonable approaches to solution, we could proceed to our laboratories and at once make a start on our newly defined research program. The same sort of rapid response is equally applicable to defining research problems that could be readily undertaken by psychologists or experimental educational institutions. However, our immediate need is not only for further research but for active programs, in the form of large-scale educational experiments, to implement what we already know. But to proceed along such lines we shall have to be concerned as much with stimulating necessary social action as with specific technical matters.

We do not now have useful techniques for predicting with comfortable reliability which individuals will turn out to be creative in the sciences or in any other field, no matter how great an investment we make in their education. Nor does it appear likely that such techniques will be developed in the immediate future; in any case, it would not seem prudent to plan national action on the assumption that they will soon be available. This means that if we are to optimize the general social use of our human resources, there is no alternative to giving as many students as can meet the minimum intelligence requirements the knowledge necessary to provide a reasonable opportunity to be productive in the sciences. However, although this level of intelligence is fairly high (estimated by some to be an IQ level of about 130) there are very large numbers of men and women, at and above this level, who do not now reach the university. This is particularly true among members of the underprivileged groups, especially Negroes. Obviously, our society is incurring a major loss in scientific productivity because of this circumstance, and ways must be found to overcome such needless national waste. As a matter of fact, it is possible to construct a very persuasive argument that our long-term national capabilities in science and technology can be more surely, and perhaps more quickly, enhanced on a large scale by providing motivation and educational opportunities for minority groups than by any other means now open to us. It would be desirable, too, for more women to seek careers in science.

Strong individual motivations for intensive intellectual training extending over many years are necessary to prepare a person for productive work at the frontiers of science and technology. Unless society's scale of values is modified to provide more generally enthusiastic approval of intellectual pursuits—including scientific creativity—we cannot expect any large proportion of those with the necessary natural endowments to begin, and to continue with persistent devotion, the rewarding but difficult labors involved. The attainment of intellectual excellence must become, when compared to other personal ambitions and accomplishments, much more generally accepted by our youth as a challenge rather than as an evidence of "squareness." But even strong motivations are not enough. Personal interest in, and devotion to, the sciences and mathematics through the early years of schooling cannot mature without appropriate learning opportunities, nor can a broad mastery of the subject matter be conveyed in the absence of imaginative and stimulating teaching. I am not suggesting any great increase in schoolwork at an early age, at least not in the better schools. Rather, I am proposing that the subject matter be real science, appropriately presented. It is as easy to present many important and basic ideas as it is to present the confusing hodgepodge often passed off as science in the lower grades. Although elementary courses will make no claim to great thoroughness, they should at least start in the right direction and include opportunities for discovery and experimentation to stimulate the curiosity and develop intellectual self-reliance. In addition to its direct contribution to superior intellectual development for future creativeness, properly planned early training might well provide a more reliable basis for selection of the unusually well endowed. It would also result in the better use of the student's time and energy, and of university resources when he reaches that level of work.

The first step toward a more effective education is to raise the level of effort in mathematics and the sciences to the level of the students' capabilities. We now believe that children can undertake serious learning at a much earlier age than we had thought previously. Experience has shown that meaningful science and mathematics can be taught in the earliest grades. Not only should science courses be started earlier but they should be part of the curriculum in each year for those who show interest and special aptitude.

Many people are impressed by the fact that the Soviet Union's ten-year cycle of primary and secondary education requires that *all* students must take five years of physics, six years of mathematics, three years of biology, and four years of chemistry, with the course content of the work during the last two years being comparable to that of the usual introductory courses in these subjects offered in our liberal arts colleges. By contrast, our corresponding school period contains twelve rather than ten years but provides on the average only one-fifth as much training in mathematics and the sciences. There is insufficient evidence to show that the intensity of early Soviet scientific training is either necessary or desirable, particularly if it involves sacrifices of some emphasis on the humanities, but it is evident that the standard program in our schools is far from optimum.

Earlier I listed the characteristics which an educational program should have if it is to develop the latent creative ability of the youngsters. The traditional high school and university science programs are very poor when judged by these criteria. Their primary accomplishment is to transfer information rather than to convey the spirit or method of science. And even much of the substance is inadequate. The typical text for physics, biology, or chemistry fails to reflect much of the understanding achieved in these fields during the past two decades. In fact many elementary texts confuse science with technology; witness the many photographs of steam engines, rockets, jet aircraft, and nuclear explosions that fill their pages. Courses for the early grades, generally limited to observation and classification of nature's objects, plants, animals, and minerals, fail to convey any feeling for the imaginative, creative character of scientific work and too often establish a dislike which can never be overcome.

We know what needs to be done. Experiments in curriculum development, in teacher-training institutes, in the enrichment of the intellectual environment for students whose homes are lacking in appropriate opportunity, in how people learn, and so forth, have charted the path for a major upgrading of elementary and secondary schools. But to reach the goals we need to apply these ideas in a determined manner. We must produce the new curricular materials; we must have more teachers, particularly teachers with a current education; we must do more research and development in the field of learning; and we must vastly improve the physical facilities of our educational system.

Fortunately an excellent beginning has already been made in curriculum development programs and teacher-training institutes sponsored by the National Science Foundation, covering biology, physics, chemistry, and mathematics. The curriculum development work so far includes only high-school courses. (Furthermore, the teacher-training institutes cannot take care of all of the teachers who would profit by participating.) Other subjects and additional grades need to be included.

Rapid progress in this sector will obviously be difficult to realize because of the present large number of students, the relative lack of involvement by the Federal Government at this educational level, and the highly fragmented character of public responsibilities for our educational system.

There are a number of outstanding high schools, such as the Bronx Science High School, that place heavy emphasis on education in the sciences. Possibly more communities, or at least individual states, should establish a science high school. Such schools could be operated under the direct control of the appropriate state universities with financial support provided, at least in part, by the Federal Government. The admission of students would be on the basis of rigorously competitive academic aptitude examinations, with the costs of attendance for those winning admission but in need of financial assistance being provided by the school through arrangements with the state and the Federal Government. Such schools could become models of educational excellence and centers for experimentation with new methods of teaching and new curricula, quickly and vigorously stimulating the advance of science and of general education throughout the country.

The need for educational reform exists at the university level, too. The shortcomings in content and method found in the elementary- and secondary-school science programs also are prevalent here, and the same opportunities exist for major improvements in teaching. I believe that the present emphasis on formal learning in the colleges and universities and the almost complete lack of contact with real research in the undergraduate years can be very harmful. The student who has had no opportunity to experiment and explore by himself before going to college often ends up bound to rigorous logical methods, afraid to experiment or indulge in flights of fancy, and quite unproductive as a working scientist or engineer. Incorporating new knowledge, eliminating the obsolete, preparing effective laboratory activities, employing teaching aids, including movies and computers, and integrating it all, are concrete steps toward improvement of college-level teaching. Groups at Cal Tech, Berkeley, Illinois, and M.I.T. are working on new college courses in the sciences, but this effort, like those at the lower grades, is just a start in a field where the opportunities (and deficiencies) are almost endless.

There is obvious need for imagination and creativity in educational innovation at the college level, but if real progress is to be achieved, a major effort must be made to attract many of our best minds to the work. The science course development programs have done this to a remarkable degree already, but there is still room for many more helpers. Incidentally, as we proceed along these lines and outstanding scientists and creative individuals from other fields join in the effort at all levels, the profession acquires a new dignity and with it a new interest for our more able youngsters. Only if this trend can be accelerated and the growing effort sustained for many years can the teaching profession succeed in meeting the educational needs of our society.

It is becoming quite clear that more rapid national progress along such lines must be evident soon if our most vital national resource, the talent of our youth, is to be provided adequate opportunity to be intellectually, and more generally, productive in tomorrow's world. That world will be more complex than it is today, will be changing more rapidly than now; and it will have jobs only for the well trained. I quote Whitehead, again, who in 1912 made a highly prescient observation in this vein:

In the conditions of modern life, the rule is absolute, the race which does not value trained intelligence is doomed. . . . Today we maintain ourselves. Tomorrow science will have moved forward one more step, and there will be no appeal from the judgment which will then be pronounced on the uneducated.

Fortunately for our future, this fact is now generally appreciated. Scholars and educators, in increasing numbers, are being drawn to creative educational activities. The government, too, as one can see from the imaginative programs President Johnson is proposing, fully recognizes the need, and there are even many signs that the Congress is prepared to back them. If this hopeful trend is sustained in future years, our educational system has a good chance of meeting the increasing demands of our complex society.

DAVID HAWKINS

The Informed Vision: An Essay on Science Education

IN SPITE of the world-transforming consequences of science, we treat it mostly as a kind of external entity or power. Corporations invest in it and governments subsidize it, but not for its inherent quality as a human interest or engrossment, not for the way it can inform the human vision. Some learned and sensitive persons, poets or metaphysicians or moralists, view it with alarm as though it were a kind of epidemic. Some, like Donne or Pascal, confess the illness in themselves as they decry it; others manage to be model outsiders. Today, it seems to me, the question of the place of science in education has a special significance. To illustrate this, let me begin by stating a sort of anthropological thesis about the mutations of culture.

The thesis is that human societies have always specialized themselves. "Specialized" is used here in the most literal sense, what biologists call speciation. Societies have been like different biological species, each of its own kind. Part of this specialization is adaptation to geography and livelihood, but that part by itself is never unique. Part of the specialization is creation rather than adaptation, the elaboration of a way of life beyond evident necessity, including much that is expressive and ornamental. A well-ordered society manages, in one or another of many ways, to hold up before itself and to dramatize, to celebrate, the means and manners of its own life. We have many expressions of this sense of involvement and commitment, this condition of happiness. One is to speak of being at home in the world. This means, of course, that we very well understand the opposite condition of non-involvement, the many moods of alienation. But even this understanding is elaborated in myths and metaphysics. Part of coming to terms, of being at home, is in the sheer familiarity of the environment and in the sureness with which one lives and walks there. In his moving account of the lives of forest Pygmies,[1] Colin Turnbull recreates the sense of the forest as home—which is so essential to Pygmy culture—and the Pygmies' veritable passion for this domesticity, reaching a high religious expression in their great forest songs. Turnbull obviously fell in love with Pygmy life, and I suppose some of the sterner sect of anthropologists accuse him of lack of objectivity. But some things are best known by falling in love with them.

It is against such a background of comparison that I wish to discuss science in our own education. The world we live in, the world we must accept as home, is a strange world, indeed, by the measures of Pygmy life or by the measures which most men of any other time and culture could supply. We have transformed the surface of nature; in a figurative as well as literal sense we have cut down the forest. But even if we do not like some aspects of our cities and their circulatory systems, we built them ourselves, and they, too, reflect a good deal of domesticity. The important kind of estrangement in our existence, or so it seems to me, is not at this level. It derives from the fact that this extraordinary technological and material evolution of the last century or two—which should be visible even from Mars!—expresses a way of life and thought that has been genuinely available only to a minority among us. To the rest it is, in essence, an alien affair. Each innovation it has produced tends to pass, therefore, from admiration to boredom, without any intervening stage of comprehension and without the enjoyment which only comprehension can release.

Examples of this can be easily found. The actual air is, in fact, a rich example. To "go by air," as so many of us increasingly do, is just that kind of deprivation if we suffer it without a certain background of experience and involvement—and we go from excitement to boredom very quickly. What is the missing ingredient? There are many, from the intuition of the symmetries of thrust and lift formulated in such beautiful simplicity in the language of mechanics, to the complex interactions of wing and atmosphere. But more rudimentary than the dynamics of flight, there is a missing intuition about the air itself, and about its fluid reality. We know from work with children (and adults) that primitive man's indecision about air is still very much with us. Is air a kind of fullness, or a kind of emptiness? Some casual experience fits the one answer, some the other. Have you ever weighed a batch of air, or played with a plastic clothing bag half full—or half empty—of the stuff? From the dearth of such experience the intuitions of air's weight or inertia are very feeble in most of us. And what of that glorious amazement that burst upon the world of the learned when Torricelli confirmed Galileo's induction of the possibility of the vacuum with his barometer, and came to the realization that we swim in an ocean of air surrounding the globe? At some upper levels we "teach meteorology" with learned words about lapse rates and dew points and the taxonomy of clouds—to people still mostly lacking any acquaintance with the rudiments. I have not meant to exhaust the esthetics of flight and atmosphere. That takes more than a note, more even than St. Exupéry. But all of it is permeated with the affections of science—cloudscape, the color gradients of the earth and atmosphere, vapor trails, the rainbowed shadow of the plane, the sight of the great solid planet revolving below, and, above all, the human involvement in a biologically alien medium, in organization, detail, decision.

Nor does the relevance of science fail when we go beyond the esthetics of flight—as we of all people must—to St. Exupéry's preoccupation with this very science as armorer of mass destruction. He loved the creativity of science but not its vision of the world. He shared, I think, the alienation that I speak of[2]—of a world that will accept science to arm its military enterprises, but not yet to inform its vision.

Another example is light—the essential element of astronomy and, in the end, of so much of physics. It has been an amazing discovery, to me at least, that many adults have no firm intuitions of even the geometry of light and shadow. Like most young children, they cannot predict a shadow before the light is turned on. Mirrors are common in our lives, yet the symmetries of reflection are but little known. And how many people have ever played with pinhole images, watched the colors in the bevel of a mirror, or seen the daytime shadows moving? How many see the moon as an illuminated sphere, and sense from it the direction of the sun? In spite of all the discussion of the marvels of space, very few of us have any instinctive orientation on the earth, let alone in the solar system. Knowing that vehicles are on their way to begin photographing Mars, how many among us can find that planet tonight in the evening sky, and spare its mysteries a thought?

Then there is the matter of scale. Astronomical intuition demands at least a sense for that hundred million miles that approximates our distance from the sun. The stretching of the intuitions of scale is one of the characteristic accomplishments of science, both toward the large and toward the small. Yet as a firm possession this sort of simple intuition is rare except among the learned. Time as well as space demands it. Suppose we were to list the sorts of happenings we knew, that required times of the order of a thousand years, a hundred thousand, ten million, a billion. They are all around us, but the book is closed to most except to loving geologic eyes. The world of the solar system, which we now are committing ourselves to explore, and thus one day to feel at home in, *demands* the intuition of such a time scale. For we and the other planets have existed together in the same sunlight for a few billions of years, but otherwise completely isolated from each other. Such is the characteristic time of our own biological development; it is an evolutionary measure, correspondingly, of our separation from the other planets. Yet we talk and act, sometimes, as though we might just move in!

The Greek dramatists defined the sin of *hubris,* the sin of men who dared to be more than men, to go beyond man's place in the fixed order of things. "Being at home" for them was not only a state of assurance and familiarity, but of residence at a literal cosmographic and moral address. By their standards we do, I suppose, commit the ancient sin. But there is another sin we are in danger of —I think it is the same one, with definition purified—which is that of Moral Tourism, going to new places with the firm expectation of proper accommodations and a readiness to blame the natives if it turns out not so. I mean this in relation not only to the moon or Mars, but to all those extraordinary novelties we are gaining the power to encounter in our exploration of nature: of fissions and fusions, of the ecological turmoil that follows in the wake of our economic development, of our power to modify the genetic substrata of life. Even the planetary explorations are likely to have, for all our future, the most extraordinary consequences. Yet we began them in a competitive frenzy and continue them in budgetary tranquility, without appreciable excitement or debate. Because of the lack of any intervening comprehension, the idea of the space vehicle, like that of the airplane, will, I am afraid, pass too quickly from the stage of romance to that of ennui or alienation. And in this state we are, as St. Exupéry said, dangerous.

Some will object, perhaps, that this is all a gross exaggeration. By now there are many among us, a few per cent at least, who fully grasp and prize the way of science. The rest of us can trust them for advice and education. They are "experts." The word used to be a term of state, the state of being taught by experience—as a qualified technical witness, for example, in the courts. Now it has become a term of status. The scientific expert is still described as a person of purely technical competence, a knower of means rather than an adjudicator of ends. But increasingly and inevitably he is thrust into the latter position. Sometimes from vanity, I suppose, but certainly often from a heavy sense of social responsibility, he becomes a definer and a proponent of new social goals that science itself has made possible. Yet everything we know of history suggests that if this division in our society continues the scientific community will be subject to all the corruptions of caste and status. A world so deeply committed to science cannot survive with a vast majority of its population intellectually and esthetically alienated from science.

In my examples I have tried to imply a style of education that would permit correction, in our culture, of this basic defect. It has nothing in common with the need, so often put forward, to "produce more scientific experts." It has much more in common with the way of education described by Colin Turnbull in his account of Pygmy life. It is an education which begins in play suffused with enjoyment and evolves into an apprenticeship premised on commitment. Our needs are vastly different, I acknowledge, though it would be dangerous to assert that the Pygmy youth has learned much less. He has learned a great deal indeed, of the edible and inedible flora and the habits of deer or leopard, to walk in total silence, and to sing great songs. He could not survive, in that world, without a complex and subtle education. But what we must learn is in part more remote from the immediate environment, more abstracted and dependent on symbolic skills. And that is the challenge to our education: to recover for our world the ways of learning that are concretely involving and esthetically rewarding, that move from play toward apprenticeship in work.

To see what all of this means for us and our education I must turn to the discussion of science and what the philosophers have to say about it. I myself have spent a good many years in this occupation, which has recently developed a label for itself, the philosophy of science. But I have also been distracted from this pursuit by others. Jorge Luis Borges[3] quotes a marvelous sentence from W. H. Hudson, who said that in his youth he often undertook the study of metaphysics, but happiness always interrupted him. One of my own interruptions has been science, science unphilosophically itself; another has been science teaching and, most recently, curriculum development for elementary schools.

Attempts to characterize science, as is true of all new things, have come mainly by analogy with other occupations and their products. Exploration, food-gathering, architecture, weaving, playing games, map-making, book-keeping, composing, all have played their part as analogies in the attempt to describe the processes of science or define its product. The one I want to single out here is the analogy of art, of art taken rather generally and therefore with a good deal of internal variety. Like all the other analogies, it will break down at various places, but I have selected it because I think it does not break down in one very important place—school.

A natural association with the word "art" is the sense of an implied spontaneity in a work of art or the enjoyment of it. In one of his most important writings on education (which, incidentally, does not contain the word in its index), John Dewey says this about spontaneity of artistic expression:

Works of art often present to us an air of spontaneity, a lyric quality, as though they were the unpremeditated song of a bird. But man, whether fortunately or unfortunately, is not a bird. His most spontaneous outbursts, if expressive, are not overflows of momentary internal pressures. The spontaneous in art is complete absorption in subject matter that is fresh, the freshness of which holds and sustains emotion. Staleness of matter and obtrusion of calculation are the two enemies of spontaneity of expression.[4]

If one were to try to formulate the quality of any achievement of learning, at its best, one could hardly find a better formulation than "complete absorption in subject matter that is fresh, the freshness of which holds and sustains emotion"—or of the opposite quality, in "staleness of matter and obtrusion of calculation."

But is it really permissible to talk about spontaneous expression in science? To be sure, the approved style of scientific communication could hardly be called lyrical. But we should not forget that *human* expression, for Dewey, is no mere display or outburst; it is a synthesized achievement compatible, as Dewey goes on to say, "with any amount of labor provided the results of that labor emerge in complete fusion with an emotion that is fresh." Emotion, then: surely science is concerned with knowing, not with feeling; with expression of fact, perhaps, but not with personal expression. Science is concerned with prosaic truth, objectively defined, publicly testable and emotionally neutral. Surely I have misled myself in thinking of science as a form of art, carried away by some wild philosophical conceit.

I know the reason for my error; it is a group of recollections and anecdotes of times in school when it did seem that children, after rather complete absorption in scientific subject matter that was fresh, emerged with some unifying and spontaneous expression of insight—and surely not without emotion. I vividly recall one child, for example, who seemed to acknowledge the reality of the great sphere of the earth as though for the first time—not from a transatlantic jet, but in the schoolroom. After long absorption in the behavior of a string-and-steel-ball pendulum, he suddenly saw it as doing *something* when it was just hanging, its motion spent. "Pointing toward the center!" The little sphere and the great sphere were joined in one act of knowing, fresh and emotion-sustaining. The only comparable experience of my own I can remember now was a recent one, when in the path of eclipse totality I became emotionally very much involved with the onrushing shadow, and quite literally felt the presence and opacity of the great occulting sphere, the moon. Surely I felt this only because, as an amateur, I have spent many hours absorbed in subject matter, exploring the moon visually and learning to picture it on the scale of earth and sun. In my case the experience came late, and I prize it; in Jeff's it came at age ten and released a flood of remarkable questions and investigations that, when we last met, was carrying him straight toward the world of Isaac Newton.

Perhaps my analogy is not lost, after all. Perhaps it is just that our usual account of science is a sort of timid and official tone, correct as far as it goes, but leaving out the personal act in favor of the public process, the privately consummated experience in favor of the social achievement. And perhaps those who immerse themselves deeply in scientific pursuits do so because of their initial attraction to science and then *learn* to prize the dry, austere, and impersonal mode of expression, as one which they think best keeps a sort of subject matter fresh, and best holds and sustains the emotions appropriate to that subject matter. From this point of view there is much about the style of scientific thought, expression, and teaching that we need to reexamine. Later in *Art as Experience* Dewey refers to the fact I have already discussed above, that science

. . . as now practiced is too new to be naturalized in experience. It will be a long time before it so sinks into the subsoil of mind as to become an integral part of corporate belief and attitude. Till this happens both method and conclusions will remain the possession of specialized experts, and will exercise their general influence only by way of external and more or less disintegrating impact upon beliefs, and by equally external practical application.[5]

Is it possible that the style of scientific expression and communication depends more upon its cultural *newness* than upon the inherent necessities of the case? If we imagine a society in which what we call science has sunk deeply "into the subsoil of mind," what would be its style of expression? Would science any longer even be *called* science? The above passage occurs in the context of a discussion of the isolation of fine art from the vital centers of community life, which Dewey, like many other critics, attributes partly to the "external and more or less disintegrating impact" of science and technology upon older beliefs and ways of life. More than any other recent philosopher—except possibly A. N. Whitehead—John Dewey spent his life attempting to naturalize and humanize the scientific way of life and thought. In his educational philosophy (best stated in his non-educational writings) he saw deep affinity between the style of research in science and the natural probings and explorings of children. In his strong desire to reinforce the latter as the basis of all true education, Dewey likewise was moved by the belief that in this way the external and disintegrating influence of science would be transformed into an internal and creative one, penetrating into the subsoil of mind. Long before the current "two cultures" debate, John Dewey had formulated the dichotomy for a generation of American thinkers and school reformers and had set forth a program to heal the split. This program was to look beneath the surface of achieved scientific knowledge as dogmatically formulated in textbooks (and popularizations) to the underlying life of scientific inquiry, to the scientific method.

In good part because of the influence of Dewey, a generation of American teachers was brought up with the slogans and shibboleths of the scientific method, and in not a few centers schools were started which undertook to demonstrate the feasibility of an education centered around practical involvement of children in enquiry and creative expression. For a time, some of the public schools became more or less involved, and "progressive education" was *the* term of praise.[6]

Judged by the aspirations of the originators of the movement, very little is left today—little of the slogans, and even less of the practice. The most recent wave of educational reform has been motivated in part by a stern emphasis upon "the return to subject matter," both in the classroom and in the training of teachers. Are we to conclude, then, that the Deweyan program of education has been tried and failed? I do not believe it has really been tried; but I also do not want to declare the experiment irrelevant. At their best, the progressive schools were excellent; but the best was rare. At their worst, they may have justified the abuse heaped upon them by scornful critics. There are, I believe, two conclusions which can be extracted from the history of this institutional movement. One is a conclusion of theory, one of practice.

The theoretical conclusion I would urge is that the key conception of scientific method, of what Dewey called "the supremacy of method," is subtly wrong. Those who have read Dewey's more philosophical and less propagandistic writings will know that he is not always guilty of any real separation of "method" from "content." But there are some truths that require at least *two* sentences for their utterance, and slogans are generally expressed in one. The first truth may well be that the art of scientific inquiry is educationally more fundamental than the facts and principles established by that practice. But the second truth, no less important, is that the art cannot grow except by what it feeds on; and what method feeds one, the whole source of its power and authority, is the very order and organization of the world it investigates. The mind equipped with method and no content is not more than the grin of a Cheshire Cat, an absurdity of misplaced abstractions. Dewey knew this, but he did not relish and emphasize it. So now we are in danger of new slogans, which in the re-emphasis on content will assume that method grows spontaneously out of improved "subject matter."

Try as I may, I cannot put it all in one simple sentence. "Method is the *use* of knowledge to *extend* knowledge." But then I must add, with the John Dewey of *Art as Experience*, ". . . through complete absorption in subject matter that is fresh." And this leads me to my practical conclusion from the failure of progressive education to win its way into a permanent place in education. Where that movement succeeded, it did so because the world of children's exploration was amply provisioned with subject matter they could explore well, could penetrate deeply. Where it failed, it did so because the freedom for active involvement was inadequately provisioned. This inadequacy was often concealed by a preoccupation, illegitimate in the *absence* of provisioning, with the maturation of the child personality. "Freedom of expression" was often seen as a good in itself, unmindful of the fact "that man, fortunately or unfortunately, is not a bird." Faced with the all-too-real maladies of psychic development in our children, and influenced by popular Freudian beliefs about the curative effects of "permissive" adult behavior, some few schools no doubt earned that indignant reflex utterance that "freedom is not license!"

It is my impression that the success of the progressive education movement was greatest for the earliest years, where its ideas and programs merged with the already solidly-based practical tradition of the kindergarten, imported to these shores a half-century before, with philosophic roots, many of them, common to Dewey's own background. Here there was not only a style of teaching that involved children deeply in subject matter, but the subject matter grew with the style—water, sand, clay, paint, good infant literature, the cultivation of story and song, carpentry, lenses, prisms, magnets, blocks, the house of packing boxes and orange crates, soil and seeds, animals, the dance, and all the rest. I do not believe that this tradition failed at all; its influence has been reduced by erosion (sometimes to the vanishing point), by pressures for thin mechanical programs of "reading readiness," "number experience," and the like, most of which tend to reduce the very readiness they seek to cultivate.

The moral, then, is that absorption in subject matter requires a major effort of provisioning for that subject matter. If children are going to emerge from our schools secure in the practice and enjoyment of the arts of inquiry, it will be only because they have long practiced those arts, in engagement with the world around. In relation to science, this means that their involvement with it will have been of a kind such that we can truly say it has penetrated the subsoil of their minds and earned their loyalty because it has liberated them from the boredom and sophistication that come with living in an unexamined world, because it preserves the freshness of subject matter and sustains emotion.

In my own way, then, I agree with the present emphasis on a "return to subject matter." In the newer science curriculum developments, there has often been an emphasis on individual work, by children, that is laboratory-like in its style. This seems to me to be of very great importance. It constitutes a delayed recognition that the subject matter of science is not, except in a derivate sense, to be found in books. The subject matter of "the liquid state of matter" is the liquid state of matter, and we had better sometimes have some of it in the classroom. Along with aprons and mops as needed! The subject matter of sea animals may make more sense for coastal schools than inland, but if it makes sense inland it will be because the provisioning of salt-water aquaria has been reduced to a simple routine that schools can and will maintain. The subject matter of atoms is a puzzle. There are plenty of them, of course, in every classroom, but there must be a long course of evolution, and much penetration of experience into the subsoil of the mind, before the world of atoms will prove to be fresh and absorbing subject matter.

The beginnings are there in the kindergarten, in sand and saw-dust worked with, and then seen with magnifiers. They are there in the drops of food-coloring billowing out into the water. Do the dye and the water really *mix,* or is it like a tangle of colored threads that just get thinner and more numerous until you can't see them any more? An honest answer is not yet available from nature, at the elementary laboratory level of investigation. But what a question! Later there is more, in the disciplined use of serial dilution, of saccharin and quinine and vinegar, of dyes and yeast suspensions, or Chlorella. Still later come the beginnings of simple quantitative chemistry, after the uses of quantity have been elaborated in other and more urgent contexts, and after the hand-lens and microscope have led to Lilliput and even smaller worlds. The direct evidence of chemical atomicity is not to be found in the elementary-school laboratory. Radioactive scintillations from a watch-dial? Perhaps, but what absorption in previous subject matter is implied, to see these as atomic events! The philosopher and physicist Ernst Mach disbelieved in atoms through all the evidence of nineteenth-century chemistry. What convinced him, in his old age, were the phenomena of radioactivity. I would not demand this much for children. Mach was stubborn. The important thing is not to *prove* the reality of atoms, but to bring them alive in the imagination and intellect. Otherwise, why push? To please parents with the appearance of understanding? Or is this high-school-chemistry-readiness?

I have tried to suggest what laboratory style might mean in elementary-school contexts. Peter the Great said he would open a window onto the West, and the elementary-school laboratory might do as much, onto the world. But nowadays the pressures are toward the windowless school, and I have very honest doubts. The laboratory traditions, in college and high school, are in many ways not encouraging. Nor do I wish to underestimate the difficulties in avoiding a style of laboratory work limited, as in fact our laboratory traditions mainly are, to the attempt to certify the truth of previously announced propositions, not yet *understood* by the majority of students who, recipe book in hand, dutifully perform.

I know the difficulties are real because I have perpetrated the crime myself as a college science teacher, and I have done it often rather than seldom. It is certainly possible to program work, in some kinds of laboratory science, so as to rob it of almost all romance and reduce it, nearly, to the status of rote—perhaps not quite, if only because a student very soon discovers that the experiment seldom works the way he has been told it will, that the "best" answers still come from the book rather than from his data. In some secret way, perhaps, he learns to mistrust the book. Or does he draw the opposite conclusion, that, in this great world he is being educated into, nature is to be taken with a grain of salt?

A partial explanation of these difficulties can be found, I think, in the psychology of us who teach science. In some measure, by some accidental pathways not commonly followed in our age, the culture of science has penetrated at least a little into the subsoil of our minds; we have pursued it much beyond the average. But from this there are two results, contradictory to each other. One is that we have some art in scientific inquiry; we have been absorbed in scientific subject matter and we know the fruits in our enjoyment of them. The other is that we have proven or declared ourselves, and are certified to teach. The consequence is social caste. We are the knowers, the explainers. Nothing moves us to such generous efforts as to be asked for explanations. Shrewd children, even shrewd adults, learn to ask these flattering questions, though their interest is slight and passing. For the deeper the perplexity, the more burning the curiosity, the less children or adults seek prompt explanation. When you have exhausted your own resources and still fail, *then* you will go for help. If you go too soon to an explainer, he does best to turn you back on your own resources, or to direct you toward acquisition of new ones.

What is true of the initiates is true, also, of those whose misfortune it is to teach science without any conviction of inner illumination. Here is the book, they are told, or the syllabus, or the teachers' guide. Now teach! The style is set for them; they know they are supposed to teach, to give explanations. And we, alas, the devotees, the mystics, have set that style.

I mean no offence to men, only to methods. There is of course a place for explanations, for didacticism in all its plumage. In the last part of the curriculum, in the homestretch toward professional degrees, we may even glory in it. The apprentice has made his decision, and we must make a tough professional of him and try him by ordeal. But our motives are still suspect, and even here, I think, there can be radical improvement. What distinguishes science from the personalized arts—as poetry, or painting—is the essentially social nature of its product. The cathedral that took a century to build is more nearly the model. No single architect planned it, though the mark of individuality is everywhere, of craftsmen absorbed in a common subject matter, whose expression sustains collective emotion. But here none of the analogies is really good. The art that is science is a distinct genre. Its constructions are not buildings, not machines, not instruments, though these may be among its modes of expression—as may be the textbook and the syllabus. The essential construction of science is a personal way of being related to the universe. This way has many expressions and can have many more, in conduct, artifact, or text; but it is primarily a way of knowing, and the knower is always the artisan of his personal knowledge. The social character of science is misrepresented when we forget this artist, pretending that the depersonalized social expression is the essence. Every art has its constraints and disciplines, and one of the disciplines of science is the demand for logically coherent formulation and noise-free communication. Hence the syllabus and text, hence the refinement of terminology. Yet, ironically and sadly, it is this very discipline which raises the barriers to communication in our schools. The letter of the discipline has too often been taken to be its substance. Here as always the letter kills, especially in the early and crucial years. The tight formulation and logical sequencing must be learned, but they cannot be learned first. They will be learned only when a knower comes to prize them for their power of liberation and guidance. What comes first is absorption in subject matter. No one learns by being led blind along a path he cannot begin very soon to see for himself.

And here I come to what seems to me to be the crucial and largely unsolved problem of science education (or of any education). Method consists in using knowledge to gain further knowledge. Yet what each individual knows that he can use in this way is, at any moment, a highly individual affair. In reducing our experience to order, the distance we must travel to achieve any component of this order is not a well-defined quantity; for there are many paths to a goal of understanding, and along any path there are *many* available important goals. Logically considered, the relations among the ideas which bring order to our experience constitute a complex network; ideas are not stations along a single road. In this psychological world, what we mean by distance along a given path can be measured by the number of probings and testings, of discriminations, we must make to traverse it. Paths already well-trodden are short *because* they are well-trodden. For this reason the patterns of optimal learning are highly individual. In the early and deep learning that goes with play, some of the conditions for approximating these individual optima are present. Since there are so many important things to be learned, the direction of exploration is not critical. What is learned will add to the power of later learning. What is important is the confrontation with materials which play can exploit and incorporate—absorption in fresh subject matter! From what we now know of informational processes, even machines designed for pattern recognition and classification will function most efficiently—when dealing with a very complex system of data—if they are deliberately programed for such "nondirective," in some respects even random, "Monte Carlo" exploratory behavior. In spite of the anxieties about machines in our culture, it may be that the machine designers are closer to an appreciation of what is involved in human learning than are those circumscribed by the simplistic traditions of behavioristic psychology and "programed learning."

But there comes a time for harvesting, gathering, organizing, even programing, and here individual learners must be drawn together under a common discipline. In our schools, this time comes much too early. Or better, it is too little preceded and followed by periods—long periods—of individualized and diversified work of a more exploratory and self-directed kind. In being so critical of the prevailing style, however, I do not want to make an opposite error, of forgetting that apprenticeship phase of their education when the young Pygmies go out on their first hunts or build their first houses under adult direction. It seems to me that in our context the great teaching art must prove to be the art of combination. We must learn better to instruct children when, after absorption in subject matter, they communicate by their behavior those directions which they are prepared to find meaningful because they themselves have begun to define and seek them. And then there is the opposite transition, when formal instruction has brought children to new levels of understanding and interpretation: to open again the door to less directed probing and testing at these new levels—and thus to consolidate what has been learned, to use it for further learning.

There are certainly some superbly resourceful teachers among us who practice and understand this art, although perhaps they are not articulate about it in the context of educational discourse. Can we identify them, we who want to know the art better? And can we go and watch, and thus learn? And can we, after watching, begin to help them with the provisioning, with plants and animals and laboratory equipment—and ideas! Can we then find ways to resonate, to amplify, to strengthen the apprenticeship of other teachers? The job is not easy on any scale. On the scale I have tried to suggest, that of a whole society in which the esthetic meaning of our commitment to science will have penetrated the subsoil of the human mind, it is difficult indeed. But on this scale the motivation should also be strong to find meeting places where these present realities of our future, children and science, may be brought more happily together.

REFERENCES

1. Colin M. Turnbull, *The Forest People* (Garden City, N. Y., 1962).

2. In some disagreement with Harcourt Brown's careful discussion in "Tensions and Anxieties," *Science and the Creative Spirit* (Toronto, 1958).

3. *Other Inquisitions*, tr. by Ruth L. C. Simms (Austin, Tex., 1964), p. 144.

4. John Dewey, *Art as Experience* (New York, 1934), p. 70.

5. *Ibid.*, p. 338.

6. Lawrence A. Cremin, *The Transformation of the School, Progressivism in American Education* (New York, 1961).

LAWRENCE S. KUBIE

Unsolved Problems of Scientific Education

I. *Preconscious Learning and the Neurotic Process*

ALTHOUGH FOR the most part we are aware only of the conscious
component of our mental processes, we neither think nor learn consciously. In fact, conscious symbolic processes are not the major instrument for acquiring new information, for processing it in the
brain, which is man's communications machine. Nor are conscious
processes ever active alone. Day and night, sleeping and waking,
there is an incessant interplay among three psychological systems
(or "levels"), for which "conscious," "preconscious," and "unconscious" are familiar, recognizable, and not too inaccurate designa-
tions. The summated effects of the interplay among them implement
all behavior, thought, purpose, and feeling in human life. There is
abundant evidence, largely overlooked, that among these three the
more pervasive, continuous, and dynamic is neither conscious nor
unconscious, but *preconscious.*

This consists of a continuous and remarkably rapid stream of
afferent, integrative, creative, and efferent activity, mediated by
coded cues and signals, but without fully developed symbolic representation. It is what the Wurzburg school[1] used to call "imageless
thought." It has also been called "paraconscious," "coconscious," "subliminal," the "fringe of consciousness," and finally "preconscious."
This preconscious stream is fed by an incessant bombardment of
afferent signals which arise both in the body and in the world
outside. Only a fragment of these signals consists of conscious
sensations; most are subliminal. Another source of data for the preconscious stream consists of active residual imprints from prior
experiences. All afferent signals feed into the stream of preconscious
internal processing, out of which come all actions, thoughts, memories, feelings, and anticipatory planning.

118

Conscious symbolic processes sample all of this activity: that is, the incoming signals, the preconscious processing, and the outgoing products. By means of conscious symbols we generalize from individual bits of data, assemble them into patterns, and make abstractions from them by scanning, ordering, and arranging temporal and spatial sequences, and so forth. Throughout life this goes on unceasingly. Relatively speaking, the processes of conscious symbolic sampling are slow and limited, and provide only weighted fragments of preconscious activity, to make up what is erroneously referred to as "conscious thought."

In sleep, preconscious processing constitutes a variable but apparently continuous dream flow. Of this, "the dream," as we ordinarily think of it, is only a condensed fragment, a weighted sample, expressed predominantly through visual imagery—a cluster of visual hieroglyphics with multiple simultaneous implications on all three levels.

Unconscious processes constitute a distorted and even more fragmentary symbolic sample of conscious samples. Note in this connection that it is never the symbolic image, thought, or act which is unconscious, but its relation to that which it is supposed to represent, but masks instead.

It is possible only to outline here this working hypothesis concerning the nature of human mentation. Its implications for the learning process will be considered next.[2]

How we learn. Preconscious learning is both effective and effortless when it operates without interference. It is not easy, however, to attain this. The preconscious stream may be hampered first by the process of conscious sampling. Yet conscious sampling is needed for communicating to others and also to ourselves (that is, ruminating), for creating multiple associative linkages, and for testing the products of the preconscious stream against reality. These are essential ingredients in all mentation and in all learning; but they should not be confused with the acquisition and mastery of new data, nor with thinking, nor with the rearranging of data into new combinations (that is, creative thinking). Furthermore conscious sampling is slow, labored, digital, and literal. Preconscious activity on the other hand is an analogic process and proceeds at a speed far greater than the pedestrian pace of conscious symbolic processes and with greater fluidity. Consequently, even the spontaneous acquisition of symbolic processes which occurs in early childhood slows up and inhibits the child's free play of preconscious creativity. From early years, therefore, the conscious ingredients in the learning process hamper the preconscious processing of data.

When we come to formal education we find that conscious drill and grill constitute a large part of conventional educational techniques. Their premature use in the educational scene increases the hampering influence of conscious processes, jeopardizing, distorting, and inhibiting our processes of preconscious learning, instead of reenforcing, sustaining, and protecting them. Educational research today should attempt to discover how to protect preconscious functions in all education, but especially in education for creativity.[3] Except for isolated pioneers among them, educators have not begun to study this. If engineering educators will turn their attention to this problem and can solve it, they will solve one of the basic problems not merely of engineering education alone but of all education.[4]

The neurotic process in education. There is a further distortion of the educational process by concurrent neurotic processes. This challenges us with the question of whether established educational procedures intensify or lessen the activity of the ubiquitous masked neurotic ingredients in human development. This requires a condensed statement of a working hypothesis concerning the neurotic process.[5]

There is a universal neurotic potential in all men who are not so defective mentally as to be unable to represent inner and outer experience by means of conscious symbols. The capacity to sample the preconscious stream by means of conscious symbols is essential for man's unique psychological activities; yet the process of symbolic sampling is itself vulnerable to two kinds of dissociation. The symbol can be dissociated (a) from the memory traces of the events which it was intended to represent and (b) from the affects which are appropriate to the experience. Such dissociations are the origin of what is known as "repression," that is, the interposition of a barrier between the symbol and its roots. Note that the symbols themselves never become unconscious, but that in the process of dissociation their links to originating experiences and to the associated affects can be distorted or severed. Such dissociations occur under the influence of painful conflicts; and when this occurs it interrupts the associative and symbolic links to the underlying conflicts. In this way the conflicts themselves become "unconscious," and can no longer be dealt with by conscious deliberation, yet continue nonetheless to impede and distort both the stream of preconscious activity and its symbolic representation. This is the inception of a continuing neurotic process, because all subsequent thoughts, feelings, and behavior acquire some of the quality of neurotic symptoms and represent the unconscious conflicts. Sooner or later, these symptoms have new destructive secondary effects on the individual's life, which produce new crops of symptoms, which in turn produce tertiary distortions, and so on. Thus the neurotic process consists of a cybernetic or reverberating chain of symptoms which produce distortions which produce fresh symptoms which produce fresh distortions, and so forth.

There is no culture of which we have any knowledge which has solved the problem of how to bring up its children free from neurotic distortions. These may vary, but they are always present to make up the universal masked neurotic components of what we euphemistically call "normal" human psychology.[6] Their influence on all education is destructive, but especially on that education which aims to inform while protecting and preserving potential creativity.

Man's development has always been limited by the fact that his preconscious functions become trapped between, on the one hand, the pedestrian, halting, earth-bound, reality-oriented processes of conscious symbolic representation, and, on the other, the neurotic distortions of symbolic processes which are imposed by unconscious conflicts and their secondary and tertiary consequences. Education itself is caught between the two.

Developmental distortions. If we are to do anything about this problem we must view it ontogenetically, starting perhaps by acknowledging our past culpable indifference to the implications of the child's early loss of free and spontaneous creative zest. The small child manifests his latent and potential creativity in his imaginative use of bodily movement, gestures, facial mimicry, sounds, words, images, color, design, and tone. When he learns to use words, even before formal education starts, he becomes less free, because words themselves confine the preconscious stream. Yet if he is to become educated, the child must master these essential symbolic tools.

If we acknowledge this, we may search out ways to protect our essential preconscious processes from this inhibiting by-product of the equally essential conscious symbolic processes. Instead, we make use of educational procedures which intensify the inhibitory impact of conscious processes, reenforcing at the same time the play of neurotogenic influences. The result is that even the highly gifted child suffers a progressive attrition of his potential creativity.[7]

Before formal schooling is begun, the acquisition of symbolic tools occurs, largely through the child's preconscious imitation of others (technically called "identification"). Consequently the quality of the emotional feedback from older people has a powerful influence (either supportive and creative, or else deforming and blocking) on the steps by which symbolic tools are acquired. It is no accident that the neglected child who is starved for the attention of loving adult models is often unable to read or write, even when he has a high IQ.

Even under more favorable circumstances, the process of symbolic learning goes through at least three critical steps in human development, during each of which it again becomes vulnerable: (a) during earliest childhood as already described; (b) in the emotionally charged transition from puberty into early adolescence; and (c) during the long years of higher education, when the student must face the imminent challenges of maturity. Each of these phases of change and growth is charged with hidden rivalries, hates, lusts, and conflicts, many of which are unconscious. The unresolved residues of each critical phase are buried but not eliminated; and in subsequent phases they are expressed in new symptomatic forms, which make use of the recently acquired symbolic tools and processes. This produces further distortions in the symbolic process itself, which is another manifestation of the chain of cybernetic processes by which the neurotogenic distortions of our symbolic tools attach themselves to and ultimately frustrate the learning process.

Again during the upper reaches of higher education—that long-drawn-out period of developmental and educational stress—conflicts arise over accepting the full implications of maturity (intellectual, sexual, economic, marital, parental, professional) with a reactivation of unresolved sources of self-doubt, jealousy, hostility, terror, and so forth. These distortions of symbolic function influence the perception, imprinting, recording, ordering, storing, scanning, and processing of bits of information and their accessibility for use and recall. They influence also the free use of preconscious processes for creative purposes, that is, for taking apart bits of data and putting them together into new combinations. None of these essential processes is isolated from the influence of concurrent unconscious processes. Even our primary perceptions are vulnerable. Therefore, the play of hidden neurotic forces can disturb the education of even the most gifted student. It can also defeat, deflect, and distort the creative productivity of highly trained and technically mature scientists of proven gifts. Such neurotogenic defeats occur at every level in the training and utilization of engineering skills, from the first year as a student on through those later years which should be a period of maximum creativity in the life of the mature scientist.

Neurophysiological variables. Also influencing and sometimes distorting the learning process are variables which depend upon neurophysiological idiosyncrasies of the human central nervous system. Among these are the conflict between the storing and preconscious processing of data, the effects of input-overload on preconscious creativity, the effects of the lengthening span of student life on the retarding of emotional maturity, and the effects of this aspect of the life of the engineering student on his freedom to grow, to create, and to produce.

I have already touched on the fact that, in all educational settings, rivalry plays a role in the activation of latent neurotogenic processes. Such rivalry can also be intensified by the excessive and premature emphasis on drill and grill, based as it is on a fallacious assumption concerning the role of conscious processes in learning. Destructive rivalries can also be intensified by the injudicious and over-enthusiastic use of testing procedures. The effects of these and other conventional "educational" techniques should be subjected to comparative studies, specifically with regard to their interaction with neurotogenic processes.[8]

The consequences of universal, concealed, neurotic processes for the education of engineers and for their subsequent creative productivity are matters of urgent concern. This is not because there is any evidence that engineering education is more vulnerable than education in other fields; but rather because science is the most basic discipline among the humanities. Therefore the illumination of this problem in engineering would throw light on its significance in less precise fields of education and therefore on the educational process in general. It is of further importance to solve this in engineering because of the high cost of engineering education and its practical importance.

II. *The Problem at the Student Level*

Departmental heads and administrative officers from various institutes in the engineering sciences emphasize the fact that students and faculty as well are carefully screened, both before coming to them and continuously thereafter as the progress of screening moves through a progressively finer mesh. All agree (and on this their testimony is remarkably consistent) that wide discrepancies between earlier records and later performances are frequent, and that these discrepancies occur among undergraduate students, graduate students, research fellows, and the faculty as well. There is further agreement that because of the frequency of these discrepancies the productivity of the group as a whole is far below that which one could justifiably expect from such concentrations of outstanding talent.

Recently the dean of a major school of engineering said that he had become convinced of several things: that of this selected student body not more than five to ten per cent become creatively productive; that there are some who demonstrate a high absorptive capacity, but never produce ideas of their own; that there is little correlation between creativity and high marks, or even between creativity and the mere fact of survival through the engineering course; that forty to sixty per cent of all students leave because of failure or else drop out voluntarily in spite of passing grades, and that together these two categories of "drop-outs" include a major share of those with high potential creativity; and that our educational processes tend to destroy the creative potential of a large share of those who survive.

My own observations in other educational fields point to similar generalizations. Yet I cannot pretend that I have conclusive evidence for the truth of this; nor has my friend, nor anyone else. For many reasons, however, I believe that it is possible to study this problem with special precision in engineering, and that a solution here would contribute to its solution in general.

Many scientific schools emphasize also that the later productivity of their faculties cannot be predicted reliably on the basis of their earlier effectiveness in graduate school or in previous academic posts. Thus, even in the upper echelons, men of high initial "yield" may grind slowly to a stop and become unproductive. There would seem to be some "X" factor in education which plays an important role and which we have not yet learned to recognize or to measure.

The converse of all of this also occurs with a frequency which is still less clearly determined. Some men of little early promise become unexpectedly fecund. Among students at all levels are men whose performances on examinations had been low but who prove in the end to be creative. Some illustrious scientists failed examinations repeatedly (for example, Pasteur). Still others performed either up to or down to the expectations which their early tests and performances had aroused. Finally there are the irregular profiles of men whose performances at different stages of their lives and in different yet related fields revealed wide discrepancies.

Some experienced scientific and engineering educators believe that their educational processes and their students are especially vulnerable. Although scientific education is not exempt, these pessimistic impressions are not the outcome either of precise studies of engineering education or of comparative studies of the nature, the extent, the quality, and the quantity of the discrepancies which occur in these and other disciplines. If such studies are to be carried out, samples should be assembled for study by new and special methods.

A few examples of the consequences of neglecting these problems may make their importance clear.[9] There are students who perform and even produce brilliantly but only up to the point of graduation (or of receiving advanced degrees). There are the flash-in-the-pan investigators who turn out one or two creative jobs early in their careers, but thereafter become so paralyzed by inner conflicts that they never produce again. There are others who seem to acquire creative freedom only slowly and relatively late in life, as they gather the courage which is needed for that free use of preconscious processing on which creativity depends.[10] From earlier studies it appears to be true in general that this freedom must wait upon the resolution of pre-existing conflicts, which may have manifested themselves only in seemingly unrelated symptoms.[11] There are those who are highly successful and productive for many years, but who become increasingly despondent and dissatisfied in spite of success. There are others who remain relatively unproductive, yet seem content almost to the point of complacency. Some young scientists will cease being productive after marriage. For others, precisely the reverse occurs. There are men whose productivity is intermittent, and who go through long periods in which they are totally barren. Sometimes these prove to be enriching years of lying fallow. For others these are catastrophic years, from which their creative talents never recover. For Mark Twain, one such period lasted for ten desperate and nearly suicidal years before he could finish *Huckleberry Finn*.[12] For Beethoven, this occurred repeatedly with the waxing and waning of his psychopathy.[13] The scientist and the student of science are not immune to processes to which their creative counterparts in these other fields are vulnerable.

Related to these blocked periods is the drive of those who are slaves to an insatiable need, sometimes spoken of euphemistically as a "hunger for knowledge." Subjectively it is more often felt as a tense, irritable, angry, restless discontent; and its unconscious roots make it as compulsive as compulsive eating (which has its roots not in the body's recurring need for food, but in an array of unconscious processes). The same neurotic distortion of normal curiosity can distort the search for knowledge and for the mastery of any field. In considering this surprising analogy, it is important to remember the clinically well-known fact that compulsive eating can turn suddenly into a total refusal of food. In a precisely similar way, when the drive for knowledge has major roots in unconscious symbolic processes, an insatiable "hunger" can turn almost overnight into an equally obstinate rejection of knowledge and an inhibition of learning and indeed of intellectual activity of every kind. Unhappily such reversals from voracious learning to rejection occur frequently and at any age. This has been happening for centuries under the eyes of educators; yet no serious investigation has been made of its roots, causes, or precise frequency.

Instead the driven student or scientist who becomes blocked is usually assailed by epithets such as "recalcitrant" and "lazy," because the neurotogenic nature of his reaction is generally overlooked. This is one of the elementary neurotic distortions of creative learning; and because every intergrade occurs between the extreme poles of compulsive over-drive and phobic inhibition, a study of the pathological extremes will throw light on the "normal" shades of gray. The whole range of the spectrum is a necessary field for fruitful investigation.

The entire course of a student's productive life may be determined by the age at which there is a change from over-drive to inhibition or, in the reverse direction, from inhibition to release and even to over-drive. A shift in either direction may occur upon changing from one classroom to another, from one teacher to another, from one school to another. It may happen the first time a youngster goes either to a mono-educational or to a co-educational school; or the first time he goes away from home to school or college. I have seen one youngster drop from top to bottom of his class and another leap from the bottom to the top on being sent away to a boys' preparatory school—in one such instance away from the aura of a brilliant and favored sister.

Another example is the depression which may account for sudden slumps, yet may go unrecognized from kindergarten to the highest reaches of postgraduate training. Many who seem to be day-dreaming are actually in masked depressions. Release from such paralyzing depressions can occur with equal suddenness, and with a dramatic but transitory increase in the effective use of latent creative capacity. The frequency of these changes during the period of engineering education or later, and how often they remain unrecognized for years are important facts to determine. If a slump occurs early and lasts for several months it may block a gifted youngster's whole further career and development. Not only can the experience be so painful that he may never be able to return to the study of science, or indeed anything else; but it can also close all academic doors to him. When it happens at a critical phase in a young scientist's career, it may hamper his entire lifework. When it occurs later in the career of a man who has already achieved tenure, the consequences will be different and less dramatic, but no less serious. Such a scientist may save himself from feelings of defeat by devoting himself to teaching, to administrative positions, to useful service to foundations, or to college presidencies. This in turn creates its own chain reaction of consequences for our educational and research institutions and foundations. Is it for this reason that even leading educators find excuses for not investigating these problems? Do they come too close to some of us for comfort? Yet since all productive and creative people and their activities are vulnerable to neurotogenic distortions, the problem is of general significance. Any investigation of this problem would set out to ascertain how and when such transformations of a normal work drive into compulsive over-drive occur; and how often an obsessional work block is the delayed aftermath of such compulsive work drives. Tracing the natural history of the process would include a study of how these changes were interrelated with disturbances in other fields of interest and activity, both instinctual and general.

Another form of neurotogenic distortion is equally familiar. It concerns the promptness with which work is done. There is the man whose anxieties compel him always to rush, always to be ahead of time. This is the man who gets to every train not only on time but early, the student or investigator or lecturer whose work is always done long before it is necessary. In his hurry such a man can rarely stop to think, to read, to digest, to lie fallow. His opposite number gets to the train only as it is pulling out of the station. He is the student who barely gets his themes in on time or consistently brings them in late. He can never think about a problem (much less work on it) until he is under last-minute pressure. Therefore although he can sleep and daydream, he cannot lie fallow either. Thus neither the compulsive rusher nor the obsessional dawdler can allow his associative processes to drift creatively and freely. What chance then has either for that play of free-wheeling preconscious processing which is indispensable for creative activity of any kind? Again these patterns of compulsive rushing and obsessional dawdling are observable from the kindergarten throughout the graduate years. At the start they are equally neurotogenic in origin; but the dawdler is penalized from the onset, whereas in his early years the rusher is rewarded for his neurosis. It is only later that the tax collector catches up with him. Thus at every stage these differences can exercise a distorting influence on all processes of study, of perceiving, recording, and reporting experiences and observation, of imaginative rumination, and of creative experimentation.

The challenge of prediction is another variable which adds its dimensions to the problem. All scientific hypotheses and experiments carry the implication of a prediction. Yet scientists vary in the courage with which they are willing to venture to commit themselves by making explicit the predictions which are always implicit in their work. To venture a prediction is to expose oneself in a special way to being proven right or wrong. Predictions which remain unspoken leave us safely under cover. In our lurking fantasies this can have many highly charged implications. There is an important difference in the neurotic forces concealed in the scientist who ventures to make his predictions openly and the scientist who hides them. (Predictions also challenge us to develop some way of scoring certain critical ratios: (a) the ratio of implicit to explicit predictions in general and (b) the ratio of correct to incorrect predictions among both implicit and explicit predictions.)

There are many other revealing clues to pursue. The emotional implications to a man of his own scientific work may be betrayed by an inability to lie fallow without anxiety, either after successful work or during the frustrating interludes of inhibited struggle. The ability to work effectively both alone and in collaboration with others is another indicator of the extent to which creative processes are relatively free of interference from neurotic distortion and control. Indirect reflections of these traits may be found in the quality of the scientist's relationships to his own family and to his students and colleagues during various phases of his work.

Even a preliminary survey would bring to light other clusters of working traits, which subsequently could be used in the classification of data into relevant subgroups. These examples are only a few of the many neurotic patterns which one would expect to encounter in studies of the working patterns of established scientists and students of science, and in comparisons of representative samples from contrasting groups.

There are neurophysiological variables as well which influence the learning process and are interwoven with the effects of neurotogenic processes. However, only limited gains in education can be attained by improvements which are made solely in neurophysiological techniques and procedures; the neurotic process, which is universal, must simultaneously be brought under some measure of control and resolution. For instance, there is evidence that anomalies in the organization of the connections between certain areas in the brain can cause reading, writing, spelling, and calculating difficulties, which are due in part to reversal of the spatial sequence of visual and kinesthetic bits of information, and perhaps temporal reversals of auditory data as well. Thus "saw" may be read as "was." Or there may be a confusing superimposition or alternation of reversed sequences or images. This was demonstrated by the late Dr. Samuel T. Orton,[14] who called it "Strephosymbolia" and developed ingenious methods for training students who were handicapped in this way, even though in all other respects they might be exceptionally bright. It became clear to him that the effectiveness of these special techniques was limited unless steps were taken simultaneously to bring psychotherapy to bear on the concurrent affective and neurotic problems of the student.

Other studies of educational processes have shown that it is only at the upper and lower extremes of the normal curve of distribution that the IQ and special aptitudes play a dominant role in determining scholastic and creative achievement. For the so-called "bright normal" students, who make up the vast majority, limits are set rather by the play of concealed neurotic processes. The Air Force studies of "Stanine" scores demonstrated the same fact.[15]

III. *The Problem at the Graduate and Faculty Level*

Operational concepts about productivity. Any attempt to foster productivity implies an ability to recognize latent productive talent, variations in its quality and quantity and also in its freedom to emerge as manifest creative productivity, plus qualitative and quantitative variations in the products in which it is expressed. None of this is easy; but it is not impossible.

The mere volume of a man's output is not a sure measure of his scientific "product," whether the number of investigations, of published and unpublished papers, or of honors is used as the measure. The product must also meet standards of quality which can be almost as arbitrary and ephemeral as are fashions in gowns. Fashions play a role in science as in all human pursuits; and these sometimes inflate or deflate reputations without regard to ultimate values. Furthermore the game is never over until the final score is in, which may at times take years of waiting.

How, for instance, can we estimate the relative productivity of these men? One spends twenty-five years in obscure and often defeated struggles before finally breaking through into a new frontier. Another spends the same twenty-five years publishing at least one report each year on definitive but limited investigations, some with positive and some with negative results. For the investigator who is addicted to counting, the second man has been the more productive. But this does not necessarily make his stature either greater or smaller than that of the worker who waited for twenty-five years, and whose one final discovery may furnish many others with a lifetime of problems to explore, techniques to use, and principles and theories to test. Still another may turn out skillful, erudite, and precise yearly experiments which yielded negative results, which prove only that some hypothesis has been wrong. This may not have been directly productive of new knowledge; but it may have cleared the way for another's breakthrough. Indeed without the dedicated labors of countless obscure men who proved only that certain clues had been misleading, many winners of Nobel prizes would have missed their objectives. Even great scientific intelligence and imagination may fail at any particular period in the evolution of science, because of the lack of specific scientific techniques or theory at that time. Therefore the erudition, imagination, skill, and devotion of the man who corrects the errors of others, or who doggedly and skillfully pursues false clues into their ultimate blind alleys, may be as great as that of a man who uncovers a new fact or principle. These are the unknown and unrewarded heroes of science, its many "expendables." They are no less essential than are the few who reach their goals. Indeed one of the unique honors of science is the humility and honesty with which it constantly struggles to correct its own errors. It is this which makes science great among the humanities. This also is why the autopsy table is one of the proud events of human culture.[16] Our thinking about the education of the scientist must include the less spectacular but equally vital achievements of those who disprove the false.

There is also the man who says of himself that he always loses his way in experimental work. By his own statement, such a man was the late Dr. W. H. Welch.[17] Yet his critical judgment was so acute and informed that he guided the work and the development of a whole group of younger associates.

For such reasons as these, even after many years had passed it would still be hard to say which of these men had had the greater impact on scientific knowledge. Consequently potential productivity cannot be measured only by immediate or deferred positive achievements. Neither will give us a rounded understanding of the creative process in science, nor in the long run improve our methods of choosing men or of nurturing their talents.

An initial problem then is how to recognize and estimate relative degrees of productivity in its several forms: (a) among the quick and immediate "producers"; (b) among those whose work bears fruit only slowly and less predictably; (c) among those many students (and faculty) who fail to achieve spectacular positive results, but who make their contributions by the definitive precision and even the brilliance of the "failures" by which they disprove errors; and (d) finally among those highly gifted thinkers and critics who do little or no work themselves, but who inspire and guide the productive careers of many others.

Thus there seem to be at least four kinds or qualities of useful scientific productivity. Actually there are even more, and one may find all of them in the lifework of one man either at the same time or in different phases of his career. In these differences and in their fluctuations during any one man's life, both healthy and neurotic forces exercise concurrent determining influences and will determine the freedom with which a man will use his latent gifts.

A mature program of scientific education would take all of this into consideration, and also what it means emotionally to the student or to the mature scientist to be one of the "expendables," instead of one of those who triumph. With this in mind the education of scientists should include measures for maturing and strengthening them, so that disappointments will not embitter or destroy. This is not solely for humanitarian reasons. It is also for the sake of scientific progress as a whole. The thinking of the scientist who is embittered becomes distorted and feeds fresh distortions back into his own further creative efforts and into his influence on his students and their work. Thus one man's bitterness can produce distortions which may propagate themselves in future scientific generations.

Creativity: operational concepts and research. We must attempt to characterize more precisely not only the process which leads to a manifest creative act, but also what is implied by latent creative potential. Operational concepts about this are still tentative; and even if our characterization of such a potential is reasonably accurate, we may not yet be able to assign to it specific quantity values. We may have to content ourselves with the simpler judgment of "present" or "absent."

The uncovering of new relationships among both new and old data is not the whole of creativity; but it is what the creative process adds to the mastery of established data.[18] Thus creativity implies invention: the development of new machines or processes by placing old facts and principles in new combinations, and then uncovering through them still newer facts in new combinations, thus synthesizing new patterns out of data whose interdependence and mutual relevance had hitherto gone unnoted and unused. This requires both "Cogitation and Intelligence":[19] that is, "Cogito"—shaking things up, rolling the bones of one's ideas, memories, and feelings, taking them apart into bits to make new combinations; plus the superimposed process of "Intelligo"—consciously, self-critically but retrospectively going through an after-the-act process of choosing from among unanticipated combinations those patterns which have new significance. It is the sum of these steps which constitutes creative activity. The critical psychological event is the recognition of new data and new relationships, their dissection into new bits, the assembly of these bits in new combinations, giving rise to new facts and principles.

These, however, are all *preconscious* processes, not the outcome of either conscious or unconscious processes, as has been claimed mistakenly both before Freud and since. Therefore, what we must learn to assay is the potential freedom of preconscious processes to operate relatively unhampered by concurrent conscious or unconscious co-determinants. In essence, this is identical with the ability to identify relative freedom from neurosis, an equally elusive task.

Conscious processes deal only with the finished product of creative preconscious thinking. They sample the stream of preconscious activity in a somewhat pedestrian fashion, and then check and test the sample, anchor it to reality, and communicate about it to others and also to one's self in rumination. If introduced prematurely, they confine, limit, slow up, and restrict the play of preconscious processing. The influence of unconscious process is both to distort and to render rigidly repetitive the sampling of the preconscious stream by our conscious symbolic process thus limiting the free creative preconscious flow. An inquiry into the influence of any educational procedure on the creative potential of men should study the impact of the two concurrent processes, conscious and unconscious, on the preconscious imprinting of percepts and on the free play of preconscious processing.

Even before formal education starts, the small child begins to lose his spontaneous creative freedom as he acquires the power to sample the preconscious stream by means of conscious symbolic devices. This imprisonment of preconscious processing occurs precisely because the process of conscious sampling, essential though it is, is both slow and literal, making little or no use of analogic relationships. At this point our problem is to understand how the later imposition of conventional educational methods increases this imprisonment and how to educate for freedom in the future. Such a study will confront us with the technical problem of how to estimate the degrees and areas of freedom of preconscious processes, as these operate between the pedestrian, literal, reality-anchored restrictions of our conscious sampling processes, on the one hand, and the rigid, repetitive, stereotyped, neurotogenic limitations imposed by unconscious processes on the other. Since the degree of preconscious freedom determines the latent creative potential, methods are needed by which to assay the extent to which conscious and unconscious processes are hampering potentially creative preconscious processes. A study of this would illuminate the interaction of educational processes with the ubiquitous masked neurotic process in the so-called "normal." It should also lead us to an understanding of how to protect the freedom of creative preconscious processes in education while preserving the equally essential processes of conscious sampling, ruminating, and communicating.[20] Educators must first become aware that this problem exists, and that the educational procedures which have been handed down to us over the generations tend to increase the distortions and inhibitions which conscious and unconscious processes exert on pre-conscious creativity. We will make progress here only as educators come to realize the importance of better methods for the development of creative freedom in the student of science, in the mature scientist in his later years, and in all of the humanities.

IV. *The Development of Pragmatic Criteria for the Prediction of Effective Creative Productivity*

The gradual validation of criteria of creative productivity requires that precise data on earlier tests and records be correlated with the same individual's later productivity. On the student level and in successive steps of scientific schooling, familiar items would be grades in lower schools, on admission examinations and in advanced schooling. Less easy to secure would be dependable information on promptness or delay in the completion of tasks and problems —whether there has been an early history of compulsive rushing, haste, and general over-drive or of obsessional dawdling, day-dreaming, and ruminating. Of special importance would be a complete history of any changes in such patterns, including when such changes occurred and whether they had occurred suddenly or gradually over years, as well as an account of alterations in the external life-setting and internal adjustments which led up to these changes. Much of this highly personal data could be obtained only through meticulous investigation of individuals selected as samples out of various basic groups.

Reports on the quantity and quality of independent creative work during advanced schooling would also be essential but more difficult to secure. Qualitative estimates of "originality" or "newness" would require subjective judgments of individuals about themselves to compare with the judgments of their teachers, of their peers in their respective fields, and of men of equivalent stature from other but related fields.

Descriptions of habitual patterns with respect to the use of leisure and particularly of the capacity to lie fallow without panic would be helpful, as would data on the sensitive balance between the freedom to change methods or fields of research as opposed to the ability to keep on without swerving in the face of disappointments.

Collecting such information is never easy or free from the influence of many hidden biases, of which the informants themselves are usually unaware. Therefore the evaluation of reports on these issues, whether from the individual subject or from other informants, would require the use of several investigators in order to balance the bias of any one.

A composite scoring system for so many variables is difficult but not impossible; and it is less difficult for undergraduate students than for graduate students and faculty because records of the productive performance during the three or four undergraduate years are more readily accessible.

A greater difficulty arises when any effort is made to extrapolate from the past into the future: that is, from the capacity to perform competently as an undergraduate student to the ability to create independently as a graduate student, and finally to the ultimate capacity to be creative as a self-starting and self-steering, mature, and independent scientist. Criteria for this can be developed only by placing faculty members and productive scientists in contrasting groups on the basis of their capacity for creative originality, using self-scoring and cross-scoring devices, as well as their self-image. Yet these could not serve alone as objective data. Only a few mature scientists would be able to score accurately the extent to which their creative productivity had fallen short of or exceeded their earlier expectations. Some would score themselves too low and some too high, for obscure inner needs can frequently warp self-scoring in either direction. Therefore it would be essential to determine whose self-scores are objectively accurate, whose are self-inflating, and whose self-deflating.

Another group of criteria involves such items as the ability to predict within reasonable limits how long a certain piece of research will take, and its cost in money, materials, space, and assistants. Such earthy considerations are measures of the extent to which reality molds the setting and pace of the creative effort, as contrasted with the extent to which neurotogenic processes distort it to serve secret needs.

Variations in the relative distribution of time between the production of positive creative work as compared to the amount of time devoted to corrective research would give important leads to differences in the emotional significance of all research. One type of investigator always sets out to prove that earlier work was wrong, whether his own or that of others. Another type attempts to show that he has always been right and others wrong, or that he was always wrong and others right, or that all were right. An exclusive emphasis on research which produces negative results, however significant these may be, furnishes a clue to unrecognized and therefore unacknowledged emotional biases.

It is relevant to point out that during the educational process itself, such group studies as these can also have therapeutic effects, for example, by developing a student's capacity for self-criticism and for evaluating his own attitudes toward people as expressed through his work. He may even come to recognize the point at which healthy criticism becomes overdriven and destructive, whether of himself or of others, until it finally becomes an excuse for producing or finishing nothing. I can think of three scientists of high potential in three different fields who misspent their lives creating nothing because obsessional-compulsive mechanisms took over the intrinsically useful function of criticism. They did *nothing* but criticize—today themselves, tomorrow others. The seesaw never ceased. In estimating the creative potential of any man, these considerations would have to be compared with the amount of definitive creative research which provided new data or new relationships or established new working hypotheses.

Another comparative study would be of the ratio between the amount of time spent acquiring and mastering new material, the amount of time spent in systematic trial and error, and the amount spent in lonely, desultory rumination. At one pole one thinks of the late L. J. Henderson spending weeks away from his laboratory, ruminating, dreaming, and "free-wheeling," then going to his laboratory for one short, intensive bout of research. At the other pole one thinks of the compulsive worker who must always live in a continuous flurry, rushing through the motions of trial and error every day from early to late. Or one thinks of Poincaré, Otto Loewe, and many others who did their creative thinking in states of abstraction, of sleep, and even of dreaming.

The ultimate goal is the mind well-stocked with matured data, that acquires erudition without becoming leaden, that can carry its erudition lightly, freely, imaginatively. But to define this goal is one thing; to recognize and assay its presence is another; to evaluate the influence of our educational procedures a third. We know that there are no easy formulas. For instance a concurrent grasp of the non-scientific humanities sometimes goes hand in hand with this preconscious freedom; but the pursuit of the humanities does not produce this automatically. Many scholars of the humanities are as inflexible as scientists. Here as in the sciences themselves it is the creative freedom of the pursuit which counts.

V. *Procedural, Organizational, and Financial Considerations*

In designing a project to investigate the effects of education on scientific creativity, it would be necessary to start by identifying several major groups of students and mature scientists: (a) those of high initial promise whose later performances fulfill the early promise; (b) those of low initial promise whose later achievements are what had been expected; (c) those of high early promise who fall far below this; (d) those of low initial promise who exceed all expectations; (e) those who perform well, whatever their earlier promise had been, yet drop out and disappear from the engineering field; and (f) those of low or of high earlier promise whose later performance is not consistently high or low, but scattered and irregular.

The homogeneity or heterogeneity of each of these groups could not be assumed until adequate representative sub-samples had been subjected to intensive individual, cultural, psychosocial, psychological, psychophysiological, and psychoanalytic investigation.

In addition to individual variables, the effects of school variables would have to be taken into account, that is, differences in educational policies and techniques, differences in the methods and standards which govern both the admission to each school and appointments to faculty posts or to research fellowships. These would determine the range and quality of the population which is to be studied and the general level of their performance, which in turn would create the general atmosphere of expectation and pressure. Such studies would have to be paralleled by special tests carried out by a research team, which would venture predictions about the probable degrees and kinds of future creative productivity of all new undergraduate and graduate students and new faculty appointments as well, basing the predictions on appropriate ratings of past performance, special tests, personality studies, and so forth. These predictions would then have to be coded and filed away unused for many years, before significant comparisons could be made with subsequent performances. Pooled data could then be published; but no data on any individual would be revealed. By its very nature, such a study is a long one. It will have to cover more than one generation of students, research fellows, and faculty, following them through at least two decades. Moreover no one school can represent all.

Because of the need for comparative data on different schools with different techniques and different student bodies, and because of the highly personal nature of much of the information which must be gathered and the vital importance of protecting the anonymity of everyone, a group of schools will have to create an independent inter-school agency specifically for this purpose.[21]

Therefore, as a first step a group of leaders from several scientific schools, with the help of educators, behavioral scientists, and psychiatrists, would formulate a program of studies to be carried out over a period of years by an independent agency for research on engineering and scientific education.

Such a program of investigation would appeal only to those who realize that in every age and in every human culture of which we have any knowledge, something has been lacking in the processes of education,[22] and that as the span of the years of education becomes longer and as we attempt to educate more people, the price we pay for our educational errors increases.

An approximate estimate of the costs of such a project would seem to be indicated. Let us assume that a study of several representative schools would require about five teams of four each, or twenty specialists detached from their usual duties: five analytically experienced psychiatrists, five clinical psychologists, five psychiatric social workers, and five engineering educators. Their annual salary budget would be in the neighborhood of $400,000. Twenty secretaries at $5,000 would come to $100,000. Secretarial space and equipment, recording apparatus, cameras, lights, studios, and travel expenses are hard to estimate. The total cost per year might range from $600,000 to $750,000. If the study continued for a period of fifteen to twenty years, the over-all cost would be between fifteen and twenty million, including publication costs.

This is a great deal of money; yet it is estimated that the cost of educating each engineering student ranges in different schools from $25,000 to $50,000. It is estimated that voluntary drop-outs, failures, and breakdowns account for the loss of ten to fifteen per cent of all engineering students during their years of training. In addition, there is a large group who graduate but never practice engineering or who leave the profession later. These two groups represent an annual loss to engineering education of not less than one million dollars. Twenty million dollars in twenty years more than balances the estimated cost of this study; and if the application of lessons learned in the study should cut these losses at all, the study would more than pay for itself and quickly. Perhaps it would not be too expensive an undertaking after all.

To pretend that a quick and inexpensive study could be made by one or two behavioral scientists would be dishonest and deceptive. An understanding of the reasons for the failures of education in all fields and over the centuries cannot be bought at bargain rates.

VI. *Summary*

Learning, thinking, and creating are predominantly preconscious rather than conscious processes, and when left unhampered preconscious processes are effortless and effective. Yet they require translation into the language of conscious symbols in order to become usable. In one respect this process resembles the effort to translate one's thoughts into a foreign language—it slows down preconscious processes to a labored walk. The struggle between the two begins in earliest childhood as the child learns to speak, and continues through the highest reaches of education. Furthermore, our conscious symbolic tools, which are essential for the learning process and indispensable for man's highest creative functions, are peculiarly vulnerable to neurotogenic distortions. This is a second battleground.

Consequently we have to face the fact that from childhood through adolescence and on into postgraduate levels, education has to overcome two obstacles: the impact of conscious sampling on preconscious processes, and the distortions due to the neurotic process. These two struggles have always haunted human education. Only recently, however, have we begun to recognize their importance; and even today few realize that certain educational procedures tend to activate and intensify these struggles.

Many engineering educators assume that this is peculiar to engineering education, or else that it plays a larger and more destructive role in engineering than in other disciplines. Yet no conclusive evidence for this exists. Careful comparative studies of different disciplines will be of value for many reasons; but the question of whether these obstacles are more destructive in engineering education than in other disciplines is of less importance than is the mere fact that they exist, that they have been overlooked, and that they exert a generally obstructive effect on the whole process of education. If any discipline succeeds in resolving these age-old conflicts between conscious and preconscious processes and between neurosis and education, it will open the door to their solution in all.

REFERENCES

1. "The Work of the Wurzburg Group," Chapter II in George Humphrey, *Thinking, An Introduction to Experimental Psychology* (New York, 1951).

2. For details, see L. S. Kubie, "Education and the Process of Maturation," from *Today's Children are Tomorrow's World*, Associates of Bank Street Coll. of Education, Fifth Annual Conference, February 1957, New York; "Are We Educating for Maturity?" *NEA Journal*, Vol. 48, No. 1 (January 1959), pp. 58-63; "The Relation of the Conditioned Reflex to Preconscious Functions," Transactions of the 84th Annual Meeting of the American Neurological Association, Atlantic City, June 15-17, 1959, pp. 187-188; and "Research in Protecting Preconscious Functions in Education," Papers and Reports from The ASCD Seventh Curriculum Research Institute, held in Washington, D. C., on December 2, 1961, *Transactions of the Association* (April 1964), pp. 28-42.

3. L. S. Kubie, *Neurotic Distortion of the Creative Process*, Porter Lectures, Series 22 (New York, 1961); and "The Fostering of Creative Scientific Productivity," *Dædalus* (Spring 1962), pp. 294-309.

4. L. S. Kubie, "Some Unsolved Problems of the Scientific Career," *American Scientist*, Vol. 41, No. 4 (October 1953), pp. 596-613, and Vol. 42, No. 1 (January 1954), pp. 104-112.

5. L. S. Kubie, *Neurotic Distortion of the Creative Process, op. cit.*

6. L. S. Kubie, "The Concept of Normality and Neurosis," in M. Heiman (ed.), *Psychoanalysis and Social Work* (New York, 1953), pp. 3-14; and "The Forgotten Man of Education," *Harvard Alumni Bulletin*, Vol. 56, No. 8 (February 1954), pp. 349-353.

7. This thesis has been developed in detail in other publications. See, for example, L. S. Kubie, "Some Unsolved Problems of the Scientific Career," *op. cit.;* "The Search for Maturity in Pre-Professional Education," *Clinical Research*, Vol. 7, No. 2 (April 1959), pp. 177-183; and "The Spiritual Challenge of Medicine and Psychiatry to Human Culture," *Journal of Religion and Health*, Vol. 3, No. 1 (October 1963), pp. 39-55.

8. L. S. Kubie, *Neurotic Distortion of the Creative Process, op. cit.;* and "The Fostering of Creative Scientific Productivity," *op. cit.*

9. Other examples can be found in L. S. Kubie, "Some Unsolved Problems of

the Scientific Career," *op. cit.;* and "The Fostering of Creative Scientific Productivity," *op. cit.*

10. L. S. Kubie, *Neurotic Distortion of the Creative Process, op. cit.*

11. L. S. Kubie, "The Search for Maturity in Pre-Professional Education," *op. cit.;* and "Are We Educating for Maturity?" *op. cit.*

12. Bernard DeVoto, "The Precipitate," in *The World of Fiction* (Boston, 1950). Also published as "Symbols of Despair," in *Mark Twain at Work* (Cambridge, Mass., 1942).

13. Richard and Editha Sterba, *Beethoven and His Nephew* (New York, 1954).

14. Samuel T. Orton, *Reading, Writing, and Speech Problems in Children* (New York, 1937).

15. L. S. Kubie, "The Limitations of Aptitude Tests in the Selection of Air Force Personnel," *American Scientist*, Vol. 43, No. 1 (January, 1955), pp. 105-108.

16. L. S. Kubie, "The Spiritual Challenge of Medicine and Psychiatry to Human Culture," *op. cit.*

17. Simon and James F. Flexner, *William Henry Welch* (New York, 1941).

18. L. S. Kubie, *Neurotic Distortion of the Creative Process, op. cit.*

19. *Ibid.*

20. L. S. Kubie, "Research in Protecting Preconscious Functions in Education," *op. cit.*

21. The need for this was first argued by Professor Gordon Brown of MIT at a conference on engineering education in Boulder, Colorado, in 1961. My own experiences in practice bring me to the same conclusion.

22. L. S. Kubie, "The Forgotten Man of Education," *op. cit.;* and "The Search for Maturity in Pre-Professional Education," *op. cit.*

FORREST WILLIAMS

The Mystique of Unconscious Creation

A FUNDAMENTAL question concerning creativity is whether to assign creative acts to the operations of consciousness and intelligence or to a region of unconscious powers. Von Kekulé's ring conception of organic compounds, Shakespeare's "ravell'd sleave of care," Poincaré's idea for the Fuchsian functions: where, and hence by what forces, are such creative achievements enacted? And in any reply to this factual question of where to locate acts of scientific and artistic creation within the economy of the human psyche, not only important issues of psychology and aesthetics are at stake. Nothing less important than our ethical portrait of man, what he is and what he can strive to be, also seems to be at issue; for wherever our creative powers are said to reside, there, we must suppose, is found the better part of man.

A number of factors have accustomed us to suppose the answer to lie in a so-called "creative unconscious." Principally Freudian psychology, of course, but also Surrealism in the arts, much of the language of contemporary criticism, and even current conversational idiom have contributed to its prominence and diffusion. On this view, which I shall dub "the underground theory," the act of creation is enacted after a psychological *regression* from conscious agencies to an unconscious level of forces at once *more primitive* and *more creative* than the conscious mind and its more specifically intellectual powers. Our admiration for human creativity, in this event, scarcely would be a vote of confidence in the powers of consciousness, but rather, an appreciation of forces operating in a netherworld of the human psyche. Thus, the mathematician Poincaré felt logically persuaded by such an explanation of the creative act, but at the same time recoiled in dismay from its intellectually deflating implications. "What do I say?" he asked. "It [the unconscious] knows better how to divine than the conscious self since it succeeds where that has failed. In a word, is not the subliminal self superior to the conscious self? I confess that, for my part, I should hate to accept this."[1]

On the other hand, we might be said to exercise the creative act upon a mountain—or at least, a hill—on the everyday landscape of conscious experience and intelligence. On this "Parnassian" hypothesis, our natural admiration for human creativity is at the same time a compliment to the efficacy of human consciousness and the powers of lucid experience. Shakespeare's metaphor and von Kekulé's chemical discovery would spring from energies conscious in character, and thus high on the scale of evolutionary development and mental complexity.

Proponents of the underground theory are, I believe, sincere, powerful, and wrong. Their hypothesis concerning the act of creation is prima facie implausible and psychologically false. By the same token, it is seriously misleading for any ethical portrait of what man is and can be.

Unfortunately for the task of criticism and evaluation, the underground theory of creativity is frequently confused with the thesis of epiphenomenalism, from which it differs significantly by virtue of its key principle of psychological regression from conscious causes to unconscious causes. George Santayana, for example, would have freely granted that creative thinking is wholly accomplished by non-conscious forces, simply because he held that consciousness itself has no causal efficacy whatsoever. All agencies in man and throughout nature are entirely material and non-conscious. Thus, in contrast to the underground theory, the act of creation is no special case on the epiphenomenalist hypothesis. A so-called "act of consciousness" is always a mere badge, a mere sign, of certain physiological activities: a causally superfluous appearance that does nothing at all and hence explains nothing at all. The efficacious acts of animals and human beings are never themselves of the nature of consciousness, which is but a play of appearances somewhat like the insubstantial flickerings on a cinema screen. The true causes are in a physical machinery hidden from immediate experience and reflection. The empirical problem of creativity is thus to establish insofar as possible correlations between specific bodily processes and the occurrence in consciousness of certain thoughts which seem creative in character. One would naturally expect the appearance of such ideas as Shakespeare's or von Kekulé's to correlate with the most highly evolved and complex physical processes of the human nervous system or brain. The epiphenomenalism of a Santayana would thus be incompatible with the underground theory and its principle of regression to more primitive forces, and is most probably a materialist version of what I have called the Parnassian theory. It has the real merit, moreover, of being able to indicate, at least in principle, precisely what "the creative unconscious" might be, namely, certain high-level physiological processes among many other physiological processes.

A proponent of the underground theory, however, will probably point out that the epiphenomalist view is prima facie too implausible even to be taken seriously. For, as Socrates pointed out while disposing of a doctrine that the body is a vibrating lyre of which thought is merely the ineffectual sound, consciousness certainly does not *seem* to us to be a supernumerary and inefficacious emblem of bodily processes. Thinking, desiring, imagining, deciding, would seem to be *causes* within man, often assuming a leading part in human behavior, just as surely as respiration and muscular flexion.

This objection to epiphenomenalist theory of mind seems well taken. Much can be said for David Hume's dictum that, although in the natural sciences the more farfetched the explanation, the more probably true (who would have dreamed that a grain of salt contains an uncountable number of spinning systems?), in inquiries concerning the human understanding, the more farfetched the explanation, the more likely it is to be false. The underground theory, by holding that conscious forces exist, function, and have results, thus lays claim to greater prima facie plausibility than epiphenomenalism. It contends simply that when our usual powers of consciousness are unequal to a radical challenge to our ideas, we regress to infra-conscious forces, where a "creative unconscious" may at that juncture succeed in formulating the illuminating metaphor or scientific idea. During this regressive moment of inspiration, the daylight forces of conscious thought on which we generally rely merely lapse into abeyance.

The main lines of argument in favor of the underground theory repeatedly occur in the history of modern psychology and philosophy. Arthur Koestler's widely-read work, *The Act of Creation*,[2] stands as a recent and particularly enthusiastic presentation. Put forward by a science writer and novelist of his reputation, the thesis in question naturally has thereby gained increased intellectual momentum. And, interestingly enough, our opening suggestion that conceptions of the locus of creativity do have significant moral implications seems to be borne out by Koestler's theory. Believing creative acts to be accomplished by unconscious powers acknowledged to be less evolved than the activities of consciousness, and at the same time recognizing the immense value of our creative achievements, Koestler is led to espouse what may fairly be called a neo-primitivist philosophy of man. His text thus promulgates a kind of mystique of the irrational somewhat reminiscent of a D. H. Lawrence—without, of course, the dispensation of poetic license. It is, therefore, a characteristic formulation of the underground theory, not only as a psychological doctrine, but as a philosophy of human values.

Genius, as an old definition goes, is the ability to intuit previously unsuspected relations. Koestler defines this occurrence as a "bisociation of matrices." Whereas the term "association" merely signifies for him a widening of a single matrix or system along some previously indicated lines, the term "bisociation" is coined to signify heretofore incongruent or separated matrices interrelating in a fruitful and unprecedented linkage. Considerable skepticism has already been expressed by commentators about the alleged universality of this formula, which is said by Koestler to apply throughout nature.[3] But with regard to specifically human, symbolic acts of creation in art, science, and humor, which constitute our only topic here, Koestler's concept of matrix-bisociation seems perfectly sound, and is amply illustrated by telling examples. In fact, despite the new locution and some explicit denials by Koestler, symbolic matrix-bisociation could probably be shown to be a restatement and extension of the venerable and persuasive analogical theory of poetic metaphor.[4]

In acts of creation, matrices are said to "bisociate" either through a clash, as in the witticism, "I can resist anything but temptation"; through fusion, as in Archimedes' law; or through juxtaposition, as in "the ravell'd sleave of care." The matrices are previously disparate worlds of ideas, which we link in creative moments, despite the powerful polarizing tendencies of convention and habit. If we accept this notion of matrix-bisociation as essentially sound, our quarrel with Koestler and the underground theory in general begins with the answers to the related questions of *where* in man this genial ability functions and by what *kind* of forces. These turning points, these critical moments of artistic and scientific thought are, as we know, said to be an exceptional type of unconscious activity.[5]

Certainly, in one sense, no one could deny that much of the work entering into creative achievement is unconsciously performed. The same is true, for that matter, of the most routine accomplishments. A fund of sheer, unconscious habit underlies both the creative solution to an artistic or scientific challenge and the resolution of everyday problems like calculating income tax or steering in rush-hour traffic. Hard-won operations, once consciously performed, such as multiplying numbers or shifting gears or sketching a human figure, settle into a veritable unconscious of useful habits. Koestler himself insists, and rightly so, on this psychological fact. Koestler further insists, and again, rightly so, that the unconscious of habits will not, however, account for what is specifically original in the achievements of a Shakespeare or a von Kekulé. Nor by sheer chance could habits suffice for creations, as in the statistical fable of innumerable monkeys jumping on typewriters until, after eons of gibberish, a *Macbeth* or a new chemical theory happens to get written. Creative acts have an extraordinarily low order of probability. Bisociations of matrices cannot therefore be sufficiently explained either by habit or by random associations at an unconscious level. Running *counter* to habit and to sheer chance at the crucial moment, they exhibit, in the words of Poincaré, which Koestler quotes with approval, "discernment, tact, and delicacy."

If telling time, planning a trip, or arguing about the nature of creative thought may stand as examples of conscious psychological agencies at work, then creative thought or matrix-bisociation becomes, on the underground theory, a special case. In certain privileged moments, we regress to a special underground system of powers. Koestler feels justified in concluding that there must exist, besides the unconscious of habit, which is merely associative, another unconscious, which is "bisociative." This bisociating unconscious performs the act of creation, neither by habit nor by chance, and on behalf of the stalled conscious powers of the mind. The result, an original notion, then "surges up" into the light of day as a *fait accompli*. Our most valuable scientific and artistic insights are therefore minted by powers phylogenetically and ontogenetically less evolved, Koestler tells us (page 172), than the forces of consciousness responsible for more commonplace mental acts.

In criticism, the theory can be shown, to begin with, to be highly implausible. Furthermore, the two main lines of reasoning characteristic of the underground theory are logically fallacious, so that the theory, even if it were not farfetched, would remain unproven by its arguments. And finally, a perfectly plausible and unforced interpretation of creative thought lies close at hand to the very sort of evidence cited in favor of the underground theory by Koestler and others.

First, the theory is prima facie implausible. If the explanation of epiphenomenalism and of random association have been rejected by the underground theory as farfetched in the extreme, what is to be said of a thesis requiring us to believe in the existence of a set of forces at one and the same time unconscious and discerning, unconscious and pioneeringly insightful, unconscious, delicate and supremely tactful? What, indeed, are we to say of the strikingly contradictory notion peculiar to the underground theory, the notion (in Koestler's words) of an "unconscious mind's eye"?[6]

Second, its two usual lines of argument are logically fallacious. One characteristic argument consists in citing the supposed pedigree of the expression "unconscious mind" or its variants. Koestler himself invokes celebrated thinkers from Plotinus to the present who have employed some such term or idea. However, assuming for the sake of argument that most of the authorities cited, together with Koestler himself, have all meant more or less the same thing by the notion, it would be easy to cite equally illustrious counter-authorities. In fact, Koestler himself correctly names John Locke as having "boldly denied" any such thing as unconscious thought; and of course one could add Descartes, Jean-Paul Sartre, and many other eminent names. The appeal to authority is a two-edged sword, and, as usual, settles nothing.

There is no reason to suppose, in any event, that the famous names cited by Koestler as affirming an "unconscious mind" all meant anything like the same thing by this notion, much less that they countenanced the particular thing Koestler means. Such expressions have been used to refer to many different things: a penumbra of awareness; temporarily forgotten experiences (as in the opening pages of *Swann's Way*); habits taken over from once-reflective and conscious operations (as already noted); desires which we have strong motives to turn our attention away from; or perfectly conscious acts of mind which are not organized in the discursive patterns of conceptual thought and prose syntax. Clearly none of these corresponds to the notion of a "creative unconscious" as this is meant by the underground theory; although the last, namely, non-conceptually organized inquiry and understanding, is as we shall see the important alternative that proponents of the underground theory characteristically and unaccountably ignore.

The historical line of argument from authorities thus fails. It is impossible to produce a satisfactory pedigree for a patently mongrel notion. The second characteristic line of argument therefore turns directly to the facts themselves, that is, to the creative turning points in experience. The object is to reason from their observable traits to a plausible account of where and by what sort of force these turning points in art and science are effected. Since the facts are psychological events, the observations naturally consist of reflections on actual moments of insight, or at least on well-reported instances. We shall see, however, that the underground theory is only reached by passing from this legitimate introspective evidence to the conclusion by way of a complete *non sequitur*.

Let us ask with Koestler, for example, where and by what powers a von Kekulé advanced from the traditional chain theory of organic compounds to the epoch-making ring theory. The scientist reported that at a given moment, while contemplating in his mind's eye a row of gamboling atoms, he visualized the row as a snake, and then, as a snake biting its own tail. Koestler correctly identifies several important traits of this phenomenon. Its content is rather more imaginal than conceptual. Temporally, it is more or less instantaneous, rather than a succession of mental events. And its form is intuitional rather than inferential, a kind of seeing rather than a kind of arguing.

On the basis of these traits, the theory maintains that such acts are performed by an unconscious agency. This conclusion does not follow, however, except on the prior assumption that an intelligent and conscious act of mind *must* be conceptual and argumentative in type. Nor is instantaneousness a proof of unconscious origins. "*Le temps, monsieur,*" as Molière's poet protested, "*ne fait rien à l'affaire!*" For reflection plainly reports conscious and intelligent acts which do *not* plod through time in conceptual boots putting down one idea after another, as in a discursive proposition or argument (such as, for example, in these words of mine).

Let us look more closely at von Kekulé's retrospective account of his historic hypothesis. Until that turning point in modern science, the thinker had been trying, as Koestler informs us, to fit known facts of organic chemistry into the matrix of a chain theory. Suddenly, he visualized a row of atoms as a snake biting its own tail. Surely, for a mind intensely preoccupied over a long period of time with a vexing problem in chemistry, this act was clearly no idle fancy, but an immensely significant performance. Indeed, given the standard scientific notions of 1865, to imagine a row of atoms to metamorphose into a snake seizing its tail seems as fine an instance of perfectly conscious intelligence at work on a theoretical problem of chemistry as one could ever hope to find. In and by the formation of this image, the new theory was thought of. A snake bit its own tail: a chain bent back upon itself to become a ring: two matrices were bisociated: a creative idea for chemistry had been formulated.

The circumstances of von Kekulé's experience were, as it happened, rather more somnolent than wakeful. How tempting, therefore—and how easy—to invoke some "creative unconscious" to do the work. Yet his dozing experience was nonetheless a state of conscious activity. (How else, indeed, could von Kekulé have recalled it?) And it was, we may reasonably suppose, greatly advantaged by the absence of the impertinent distractions of more wakeful experience. To think *hard*, to *concentrate*, is to tune out much of the surrounding world, and is frequently facilitated by circumstances in which inhibition of such stimuli has already been accomplished by fatigue or other conditions. Fortunately for von Kekulé and for modern chemistry, no Porlockian visitor knocked on the door at that moment to summon the scientist's *consciousness*—not some unconscious—back to its more workaday world.

Thus, a plausible answer to the question of the locus of creation seems to lie ready to hand. On the scientist's own account, the creative act was performed *by* powers of intelligence *in* the full light of consciousness. Von Kekulé made the creative discovery *in* his conscious mind's eye precisely *by* the power of imagining a row of gamboling atoms to be a snake seizing its own tail. The same may be said, *pari passu*, of the felicitous metaphors of a Shelley, the witty phrases of a Wilde or a Molière, the mathematical discoveries of a Poincaré—all those acts of extraordinary "discernment, tact, and delicacy."

To conclude that because such "matrix-bisociations" are not abstract in content, nor discursive in form, nor temporally extensive, they must therefore be unconsciously performed, is surely an egregious *non sequitur*. That an activity is non-discursive in character does not imply at all that it is non-conscious—unless, of course, one has previously equated the two.

This identification or confusion of the non-discursive with the non-conscious is the key mistake of the underground theory. It might well be dubbed, for want of a conventional name, "The Prose Writer's Fallacy." For, like M. Jourdain, all of us have been talking prose most of our lives. So we seem inclined, by a kind of occupational prejudice, to equate forthwith the sum of all intelligent activities of consciousness with only one species of them: discursive thought. Anything equally knowledgeable, yet characteristically different from the discursive style of prose writing, must, we tend to suppose, proceed from an *infra-conscious* agency. The philosophic stage is then set for introducing a special kind of powerfully wise, unconscious power, to which we are then assumed to regress in moments of creation.

This confusion, and the attendant *non sequitur* regarding human creativity, are far from inevitable. The history of the subject shows that intuitive powers of intelligence, of conscious mind, have been acknowledged, examined, and characterized, by such otherwise divergent minds as, *inter alia*, Plato, Aristotle, Spinoza, Croce, Cassirer, Koffka, Merleau-Ponty, and Susanne Langer. This is not to deny, of course, that the topic of intuitive intelligence is a very difficult one. Within the common acknowledgment of such an active function of consciousness there is room for considerable disagreement. The particular place of such acts within the whole economy of consciousness, their relationships to judgments, to concepts, to analysis, their criteria of evidence, their specific symbolic form, these are much debated and difficult issues for epistemology and psychology. Furthermore, that intuitive acts of mind are not always fruitful, that they may be misleading, even obstructive, is not to be forgotten, and has already been noted. Like every effort of the mind to advance in wisdom, allegedly creative ideas must meet the test of experience. But this pragmatic requirement is nothing to the point as to their conscious or unconscious enactment.

Theories of human creativity, it was said at the outset, always have a moral. If the act of creation is, as I have claimed, a perfectly conscious exercise of a certain capacity of human intelligence, then artistic and scientific "bisociations of matrices" bespeak a human power *at least* as complex and evolved as the power of conceptualization and discursive argumentation. Indeed, beside such exhibitions of intuitive "discernment, tact, and delicacy," the discursive activities of consciousness would seem somewhat *less* complex and refined.

Thus located upon, as it were, a Mount Parnassus rising on the landscape of intelligence, creativity draws our attention and, indeed, our admiration toward human consciousness and its powers. In our various portraits of what man is and ought to be, these would seem the functions which represent the better part of man. But if the thesis of a creative unconscious be true, then we shall have to accept an irrationalist conception of human culture that depreciates the conscious life of perception, imagination, and reason to just the degree that it identifies creativity with ontogenetically and phylogenetically primitive forces operating in an infra-conscious region. This would be to say, in effect, that the *toro*, not the *torero*, makes of the *corrida* a subtle science and an expressive art.

Having been misled by an identification of the intuitive with the subconscious, Poincaré was only too understandably reluctant to abide by his own hypothesis of unconscious creation. The underground theory always bears with it an ethic of dark gods, proposing to lend an aura of scientific respectability to an atavistic mystique that, one fears, has only too sure an appeal in every time, ours being no exception. If human culture is indeed created in a pitchblack cave below the functions of perception, imagination, thought, and reasoning that empower our conscious life, then our incalculable gratitude and respect for the creative abilities of a Shakespeare, a von Kekulé, a Molière, a Poincaré, are properly owed to primitive, chthonic forces. We need not be surprised, therefore, that some of the proponents of a creative unconscious, less committed than the great French mathematician to the worth of the human intelligence, cheerfully score polemical points off clarity and thought, in the same breath that they praise creativity in the arts and sciences. Over the shoulder of the thesis of a creative unconscious, whatever its specific form, grimace sooner or later the features of a mankind wittingly or unwittingly confounding the best in itself with the least in itself.

But the thesis, we have argued, is mistaken in fact. It justifies its inevitable disparagement of man's unique and precarious organ of lucidity, human consciousness, only by ignoring a prima facie plausible interpretation of the act of creation for the sake of an implausible one, which is reached by a *non sequitur* based on a confusion.

REFERENCES

1. Arthur Koestler, *The Act of Creation* (New York, 1964), p. 164.

2. Arthur Koestler, *op. cit.*

3. D. R. Newth, *Spectator* (May 29, 1964), p. 728; P. B. Pedawar, *New Statesman* (June 19, 1964), pp. 950-952; Stephen Toulmin, *Encounter* (July 1964), pp. 58-70; Elizabeth Janeway, *Saturday Review* (October 17, 1964), pp. 35-36; Loren Eiseley, *The New York Times Book Review* (October 18, 1964), pp. 3, 40-41; and Henry D. Aiken, *New York Review of Books* (December 17, 1964), p. 22.

4. Koestler maintains that the familiar notion of analogy falls short of his concept of matrix-bisociation. Analogy, he objects on page 200, is merely "a process of reasoning from parallel causes," and "the rub is in the word 'parallel.'" He observes correctly that more than a mere parallelism is involved in a fruitful "bisociation of matrices," because a "selective emphasis" is also present. However, as a matter of historical fact, Koestler has underestimated the notion of analogical thinking. A factor of selective emphasis was traditionally included under this title; as, for example, in Aristotle, where analogies expressed in simile and metaphor were recognized as involving a determining context or limiting ground.

5. Some critics might object to Koestler's ignoring the question of public verification of such genial "bisociations of matrices." The objection would seem unfair. The topic of the act of creation, as Koestler understands it and as understood here, is the more limited one of the psychological act. Naturally, the act of creation, the "inspired conception," as it might be called, must then prove itself publicly, by reference to the artistic or scientific task at hand.

6. Arthur Koestler, *op. cit.*, p. 200.

JEROME KAGAN

Personality and the Learning Process

THE CENTRAL concern of both educator and psychologist has always revolved around the twin questions of "what is learning?" and "how does it occur?" Despite years of thought and many hundreds of laboratory investigations, we are still not able to provide logically commanding and intuitively attractive answers to these questions. The gnawing sense of bewilderment that surrounds these issues is attenuated a bit if one assumes that if a child attends to information presented to him he is most likely to learn something about it. If the child's attention toward the written or spoken symbol is guaranteed, some learning is likely to occur. Put aside any temporary complaints to this presumptuously simple proposition and consider the directive it implies. This idea leads us to inquire into those psychological factors that promote or obstruct attention to symbolic material. The focus on the child's attention rather than on the special effect of a particular book, television program, or curriculum delineates a principle that can guide the preparation of material for intellectual consumption by the child. The principle states: the learning of a new rule, word, or bond between two previously unrelated elements requires a certain level of prior cognitive resources and sustained attention to the material to be learned. The level of attention is determined by a variety of factors, many of which have been regarded traditionally as personality variables. These personality variables include concepts like motives, expectancies, sources of anxiety, defenses, and standards, each of which exerts some control over the child's distribution of attention in a problem situation and governs the initiation of and persistence with mental work. These intrapsychic forces determine how long the child will work at the learning of a new task, how difficult a task he will attempt to master, and how he will interpret success or

153

failure. The most relevant concepts are described in the sections below.

The motive for acceptance and positive evaluation by parents and parent surrogates. The desire for praise, affection, and more symbolic signs of positive evaluation from adults leads the child to work at the mastery of new skills in order to obtain and retain these rewards. To many children of four or five years of age learning is a socially motivated enterprise, especially when the tasks do not have any clear relationship to the instrumental skills the child uses every day. That is to say, learning how to play marbles and learning to ride a bicycle have strong significance for the child because of their positive valuation by peers and because the child is able to assess his progress in gaining mastery over them. However, reading, spelling, and arithmetic do not always share these extra advantages. Learning multiplication tables is intrinsically boring to many children. The child becomes interested in acquiring this skill because adults whom he admires praise and reward him for that mastery. The receipt of adult rewards for such mastery is interpreted by the child as signifying that he is appreciated by the adults who administer these favors. The value of these favors depends on the sex and age of the child and the nature of the task. In general, adult praise is more significant for girls than for boys, for younger children than for older children and most relevant when the task to be mastered is related to previously valued instrumental skills.

The motive for differentiation. There is a general human tendency, present from the preschool years on, to accrue attributes that differentiate the self from peers and siblings; to develop characteristics that allow the person to label himself in some unique way. The writer recalls young children pointing with pride to their surname in the telephone book and saying, "We are the only Brewsters in the telephone book." The child's understanding of who he is derives, in part, from the skills he has mastered. The specific skills he chooses for mastery are determined by the values of his subculture. Since our social community places heavy emphasis on intellectual mastery, most children choose this route for self-definition, and their striving for excellence in the academic situation is partially in the service of the desire for differentiation. Professor Donald MacKinnon of the University of California recently contrasted the personalities of architects and mathematicians who were judged to be extremely creative with those in the same occupation who were successful but less creative. One of the salient characteristics of the highly creative adult was his strong desire to be different from his peers, his yearning to produce a unique product.

The motivation to maximize similarity to a desirable model. Children and adults want to maximize similarity to adults who command power, status, and instrumental competence. The child desires these intangible goals but does not know how to obtain them. He believes, however, that if he made himself similar to the adult models who appear to possess these desirable resources he might share vicariously in their power, status, and competence. If these models display an interest in the mastery of intellectual skills the child will attempt to mimic such mastery in order to maximize similarity with the model and increase the probability that he will share in these intangible goals. The absence of this dynamic in many lower-class families is partially responsible for the fact that lower class children are less highly motivated to master intellectual skills. The lower-class child's inadequate performance in school is not solely the result of his parents' indifference to his school performance. Lower-class parents often exhort the child to work for grades and punish the child for failure. However, the lower-class parent is not perceived by the child as a person who values intellectual mastery. Thus the child does not view intellectual mastery as a likely way of gaining the adult resources of power and competence that he perceives his parent to possess.

It may seem inconsistent to state that the child has a strong motive for differentiation and an equally strong motive for maximizing similarity to an adult model. These two processes behave like a pair of opposing pipers that lead each individual through much of his life. One of the basic characteristics of man is his attempt to maintain a balance between the desire to differentiate himself from a larger group with less resources than he commands and an equally strong desire to make himself similar to a group who he believes possess more resources. Psychological development has a spiral form in which a child identifies with a group commanding desirable goals and, after maximizing similarity to that group, differentiates from it and passes on to the next identification, in an almost never ending seesaw struggle between maximizing similarity to one model and differentiating from another.

Expectancy of success or failure. Children quickly develop different expectations of success or failure in intellectual tasks. Unfortunately, the most frequent and prepotent reaction to an expectancy of failure is decreased involvement in the task and subsequent withdrawal. Educators have been guilty of minimizing the critical role which a child's expectancy of failure plays in shaping his behavior in a school situation. An extreme variant of the progressive movement in education assumed that the child, if left to his own devices, would seek the best possible intellectual diet. This assumption proved only partially true, for it ignored or refused to acknowledge that a child as young as six years of age is aware of his capacities, has clear expectancies of success or failure, and wishes to protect himself from the anxiety that follows failure. Many six-year-old children with a strong desire to learn to read, but with an equally strong doubt over their ability to do so, do not spontaneously approach books, but withdraw to the less threatening tasks of coloring and pasting. The child's motives are contingent upon expectation of success or failure, and motives are sloughed or adopted with zeal, depending upon the degree to which the child believes he can attain the goals that gratify the motive. Persistence at task mastery hangs delicately on the balance between hope and fear.

Anxiety derived from conflicts over learning. There are many relevant conflicts that inhibit or facilitate the learning process. These include excessive competitiveness, desire for power over others, assumption of a passive posture with teachers, anxiety over dependency, and sex-role conflicts. Let us consider each of these briefly. The school situation, in most public-school settings, is essentially a competitive enterprise. The child who desires good grades, for whatever reason, realizes he is in competition with his peers. The teacher organizes the classroom situation as a competitive arena. In such a context the child with a strong desire for excellence will entertain wishes that those who are his closest rivals will suffer some misfortune. The child who is vulnerable to guilt over these hostile thoughts may become anxious and place some inhibition on his attempts at excellence. This conflict over the hostile flavor of competitive wishes is one reason that young adolescent girls perform less well in high school and college than they should. The female in our culture is more disposed to guilt over hostile wishes and inhibits intense academic effort as a result of this conflict.

An equally forceful conflict is experienced by boys during the elementary school years. The primary grades are characterized by a pressure for conformity and for a passive posture vis à vis the teacher. The six- or seven-year-old boy is in the process of identifying with adult males and experiences some conflict over assuming an overly conforming or passive attitude with the female teacher. The imposition of a passive role creates anxiety and conflict, and he attempts to fight assumption of this role. The unruliness, distractibility, and general mischievous behavior of second-grade boys is related, in part, to conflict over the passivity imposed by the school situation.

A final conflict is more pervasive and involves the relationship between sex-role identification and academic products. It is well documented that problems requiring analysis and reasoning, especially spatial reasoning, science, and mathematics problems, are viewed by both sexes as more appropriate for boys than for girls. As might be expected, girls perform less well on such materials. In one investigation, adolescents and adults were presented with problems involving mathematical reasoning, and the males obtained consistently higher scores. However, if the same problem dealt with "feminine" contents such as cooking or gardening, the females did much better than if the problems dealt with guns, money, or geometric designs, although the reasoning operations were identical in both problems. The typical girl believes that the ability to solve problems in geometry, physics, logic, or arithmetic is a masculine skill, and her motivation to persist with such problems is low. Her decreased involvement reflects the fact that her self-esteem is not at stake in such problems. In some cases she is potentially threatened by the possibility that she might perform with unusual competence on such tasks, for excellence is equated with a loss of femininity.

The sex-typed character of knowledge is most evident in the vocational choices of young adolescents. A recent national survey asked several thousand high-school students about their probable major in college and future occupational choice. The sex-typed character of their choices was already evident in the ninth grade where twenty-five per cent of the boys and only three per cent of the girls selected the physical or natural sciences, whereas three per cent of the boys and thirteen per cent of the girls chose elementary- or secondary-school education as future vocations. An additional reason for the lowered motivation and performance of girls in science and mathematics rests with the fact that a girl's sex-role identity is more dependent on her ability to attract and maintain a love relationship than it is on her academic skills. The male views academic excellence as a necessary antecedent to vocational success. Since such success is an essential component of the male sex-role identity we would expect the adolescent male to be more highly motivated to master those tasks that are linked to his vocational choice. A girl is more likely to work to gain the acceptance or approval of her teacher and parents, while the boy uses mastery as a test of his personal potency. More boys are oriented to figure the task, more girls to figure the teacher.

Although an intense involvement in the sciences and mathematics is more characteristic of the adolescent and adult male than female, this differential in motivation is not necessarily the case in the primary grades. In the early years, girls typically out-perform boys in all areas, and the ratio of boys to girls with reading problems varies from three-to-one to six-to-one. How can we understand the fact that the academic performance of girls is superior to that of boys during the primary grades but gradually becomes inferior during adolescence and adulthood? Two reasons have been mentioned: boys eventually link vocational success with academic performance and their lower anxiety over competitiveness leaves them freer to strive for superiority over their peers. A final reason for the increasing academic superiority of boys rests with the change in perception of the sex-typed character of school and academic work. First- and second-grade boys have more difficulty than girls in mastering reading and arithmetic because the boy perceives the school atmosphere as essentially feminine. The six-year-old boy is striving to develop a masculine sex-role identification, and he resists involvement in feminine acts. By the time the boy is ten or eleven, he recognizes the relationship between a vocation and school work, and his resistance lessens. The atmosphere of the primary grades is generally viewed as feminine because the child's introduction to school is mediated by females who initiate the activities of painting, coloring, and singing. Most teachers place a premium on obedience, decorum, and inhibition of aggression and restless motoricity. These values are better tailored to girls than to boys and it is not surprising that children view the school situation as more feminine than masculine. Also, there are strong semantic associations between the dimensions of "masculinity" and "femininity" and specific areas of knowledge for most adult members of western culture. This is an unfortunate marriage for one would hope that knowledge would retain some neutrality amidst the warring factions of the mind. It may be possible, however, to alter this associational link between domain of knowledge and the sex roles through modifications in the procedures and atmosphere in the elementary schools.

Standards of performance with respect to intellectual tasks. Children differ dramatically in the standards of performance which they set for themselves. Some children decide that performance just a bit above average for their class is adequate to meet their standards; others demand of themselves the top position in the class. The child's commitment to work and persevere will be a function of the standard that satisfies him.

Preferred modes of dealing with hypotheses and information. A final construct of relevance involves individual differences in the speed with which hypotheses are selected and information is processed. It has been established that the tendency to be impulsive or reflective in selecting ideas for action is an extremely stable trait that generalizes across a wide variety of tasks. When faced with a problem suggesting multiple possibilities for solution, some children select the first answer that occurs to them, and, in many cases, their solution is incorrect. Others tend to brood a longer period of time, considering the differential validity of the various solution hypotheses that occur to them. These children are called reflective, and they are usually more accurate in their first reply. It should not be surprising that reflective children do better on problems of inductive reasoning, make fewer errors when learning to read, and are regarded by the teacher as inhibited.

These constructs deal with some of the major forces that exert strong control over the involvement of children in learning new materials. Now let us turn to the ways in which these ideas can help resolve the question of whether discovery learning, that is, learning through inductive reasoning, is more effective than teaching through exposition. Should the teacher give the child examples and allow him to infer the rule or should she present the rule first and allow the child to explore the relevant examples?

A common strategy in polarized debates of this type is to reply, "It depends on the child, his sex, his age, his personality." This reply is offered not because we wish to evade the issue, but because it appears to be the most reasonable posture. Individual differences in behavior are the rule rather than the exception, and there are few environmental intrusions that have the same effect on all children. There is always interaction between method of presentation in the classroom and the psychology of the child with respect to the mastery of intellectual material. Let us consider, therefore, the pros and cons of an inferential *versus* a deductive approach to the presentation of learning materials to children.

The following arguments are often presented in support of the inferential or discovery method of teaching:

Discovery learning requires more involvement on the part of the child and therefore greater attention to the component materials being presented. Since the discovery strategy creates maximum attention and involvement it should lead to more efficient learning.

Discovery learning requires the child to make an intellectual effort, and this effort leads to an increase in the value of the task. It is reasonable to assume that activities become valuable to the degree to which effort is expended. In fact, many of us have had the experience of being more involved in a set of data we collected personally than in data we might regard as more "significant" scientifically but which were collected by other people. Effort increases the incentive value of the enterprise, and motivation is created or increased.

Inferential learning is likely to increase the child's expectancy that he is able to solve problems autonomously. The discovery method maximizes the likelihood that the child will learn a self-descriptive statement having the following content: "I can think." One of the primary aims of education is not only to teach the child some particular set of cognitive rules or structures, but also to teach him confidence in his ability to think creatively about intellectual problems. The method of discovery is more likely to accomplish this end because it requires the child to infer a major principle without excessive guidance from an external agent.

The method of inferential learning helps children who have a passive-dependency conflict with respect to the teacher. Some children, especially boys, have difficulty in a traditional school setting because of their strong conflict over a dependent orientation toward the teacher. Since the culture promotes independence in boys and creates a standard for independent activity, many boys experience discomfort and anxiety over a passive posture with female adults. The method of inferential learning requires and promotes a more independent attitude on the part of the child and should help those boys who are experiencing high conflict over passivity.

These are four possible advantages of the inferential method. But before being persuaded by these arguments, consider the equally compelling arguments against this method of presentation:

Many children do not have the initial motivation to exert the effort required to make inferences. The method of discovery requires a period of five or ten minutes or even longer during which the child is attempting to tease out a simplifying rule. For children who enter the task with high motivation this delay is not of much import. But for children of lower IQ and/or lower motivation who do not place high value upon intellectual mastery, the requirement of even three minutes of involvement without reward is too burdensome, and they are apt to withdraw from the task if success is not immediate. I have watched children with lower motivation in a discovery atmosphere, and their low threshold for distractibility is painful to witness. The method of discovery is minimally appropriate for children who enter the problem with low motivation.

Young children, especially five to seven years of age, do not have a sufficient appreciation of what a problem is or what a solution is, and the incentive value of making discoveries is not very strong. I refer here to an important developmental difference in the attractiveness of making inferences. Twelve-year-old children have already learned the joy of discovery, and for them the inferential method is inherently attractive. The seven-year-old is still acquiring the value of this activity, and many have not even learned to appreciate the nature of a problem. As a result they do not remain within the constraints of the problem and bring in aspects of reality which interfere with the problem solving process. The tendency to confuse reality with the artificial constraints of the problem is serious when one is trying to teach principles by the discovery method.

Impulsive children are apt to settle on the wrong conclusion in the inferential method and become vulnerable to developing feelings of inadequacy. The impulsive child does not reflect on the validity or probable accuracy of his hypotheses before offering them to the teacher, either orally or on paper. Since these impulsively derived hypotheses are apt to be incorrect, the impulsive child encounters a series of humiliating failures and eventually withdraws involvement from school tasks. The method of discovery is more appropriate for children who normally reflect on the validity of their hypotheses.

In sum, the method of discovery is most appropriate for highly motivated older children who might have high dependency conflict and who are inclined to use a reflective strategy. This method is least appropriate for younger children, especially those below the age of nine, who do not have high motivation to master intellectual tasks and who tend to be impulsive. Some aspects of these recommendations have research support, others must be tested in the laboratory, but each is a reasonable proposition.

There is not only interaction between the psychological organization of the child and the method of presentation, but also between the substantive content and the method of presentation. It would seem that contents that are tailored for discovery learning are disciplines containing principles that are usually induced through the proliferation of hypotheses. The proliferation requires a rich cognitive structure upon which the child can draw. The natural sciences and history are the best exemplars in this regard. Content areas for which the principles tend to be less obvious and for which the child does not initially have a rich set of cognitive structures gain less from discovery procedures; early mathematics is the best exemplar of this class. Considerable structure must be accumulated before the discovery method can work with profit.

Attention and the role of novelty. The theme of this discussion has centered on the directive role of intrapsychic processes within the child, processes which determine how much attention shall be invested in the mastery of particular skills. The organization and strength of these forces are highly variable among children, and this variability helps to account for the broad spectrum of intellectual competencies present in every school.

There is, however, one event that usually captures the attention of all children—at least temporarily—and the critical quality of that event is surprise. Novelty is one of the educator's most effective weapons in the battle against pupil apathy, for surprise temporarily recharges the attentional system.

The contemporary educational scene has generated palpable excitement over the benefits to be secured from manipulation of materials, books, curricula, and visual presentations, and there is a strong hope and unshakable faith among many who are exerting much effort and wisdom that herein lies a major solution to the ills that plague educational practices in our schools. In many instances the major catalyst behind improved performance is the novelty implicit in the change. Perhaps it is strategic to present the child with a method he does not expect, to pose a series of surprises along his educational itinerary, to violate his anticipation of what is to come—gently rather than with hammer blows—in order to keep his vigilance perennially high. A dean at a leading liberal arts college facetiously summarized this notion when I mentioned my apprehension about a recent radical change in the educational procedures of his institution. He replied to my ingenuous attitude with a reassuring laugh: "Don't worry, the novelty effect will bail us out." It would be unwise to derogate the role of novelty or to develop a coolness toward revision of instructional procedures because novelty rather than an abstract theoretical consideration provided the impetus for growth. We all seek the same goal—to teach the child the desire to sharpen his intellectual tools. We know too little about this delicate process to reject any tactic that might pierce the nightshade of ignorance that envelops the problem of why and how a mind grows.

Preparation of this paper was supported, in part, by research grant MH-8792 from the National Institute of Mental Health, U. S. Public Health Service.

J. DOUGLAS BROWN

The Development of Creative Teacher-Scholars

ALTHOUGH THE general public, and even Congress, may accept the assumption that quantity and quality move in parallel, anyone with responsibility for the assurance of excellence in any human endeavor soon learns that size and quantity are very mixed blessings in fulfilling their purpose. There is no area in which this is more true than in the development of creative talent for the learned professions. More specifically, size and quantity will not ease the task of providing creative teacher-scholars to man the faculties of our liberal universities in the face of rapidly increasing enrollments.

The difficulty of developing creative teacher-scholars in adequate supply lies in the nature of the persons potentially qualified to assume the role. We have no reason to believe that there is a fixed proportion of candidates per hundred-thousand live births, let alone an *increasing* proportion as the needs of the world expand. It is necessary, therefore, to learn how to nurture with the greatest possible insight the precious flow of potential talent which is discovered and started upon the long road to full productivity. In considering this problem, it may be helpful at the outset to examine the nature of the creative teacher-scholar. Since most of the subjects to be analyzed are too busy in their chosen disciplines to examine themselves, it falls to a dean of faculty who has observed them for many years to present some conclusions on the attributes of the creative teacher-scholar.

A distinction should be made at the outset between the creative teacher-scholars who provide the vital core of a dynamic teaching university and those very learned persons who spend their lives in accumulating vast erudition for its own sake. A creative scholar provides a flow of new ideas, drawing upon deep resources of accumulated knowledge. Further, the art of teaching is itself creative, if well performed. The teacher must constantly find new ways to communicate old ideas and new ideas and to nurture the development of ideas and understanding in his students. The excitement of the teacher-scholar in the creative process and ideas carries over into the excitement of helping others to gain deeper insights. The scholar who is not also an active teacher may become very learned but, without the stimulation of the teaching situation, often comes to respect the authority of past scholars at the expense of his own creativity. It is true that fields of knowledge vary in respect to the degree to which new ideas and new approaches can be developed, but the creative teacher-scholar can be distinguished from the merely "accumulative" scholar in any field.

A further premise should be made clear. Since the distinguishing qualities of the creative teacher-scholar are essentially *subjective* in nature, it is most difficult, and perhaps futile, to attempt to design a research project in which these qualities must be precisely determined and validated. The determination of a single attribute in the person studied would be no better than the judgment of the investigator. Dependent upon the response of the subject in the presence of the observer, the evidence may become self-consciously autobiographical and impressionistic rather than scientific. When a mixture of attributes developing over a whole life span is involved, the problems of validation become enormous. Few people can understand or remember just how they became what they are. Therefore, the following propositions are based on the *judgment* of a single observer whose chief responsibility for many years has been to help in the selection and evaluation of creative teacher-scholars.

I. *The Attributes of the Creative Teacher-Scholar*

An inquiring mind. This is a native quality in the creative teacher-scholar, enhanced from earliest education onward. It is a tone of attack stimulated by both informal and formal education in all areas of interest. If the native quality exists in high degree beyond the natural curiosity of the child, family influences may have much to do with its early maturing. The fact that many creative scholars grew up in academic families is not an accident. Both heredity and environment have had their effect. In the young person of inquiring mind, the "why" must be answered as well as the "how," and the parent or teacher who is also interested in the "why" reinforces a growing hunger for knowledge.

The nature of the essential drives which cause a high degree of motivation toward inquiry in some individuals of apparently similar backgrounds and not others remains a fascinating mystery. A desire for status or evident accomplishment is often present. But the love of inquiry in the truly creative scholar is what carries him to a level of high competency and lifts him to the sustained exploration of the great unknowns. Since the early environment of creative men varies so widely, one is led to believe that the larger share of elements which bring success are in the person himself and can be developed only in an atmosphere of a specific and individually appropriate kind. This suggests that there may be a strictly limited number of persons of high creative potential and that not all will become effective unless they receive the individual attention of an inspiring teacher. This would explain the marked success of a number of smaller colleges in starting able young scholars on their way.

That a high potential for mathematical analysis appears earlier than other aptitudes is fortunate in an age when creative mathematicians are greatly needed. It would be a serious loss, however, if the early maturation of interest in mathematics, or even in science generally, channeled individuals into the field of their first love when they might contribute even more in the social sciences or the humanities. It is a function of liberal education to give opportunity for range and excitement in inquiry in many fields and for understanding the diverse approaches in seeking knowledge and understanding. Time and again an underclassman who has excelled in mathematics, physics, or chemistry finds economics, history, or philosophy even more exciting. The same love of analysis which made mathematics a challenge carries over into less abstract disciplines as the individual realizes the complexity of human affairs. Liberal education in breadth is necessary to help students of high potential to find the field in which they have a comparative advantage, even though they could succeed in several. It is also valuable for society in spreading talent over the many areas in which creative persons are needed.

It is my experience in dealing with many creative scholars that liberal education serves to sustain the drives toward inquiry through life. Years of specialization in a narrow field of learning sometimes cause an individual to "go stale" if a broad resource of interests does not exist. Such breadth of interests is more likely to develop early in one's education. If opportunity has not been given to or accepted by the talented person at this time, he may lose in later years the stimulation of mind and spirit and the catholicity of appreciation which sustains the truly creative teacher-scholar through the forties when many able men level out. A sabbatical leave will not overcome the staleness of long overspecialization. This, I believe, is a special problem in mathematics. Physicists have sometimes welcomed involvement in national policy as an antidote to long-continued concentration in theoretical analysis.

The powers of analysis and accumulation. This is the ability to acquire, understand, evaluate, and retain knowledge in an orderly manner. The human mind has tremendous powers of assimilation of experience in all its forms. Unlike the animal, it can far outreach in its retentive powers the range of experience which is useful in day-to-day survival. The important difference which marks the creative teacher-scholar is that his experience or new knowledge, at least in significant areas, is not merely acquired like impressions of a passing landscape or a moving picture, but is by habit analyzed, evaluated, and understood at the time it becomes a part of his mental resources. A potential teacher-scholar unconsciously or consciously is attempting to create within himself an orderly library of knowledge from which retrieval is facilitated by sustained self-training.

In the maturing teacher-scholar, analysis and accumulation become a way of life—an intellectual habit. This approach is strengthened by education and training under conditions which question hasty or partial answers to difficult questions and which demand an organized and responsible consolidation of knowledge. This is why the education of the teacher-scholar of high potential can seldom be effective in an environment stressing only accumulation of knowledge and not interaction among colleagues. Analysis can be carried part of the way by the solitary, inquiring person, but he also has a great need for the teacher who questions easy answers, or fellow students who make him defend his position.

Unfortunately for those who propose new economies in higher education, constant, vigorous interaction between minds is not consistent with mass instruction. Like TV or movies, lectures can communicate a great deal of knowledge to large audiences. But lectures are no substitute for the expensive process of helping the individual student hammer out an analysis of values, relationships, judgments, and proofs in his own mind. This is true education. It is an essential element in the development of the creative teacher-scholar, and some institutions must assure its availability no matter how expensive it may become as students flood our colleges and universities.

The need for constant interaction of inquiring minds does not stop with the attainment of the Ph.D. University faculties, to be productive, must provide a climate and process of mutual interaction to assist each member in his life-long career of analysis and accumulation. Easy answers are not the monopoly of the unenlightened. The physicist, the economist, and the classicist need the cross-criticism of colleagues and the polite doubts of students to prevent mastery from becoming arrogance. This introduces the problem of critical mass in the developing of sources for new creative teacher-scholars. Unfortunately for those who seek a rapid expansion of supply, the university environment which produces teacher-scholars of high talent must itself have a critical mass of both able teachers and able students.

The absence of a critical mass in some fields of learning has constituted a problem for many universities. Until recent years, astronomy suffered from the relative isolation of the few professors which each university could afford. In an attempt to compensate for this, the discipline developed arrangements for intercommunication between universities, and visits to the great telescopes became a normal way of life. Despite this, the profession was not able to attract and develop any considerable stream of new talent until recent governmental interest in astrophysical sciences provided support for a much larger group of teachers and advanced students. At the other end of the spectrum of knowledge, the ancient languages continue to need the dedicated efforts of a few universities to assure an adequate flow of new scholars. The teaching of the classics in translation has helped to justify costs, and also to prevent professors from becoming "accumulative" scholars alone.

It would be a fortunate development if isolated research centers which are organized to produce immediately useful findings could be relied upon to develop a flow of creative talent to augment that provided by the universities. While exceptions such as the Bell Laboratories exist, it is becoming apparent that such research centers usually absorb more talent than they produce. A university, no matter how productive its faculty may be in contributing new knowledge, remains essentially man-centered. An industrial or governmental laboratory must be product- or mission-centered to justify its costs. The development of creative talent seems to require the climate of academic freedom in which teaching is as important as learning, and where the process of discovery is as important as its product. Even in the most carefully planned institutes for advanced study, the absence of a teacher-scholar relationship appears to be a handicap rather than an asset except for the short-term visitor on sabbatical from teaching.

The attribute of intuition. This is what makes a truly creative teacher-scholar. It is a mysterious quality of subconscious association of ideas—the combination of ideas to form new ideas. It is, however, creation *from* and not *against*. It requires a vast complex of accumulated knowledge and ideas which have been assembled by an inquiring mind. A great body of such knowledge and ideas, especially in one's discipline, must have been analyzed and evaluated over past years. But it is important to recognize that by no means all, or perhaps even a major part, are the ideas in a narrow segment of knowledge or experience. Creativity is a mysterious process. It involves discovery and not logic alone. It grows out of accumulated experience, but it transcends the conscious analysis which made that experience useful.

The intuitive instinct in a potentially creative teacher-scholar can be dulled by his own habits of mind or by his environment. To range widely requires the courage to break with convention, to avoid undue respect for authority, to keep logic in its proper place, and, above all, to avoid over-concentration in a single field of experience. A firm basis of liberal education is a vital resource for a creative person. The interplay of ideas and approaches from many fields of learning and human experience enriches and strengthens the resources for creativity.

Environmental factors militating against sustained creativity among teacher-scholars are all too common. Intuition can be crowded out by immediate personal concerns, detailed administrative tasks, frustrating responsibilities, and demands for too-early demonstration of results. Academic freedom, in the last analysis, is the freedom to think intuitively about all possible answers to man's questions about the unknown or the unresolved. Logical analysis may provide the basis for lectures and for many of the published papers which fill the journals. Free-ranging intuition takes time and may show limited results. The liberal university should provide the time and the freedom for it, once the teacher-scholar has indicated potential talent. This involves not only many practical arrangements in daily existence, but also a propitious climate which evolves over many years.

The great emphasis which I have placed upon the attribute of intuition in creative teacher-scholars may suggest that I am limiting this category of persons to a small but precious minority of those holding professional rank in American universities. If one is looking for the complete and balanced model, this is true. Few professors attain the intuitive brilliance of a John von Neumann. But there are many others who in their own way and time demonstrate the intuitive qualities which lift them above the rank and file of the larger number of solidly competent teachers and scholars who make higher education feasible on the American scale.

But excellence in teaching as well as excellence in scholarship requires intuition. A liberal university is always seeking men who have this quality, even though the precise term is seldom used. Perhaps it is the pragmatic strain in American culture which reserves "intuition" for poets and women, and assumes that those responsible for the important affairs of the world should be logical at all times. All one can counter is that the discovery of most of the great ideas of the world and the contributions of its most influential leaders involved intuition and not logic alone. A university can disregard this fact only at the risk of losing the excitement and vitality which are its peculiar heritage.

The attribute of self-discipline. In the cycle of creative work, the freedom of mind and spirit which enhances intuition must be preceded by *and* followed by sustained concentration—*before,* to prepare oneself, and *after,* to distill and re-distill, test and retest the new idea which intuition has produced. This requires a persistent quality of self-discipline, an ability to change mental gears from analysis to intuition to analysis again. It separates the truly creative scholar from the brilliant "idea man." It marks the scholar whose efforts provide an essential contribution to the general body of knowledge rather than remain interesting hypotheses. The testing of ideas may be reinforced by the anticipation of criticism by others, but in the truly creative teacher-scholar it involves a sustained quality of self-criticism.

At its best, the doctoral dissertation is an excellent example of the analysis-intuition-analysis cycle in the process of creative scholarship. At its worse, it becomes a tortured accumulation of material on some minor item in the encyclopedia of knowledge. In any case, it requires self-discipline on the part of the prospective scholar. Universities have been criticized for making the doctorate a union card for membership on their faculties. So far, no one has invented a better method of discovering whether a candidate possesses the required quality of scholarship. Whether the doctoral dissertation is the first or the last experience in protracted, analytical self-discipline divides the creative scholars from the pack. The element of excitement which intuition brings to the cycle of scholarship seems to make the difference. Where this exists, the goal becomes worth the effort, not once, but repeatedly throughout life.

A tendency toward perfectionism. It has been said that the final test of truth is esthetic. In the universe of knowledge, there is no great master-teacher on this earth who corrects and grades the papers. A creative discovery in any field, it seems, must have elegance, simplicity, symmetry, or "perfection." A teacher-scholar must have faith that there is order in truth, once the many complexities are understood. In seeking that order, he comes to reflect his goal. He becomes a perfectionist not only in his chosen discipline, but in other areas of living, sometimes to the point of irritation for those who want him to be practical. Unfortunately, at times, the teacher-scholar in a more abstract discipline fails to realize that university operations, like those in all human organizations, require compromise and mutual accommodation.

It appears to be necessary for deans and departmental chairmen in dealing with the creative teacher-scholar to remember that, in their official capacity, they do not have the privilege of private irritation. The unconscious assumption that space, staff, library services, and equipment should be available in neat balance as the scholar needs them can be exasperating when budgets have been disregarded and practical limitations discounted. But the true perfectionist is not dismayed and persists in expecting rare foresight and generosity in all those who support his work.

A tendency toward introspection. The most complex and productive laboratory in the world is the human mind. Those who work in that laboratory most intensively are likely to determine many of their judgments and attitudes for themselves, even to the point of stubbornness, rather than depend upon the views of others. This is not always a source of happiness, especially in the perfectionist, the self-critic, and the person of intuition. It is not always helpful in one's personal affairs. There is concern about where one stands and about one's accomplishments.

It is a part of the function of a university to provide a sense of security and status for creative teacher-scholars. The attitude of the general public toward professors has changed greatly since their contribution to scientific and engineering progress has been made apparent. Economists are beginning to be recognized as useful in public policy. But there remains a large proportion of the disciplines on any campus in which men will study and teach throughout life without benefit of public notice. The status of professor in the particular university will be recognized both in the academic world and in that segment of the public which is most meaningful to him. The separate ranks of assistant, associate, and full professor may seem unnecessary refinements to those outside academia, but within, they are a means not only of encouraging achievement but of registering it so that all may see. The creative teacher-scholar whose subject does not lend itself to textbook-writing or consulting must depend upon recognition by his peers and upon the regard of those few outside the academic community who can understand his work. As an introspective person, he needs some formal recognition of status within the university in those times in life when new intellectual accomplishments are not obvious, even to those close by.

A tendency to resist external authority. The creative scholar tends to resist the judgments, standards, and criticisms of others unless he respects their previous contributions. This leads to a more or less conscious discounting of advice from any authority based on hierarchical status alone, whether in the university, industry, or government. As all presidents and deans well know, there are strict limits to their authority, once a faculty member attains tenure. Large areas of university operation depend upon colleague authority for direction and control, for universities are essentially systems of partnerships, housed, financed, and kept out of serious trouble by patience and understanding.

To avoid the impression that university administrators are passive servants arranging things to make life simple for great minds, it may be well to remember that the majority of effective presidents and deans are also teacher-scholars, or were at one time. From their own experience, they understand why their colleagues act the way they do and are convinced, at least in their more philosophical moments, this this is for the best if the creative work of the world is to be done. Yet, there are innumerable decisions in the development and functioning of a faculty which cannot be left to protracted and undisturbed analysis, to intuition, or to uncompromising perfectionism. Fortunately, most teacher-scholars recognize this, especially in an institution which must educate thousands of young persons, provide salaries, plan buildings, and support research.

It is also true that university administrations in America have developed a body of experience—one is tempted to say an art— in creating an environment for creative teacher-scholars which justifies, in some institutions at least, the respect of a large segment of the faculty. The more useful elements of this experience have evolved out of years of interaction between members of faculties who remain teacher-scholars and those teacher-scholars who try their hand at administration. Not infrequently, a lawyer or industrialist takes on the arduous task of presiding over a university. Some have performed miracles of organization. Others, like the invaders of China, have been absorbed into the faculty way of thinking. Still others, to the relief of all concerned, have moved on to less demanding positions. It appears that some service as a professor provides insights, or at least good hunches, which enhance survival.

II. *The Development of a Faculty of Creative Teacher-Scholars.*

Neither space nor ingenuity permits a precise demonstration of the way in which a faculty of creative teacher-scholars can be developed and nurtured. Several approaches or means can be suggested, but the best way to learn how to administer a university is to take charge of one.

As has been suggested, the nurture of a creative teacher-scholar begins in childhood and is carried forward in school and college. The succeeding levels of education provide not only a preparation for creative work but a continuing system of tests of motivation and attainment. The crucial screening comes in the last years of college and the first years of graduate work. It is at this point that accumulation gives way to independent creative skirmishes with ideas and approaches. There is a cycle of education in *conformity,* of learning what is already known, which is succeeded by education in *creativity,* of seeking to find out what is still to be discovered. The best institutions of higher education, and the best teachers, wherever they are, sense this difference clearly and recognize the need of the student of high potential to move ahead into the more challenging period of a creative approach to self-education.

It is for this reason that the recruitment of potentially creative teacher-scholars depends heavily on the recruitment of young people by good universities from good colleges whether within universities or not. The student-teacher relationship is the catalytic agent which continues to be important until the doctorate has been completed. If teachers have little contact with individual students, the latter are far less likely to gain the help and the motivation necessary to persist along the road to excellence. Moreover, with little individual contact, the teacher is ill-prepared to perform his part in the highly selective process of judging both the mind and the spirit of the young person who has potential for creative scholarly work and should be urged to invest years in graduate study.

Once the Ph.D. is attained, the recruitment process in building a faculty of creative teacher-scholars becomes the joint task of the peer group in a discipline and of the central administration of the university. The peer group in a good university is on a constant quest for exceptional talent and should have an appetite limited only by the administration's sense of economy and balance. The peer group must emphasize potential ability as well as achievement, willingness to cooperate on a team as well as to work alone, and a desire to teach as well as to learn. The central administration, besides assuring means, need, and balance, has a basic obligation to make certain in each individual appointment that the candidate, as a person, understands and accepts the obligations of membership in this sensitive, self-administering human organization. If a university needs both good laws and good manners to survive, the time to judge good manners in their largest sense is when a new member is appointed.

The heavy reliance upon the judgment of peer groups in the selection of new members involves countervailing pressures which must be resolved if an effective faculty is to be assured. A very natural tendency of both departments and universities is to hire established scholars of high visibility who may have passed their period of greatest contribution and who prefer to spend their remaining years undisturbed by students and less mature colleagues. This form of investment in talent for the sake of public image is expensive not only in dollars but in faculty morale. Within the peer group, and especially among younger colleagues, the aura of the "great man" wears thin as others must carry the load he avoids. Only if such a scholar serves as an exciting catalyst or a wise and patient critic is the investment worthwhile, for a creative faculty is much more than a collection of solo performers. The central administration has the obligation to question the "stamp-collecting" tendencies of an ambitious department and to exercise restraint on its own part.

On occasion, the reverse of this trend appears in peer-group selection of members for promotion to higher rank. This is the desire to be kind in a short-sighted, comfortable way. A colleague works hard, takes on many chores, and is pleasant and convenient to have around. But an impartial and incisive analysis of the member's tone of attack in creative work leaves much to be desired. While some men go through cycles of more and less productive periods in their scholarly work, it is safe to say that in the case of younger colleagues, at least, any doubts in respect to creative potential are likely to increase as years pass. Routine duties may become a compensating self-justification for lack of enthusiasm or energy for creative effort. It is no kindness to hold a man in an environment of deepening frustration when he might gain continuing satisfaction as a useful college teacher rather than as a creative teacher-scholar in a demanding university. Again, it is the obligation of the central administration to question the kindly, comfortable attitudes of peer groups and, if necessary, to seek outside evaluations not clouded by sentiment.

There is probably no aspect of faculty administration which is more certain to arouse public criticism than the attitude expressed in the slogan "publish or perish." The misunderstanding of the very important role of publication in the evaluation of creative men lies in the shift from ends to means. To the public, and to the eventual user of knowledge, whether in academia or industry, the published book or article stands as a contribution in itself. To the peer group within the university and to the central administration, the publication is a means of gaining insight into the creative powers, the tone of attack, the self-discipline, and general motivation of the author. Books and articles are only one means of "entering" a man's mind, but they have the important attribute that, through widespread distribution, they can be read critically by large numbers of people not influenced by personal association with the author. Also, in the words of Bacon, "writing maketh the exact man." Errors or sloppiness which can be covered up in oral discussion become apparent in the written statement. It is not the amount of writing, but the quality and insight shown in writing which are the true measure of publication. The pace of publication of a creative teacher-scholar is affected by many factors, but a prolonged absence of flow from the spring suggests doubts concerning the vitality of the source.

Not all disciplines lend themselves to major dependence upon publication as the test of men's minds. In some areas, such as public affairs, many contributions to knowledge and understanding are joint products in which individual authorship is submerged. Also, some scholars find their greatest satisfaction in stimulating colleagues and students and in contributing the germs of ideas for others to nourish and perfect. Criticism itself can be creative in the larger sense. Occasionally a truly creative scholar transmits most of his hard-won wisdom through consultation both within and outside the academic group. The best approach in dealing with men of diverse talents and inclinations is to seek to judge their creativity on an individual basis by the outward manifestations which occur through time. It must be admitted, however, that a creative teacher-scholar who writes little must stand the test of close scrutiny of all the other means of communication which he may find preferable.

There is no more ambiguous expression in academia than that a professor is a "good teacher." In the mouth of a freshman concerned with staying in college, a good teacher may be one who so organizes and simplifies a body of material that any mediocre student who stays awake and reviews his notes can pass the course. Or the good teacher may be the enthusiastic lecturer who, by interesting illustration, makes a subject exciting. But the true test of a good teacher is what he does to the student in the drawing forth—the education— of the student's powers of clear thinking, analysis, orderly accumulation, evaluation, and re-creation of ideas in his own terms. The good teacher changes men rather than transmits knowledge for its own sake. In the earlier stages of college or university education, there is need for good "coaches" in the learning process, in the development of tools such as language, mathematics, laboratory techniques, and the use of libraries. But in the later years of education, and especially in graduate work, there is need for teacher-scholars who, through their own zeal for thinking things anew, transmit the excitement of the process to their students. With such teachers, the man is more important than the method.

In the evaluation of the qualities of a creative teacher-scholar as a *teacher,* it is necessary to keep clearly in mind the role in which he can contribute most. There are teachers of enthusiasm and effectiveness who make the art of teaching at a more elementary level a life-long subject of study. A number of such scholars of teaching are a valuable supporting cast in any university. Their facility in attracting student interest in what is already known should not be permitted to upstage the teacher-scholar who in his drive toward discovery of new approaches and ideas in his discipline may at times leave his students breathless and confused. The ideal, of course, is the perfect blend of the dynamic scholar and the ever-lucid, ever-patient teacher; but in the absence of any large reservoir of such persons, most universities must be satisfied with the compensating attributes of a balanced team. It is the task of the university, however, to establish the assumption that the precious norm is the balanced teacher-scholar, and that one-sidedness is a shortcoming rather than a source of distinction.

Given the nature of the creative teacher-scholar and assuming some success in recruiting and evaluating individuals who appear to possess these attributes, it might be presumed that sound scholarship and effective teaching will automatically ensue. A university is more dependent upon the initiative of its members than almost any other form of organization, but it is still an organized community, sensitive to leadership, tradition, common and statute law, equity, and mutual support. The creative individual is peculiarly responsive to these aspects of his environment.

Leadership and tradition—which is the projection of leadership through time—can greatly influence the environment in which scholarship takes place. Such leadership encompasses both the administration and the senior faculty. Its manifestations include assumptions of dedication, integrity, freedom, persistence in seeking fundamental truth rather than quick and useful answers, cooperation rather than self-centered interest, and the dignity of every individual. Farsighted planning for the support of the individual scholar in library and laboratory resources, strong colleagues, good students, and effective staff are the obvious requirements which an administration must fulfill. Good departmental organization which produces results with a minimum of wasted time or friction is the product of leadership at the most immediate level.

As was suggested earlier in this essay, the truly creative scholar must possess the capacity to move through a cycle of analysis and accumulation, followed by intuitive thought and again by a period of testing and retesting of the new concepts gained. Not only is the *capacity* required, but also the time and specialized resources to use this capacity. The modern university has learned this slowly. It has also learned that scholars in different disciplines need very different patterns of time and resources. The scholar in the humanities needs blocks of time and a richly endowed library, wherever it may be. The older concept of the sabbatical year is too rigid in timing and often too long delayed. A whole battery of measures for leave or partial relief of teaching must be provided on an equitable basis which takes individual needs into consideration. Younger scholars need assurance of relief from teaching even though projects and potential are still uncertain. It is difficult to test creative potential if no time is afforded to demonstrate it. Opportunity for intensive periods of analysis and accumulation is of great help, but even more important is uninterrupted time for the intuitive kind of thinking. Most of all, perhaps, the humanistic scholar benefits from free time during the period when consolidation, testing, and writing must be done.

The social scientist in the university has turned more and more a staff-supported research and the scientist to team research with graduate students. Time, facilities, and staff must be provided. It is fortunate that the government and the foundations are now providing much support for research in these fields. But, again, a mistake is made if the day-to-day pressures of "organized" research crowd out time for intuitive thought and recharging of intellectual batteries in the creative individual. For their own survival as centers of free-ranging creative effort, the liberal universities of the country must make sure that scholarship and research by their faculties are not limited by the predispositions of government panels or foundation staffs, no matter how wise these may be. Creative scholarship can be hemmed in by undue respect for logic, whether in the individual or in the institutional setting in which he must work.

It has been suggested earlier in this analysis that creative teacher-scholars are likely to be introspective perfectionists, not disposed to respect the judgments of those outside their fields. While exceptions occur, the by-product of this attitude is often a lack of interest in the details of personal budgeting, retirement annuities, insurance, mortgages, and savings and, at the same time, a tendency to worry more than most about the risks of modern life. It is the responsibility of the university to provide a supporting framework. This is not only a reflection of the evolution of good industrial relations in progressive corporations, but a peculiarly important function in an institution whose chief asset is a body of creative men.

The wise university administration today does not leave the decision to participate in retirement programs, group life insurance, or major medical expense insurance to the individual faculty member. This is not an act of paternalism, but rather a mutually accepted bargain. The university is a perpetual institution which can average risks over time. It offers a lifetime of employment to its tenure faculty. It has learned that its faculty is more productive over the years if it is relieved of certain details of the business of living for which the university can provide expert insurance service. Whereas a storekeeper or a corporation executive may enjoy competitive taking of risks and planning to minimize loss, the creative teacher-scholar faces competition and risk in the world of ideas and in the varying reaction of students and colleagues. Uncertain of continuing success, even with sustained effort, he prefers to limit his economic risks through the help of his university.

The pattern of university salaries through a period of career service seldom matches the varying needs of the faculty member. The creative teacher-scholar usually attains his highest salary very late in life. His needs for the housing of his family and the education of his children come to a peak long before his salary does. Liberal arrangements for rental housing, for mortgage loans, and for children's college tuition are means of readjusting the pattern of compensation to the pattern of need. Such programs may seem to be little related to a climate for creative thinking until one deals with a distraught physicist who has been house-hunting for weeks or a linguist with three college-age children. The notion that creativity is sharpened by financial insecurity should be reserved for romantic stories of bygone days.

Probably the most precious source of personal security for the creative teacher-scholar is the assurance that he will receive fair and equitable treatment by his peers and his university. This does not mean that he will always get what he wants, but that he gets, over time, what he truly deserves in comparison with others. The need for sound and positive personnel administration is more critical in universities than anywhere else because of the nature of creative men. At the same time, it is a difficult and complex form of personnel administration because of the diverse and intangible qualities to be encouraged, measured, and rewarded. It is a proper field of study for all concerned in the advancement of higher education. Impersonal, bureaucratic methods which create and rigidify inequities in individual or categorical salaries or status in a university can cause more loss in morale than heavy teaching loads. To assure a creative faculty, a university should indulge in creative thinking about the way in which individuals are developed and rewarded for careers of creativity as well as for all other forms of contribution to the mission of higher education.

America has become accustomed to meeting its vastly increasing needs for goods and services by ingenious extensions of mass production and large-scale organization. There is now a sharply increased need for creative teacher-scholars to man our colleges and universities and to advance knowledge as a basis for growth and human welfare. It appears likely that this particular need will not be met easily or by any radical change in methods or organization. The reasons are that the nature of the creative teacher-scholar is such that highly individualized methods must be used to discover, recruit, and develop persons of such talent and that these methods become more difficult to sustain as organizations become larger. It behooves us, therefore, to study and perfect the arts of administration in the university of limited size as a time-tested source of high talent while experimenting with the more spectacular operations of the multi-versity. The resolution of the dichotomy of scale and quality remains an American challenge.

CLIFF W. WING, JR.

Student Selection, the Educational Environment,
and the Cultivation of Talent

WE HAVE, in American higher education, a complex, variable system
for the selection of students and an equally complex and variable
system for their instruction. While both are important for the cultivation of talent, there has, to date, been remarkably little effort made
to relate the two. Information collected by admissions offices has
recently been used to help place first-year students in courses appropriate to their ability and achievement; it has rarely served as
a source of guidance for the faculty charged with curriculum design
and instruction. Conversely, except for grades at the end of the
freshman year and records of drop-outs and failures, the results of
exposing students to various educational practices are seldom even
considered, much less related to the original selection process.

Current Status of Selection. Pressed toward objectivity by the
force of large numbers of college applicants, admissions offices have
developed actuarial tables relating the credentials of applicants to
some of their college performance. A decade or more of experience
has made possible fairly accurate prediction of freshman average
grades, for example. Techniques in popular use for the selection of
college students—systematic analyses of high school records, test
scores, and recommendations—have been of major importance in
effecting positive changes in our educational institutions. Selection
has helped raise the quality of graduating classes by identifying students who possess the general ability to succeed in given colleges;
it has decreased the rate of academic attrition by discouraging admission of those who would probably fail; and, very importantly, it
has given impetus to improvements in the academic curricula of
secondary schools. The systematic utilization of objective data has,
in short, helped to improve the average product of educational institutions at all levels. But, despite these contributions and accom-

plishments, the admissions process in American higher education remains gross, unrefined, and unsophisticated, and provides little assistance in identifying genuinely creative talent.

What is wrong with the tools currently being used for the prediction of success in college? Why do they fail to detect creativity? Norman Mackworth recently supported the view that part of the fault may lie with the composition of selection tests. They seem to favor the problem-solvers over the problem-finders, the verbal reasoners over the intuitive thinkers, though the latter are the more truly creative.

It seems clear that a second reason that creativity is not being identified is that secondary-school records and test scores do not effectively differentiate among various specific talents. There are, observation tells us, different kinds of creativity—for writing poetry, painting pictures, solving abstract mathematical problems, designing physics experiments, providing political leadership. Talent of one kind often is correlated with talent of another: Two or more may exist side by side within the same individual. It is well known, for example, that people who score high on verbal tests tend also to score high on tests of mathematical ability. The reverse, however, may also occur: an individual may have, by reason of congenital ability, specific training, or direction of motivation, a peak of talent surrounded by valleys of less or almost no talent. He may, for example, have great scientific potential, yet find it difficult to mobilize his resources to study a foreign language.

Techniques currently being used for the prediction of success in college are restricted principally to an overall view of the high-school performance—the gross measure of average grades, rank in class—so that a sterling contribution to a chemistry class is not reflected in the class rank of a pupil who happens to be inept in French. Thus, an individual with a peak-and-valley distribution of creative ability is unlikely to be pinpointed by current selection methods. Tests and grading techniques therefore need to be developed for recognizing single great talents as well as abilities that are evenly distributed and highly intercorrelated.

There are two other reasons that current selection devices often overlook the highly talented. They fail to take into account the fact that creativity develops according to individual patterns, emerging earlier for some than for others, and evolving thereafter at different rates. It is probable that talent, despite variations, typically grows at a much faster rate during the first ten years of life than during the second ten. It follows that the difficulty of developing creativity to its full potential increases with the age of the individual at the time his ability is identified. Means for identifying creativity at an early age need to be developed and utilized in the selection process.

Still another area for improvement in selection lies in increased recognition of the fact that creativity knows no social, ethnic, religious, or geographical boundaries. It can appear at any time, any place, sometimes over apparently insurmountable odds. Yet, secondary-school records and test scores, the main bases for admissions policies, tend to favor those applicants who have had an opportunity to acquire prescribed skills. A child with important latent ability may therefore be evaluated as inferior. New techniques for identifying potential creativity must be developed so that they will not discriminate, or will discriminate less, against a child from disadvantaged circumstances. There are indications that some national testing organizations are beginning to make efforts along these lines and to take cognizance of suggestive research being performed in university settings. In the meantime, it is noteworthy that increasing numbers of admissions officers now tend to evaluate the records of disadvantaged students rather differently from those of students from culturally more affluent homes, and to admit some of the former who previously would have been rejected. On the basis of these admissions, data are just beginning to be developed which might ultimately be used to help make more accurate adjustments in interpreting records for students from disadvantaged backgrounds.

If cultural biases exist, we must be aware of them and their influence so that proper compensations can be made in the selection process and so that proper educational programs can be designed to help improve the training of talent available in each subculture. In other words, we need to know about the interaction of the individual with his cultural setting in the cultivation of educational skills, abilities, and potential, as well as how the cultural setting during the early years is mediated by the individual and interacts with the stimulation of higher education.

Current Status of the Higher Education Environment. Unlike the admissions offices, which have been pressed by large numbers of applicants toward objective evaluation of the selection process, college faculties and administrative officials responsible for curriculum design and teaching have often changed courses and instruction without submitting the outcome of the changes to objective tests of effectiveness. Ideas like the "general education" curricular approach have often been introduced without developing factual information about the consequences to students. The introduction of unevaluated changes into the educational environment frequently has led us to return, like the swinging pendulum, to a position vacated only a few years before, with no record of the pendulum's course. As a result, we know very little about how to manipulate the various elements in the higher education environment to maximize the development of students' abilities.

Knowledge about the effect of the educational environment upon student development is of central and urgent importance to selection generally and to the selection and cultivation of creative talent specifically. Technically, the actuarial tables used for selection purposes are based upon college faculty assessment of students, and these assessments are formulated on the basis of student performance under the influence of a variety of curricular and instructional techniques: (1) Standard tests of aptitude, used nationally for selection, are composed of questions included because they discriminate accurately between students who will be judged successful by their college teachers, and students who will not. (2) The use of secondary-school records in selection also is highly dependent on college faculty assessments: an index shows, for instance, that a pupil who makes a B average at City High usually will maintain a B average at City College, whereas a pupil who maintains a B average at Town High will earn only a C average at City College. Admissions offices use information such as this in evaluating high-school records. Both standard aptitude tests and school grades, then, are utilized for selection purposes not in the absolute, but on the basis of their correlation with records of college assessments. It may be concluded that selection for college and effects of college environment are related in a circular fashion, and that one cannot properly be considered without the other.

The interdependence of selection and collegiate educational practices concerns us here especially in connection with the cultivation of creative ability—a process presumably involving both the selection of those with creative potential, and their educational nurture thereafter. The fact is that the current educational system fails, in general, to grant recognition to creativity. As matters now stand, we are probably losing potentially creative individuals at the college level in two ways: (1) We lose some indirectly by failing to select them for college, because selection tools are evaluated according to capacity to predict college performance and cannot be satisfactorily developed for detecting creativity without recognition of creativity at the college level. (2) We lose other students directly, because we fail to encourage them or fail to recognize their specific talents in college.

Current collegiate educational practices seem designed to do the opposite of what we should want them to do: They grant premium recognition not to creativity but to average performance. Note the many ways employed formally by our higher educational system to encourage well-roundedness and discourage specialization in a single area: For example, progress through college, graduation, and even admission to graduate school are often based on performance in all fields, not just one. A student with a C average, making all C's, gets through; a C-average student with an A in physics and an F in English does not. Official sanction is given to average achievement and withheld from peak accomplishment in one field surrounded by valleys of indifferent or poor performance in others. The present grading system also discourages single-field creativity. Using only one grade, only one kind of grade, may completely obscure the difference between the student who achieves an A by dogged persistence, good study habits, and uninspired but correct answers and another who earns his A through brilliant insights and original solutions.

Probably the most profound deterrent to the recognition and development of creativity is inflexibility in the college curriculum. There are two kinds of inflexibility. First, a sampling of courses from the sciences, social studies, humanities and arts usually is required during the first two college years, specialization allowed only later. Assuming that a liberal education is a desirable goal for everybody, including those who are enormously creative in some one field (and there are many who would challenge that assumption!), what is sacred about the first two years of college as the time for promulgating it? Yet curricular requirements around the country are almost uniformly inflexible in this regard. Second, the sequence of courses designed internally by the various departments on the college campus inhibits flexibility. Progression may be based on some agreed-upon logical ordering of the discipline itself. But what of the developmental patterns of the individual student who is concentrating in the field? Suppose he comes to a discipline highly excited about one small portion of it, and suppose he shows creativity, or unusual ability. Under present conditions, he is not allowed to probe the area of his interest but is told to wait for two years, learn the broader subject matter first, and later perhaps relate it to the current focal point. In short, inflexibility in ordering courses within a given discipline may force a creative person to grow wide before he grows tall—even though growth forced in this way may stifle talent.

Two additional points about current educational procedures and their effect upon the cultivation of talent bear mention. First, educational institutions insist upon being exceedingly vague about their purposes. Nearly all liberal arts colleges or university divisions, many junior colleges, and some institutes and technical schools state their goals so broadly that one institution is indistinguishable from the others. Over-generalized statements provide little basis for making sophisticated selections of one type of college environment in preference to another. Such statements prevent students from learning pertinent specific information—for example, that course offerings at a certain college are particularly good in chemistry and biology and in English and history. At the present time, colleges avoid specifying their departmental strengths because to do so would imply relative weakness in the departments not named. Yet it is likely that no college offers a uniformly strong faculty in all departments, does everything equally well, or remains static in its outstanding contributions.

Second, we must not lose sight of the fact that students brought together on the same campus learn from each other. Because this interaction and mutual stimulation are a significant part of each student's educational environment, it is important to have different kinds of talent on the same campus—individuals with special gifts for chemistry, poetry, and other fields of study. Currently, efforts to compose classes representing different backgrounds concentrate more upon wide geographic, social, and cultural distribution than upon representation of a variety of specific intellectual talents.

A Proposed Model for Selection. The foregoing discussion indicates that there is a chicken-or-the-egg interdependency between selection problems and educational problems related to the cultivation of talent. Techniques for identifying unusual ability need to be developed. At the same time, they need to be evaluated against tangible, explicit signs of recognition of talent within the educational system. Coupled with the needs for modification to help achieve more nearly ideal conditions are certain practical matters that also must be considered.

However complicated and intricate the problems are, there must be some way, and there are many, to begin solving them. One might start by designing a model for admitting students to selective educational institutions and then pursuing the implications such a model would have, if put into practice, both for the development of selection tools better suited to measuring potential talent and for the modification of educational offerings to stimulate more active cultivation of creativity. Today most of the reliable information available for selection purposes is confined to the gross measure of general aptitude and secondary-school achievement as related to a gross measure of progress through college. For purposes of selection and education, we seem to have extracted about all we can from this general relationship. It seems appropriate now to go beyond this essentially one-dimensional measurement device and to consider a multidimensional definition of talent, of organizational structure, and of educational purposes and procedures.

To meet the ideal as well as the practical considerations, the following selection model is designed to cultivate a full range of talents, productive in all areas of study in an institution. At the same time, the model allows for the admission of students with capabilities or characteristics not primarily associated with academic excellence.

To illustrate how an admissions model might work, let us suppose that a given college has 3,000 applicants. To begin, the college uses present-day techniques that relate the overall high-school and test performance of applicants to the overall performance expected in the freshman college year. By this means, the general qualifications of the applicants can be defined in terms of probabilities. (Each college must decide for itself which applicants are qualified, giving consideration to the kinds of talent it sets out to cultivate and to the amount of error it is willing to tolerate in its prediction. For example, a qualified candidate in one institution may be defined as a student who has a fifty-fifty chance of a C average, where the predictions are seventy-five per cent correct. Another college with the same predictive efficiency may be more conservative and demand a seventy-thirty chance for a C average.) Current gross techniques enable our college to set, with reasonable accuracy, academic minimums for the protection of both students and institution. Once the term "qualified" is defined, the college can proceed with the rest of the selection process.

Let us assume that, in our hypothetical institution, 2,000 of the original 3,000 applicants meet minimum qualifications. After eliminating the 1,000 who do not, the college must proceed with the selection of as many students as the available resources and facilities can accommodate. In this case, our college can handle an entering class of 1,000. We will further assume that every accepted applicant registers. The problem facing the institution now is to select (or reject) one of every two remaining applicants.

As previously discussed, peaks of talent are sometimes set in valleys of indifference. The opportunities in an educational environment stem from interchange among students as well as from formal curricular offerings. It is desirable to express institutional goals and structures explicitly, and they therefore should be woven into the admissions process. These three points cannot be articulated by the admissions process unless the model goes beyond the one-dimensional technique used for defining "qualified."

Let us now assume that the first responsibility of an educational institution is to train the academically talented student, and that its secondary concern is to realize some of its extracurricular and traditional aims. The first decision, then, is to establish what proportion of the class is to be admitted solely on an academic basis. Our hypothetical college sets this figure at seventy-five per cent. The first 750 students to be admitted will be chosen on this basis.

Keeping in mind the principles of seeking intellectual diversity and of expressing the organizational structure of the institution, the college views its selection problem as one of obtaining the best possible intellectual talent for the loosely federated group of departments which make up the college. To simplify the process, the departments are grouped into four general areas: hard sciences, soft sciences, humanities, and arts. Each applicant is then rated on the basis of his ability in each of the four areas. The four groups of departments draw off the best students in their respective areas. (This replaces the practice of drawing off the 750 students who have the best overall rating for work in all departments.)

Because some individuals have a wide range of abilities, they are chosen by more than one group of departments; but means are found for making equitable assignments and adjustments for losses where necessary, still drawing from the ranked order of students by departmental groups. This technique gives preference to students with peaks of talent over those with a generally good but not brilliant rating.

Once the academic quota for each area of study is filled, the remaining 1,250 applicants are grouped according to their potential contribution to extracurricular pursuits considered worthy of attention by the college, such as organizational leadership, journalism, or athletics. Here, too, quotas are assigned for candidates whose families have traditional affiliations with the institution or other notable connections. Finally, the admissions office is allowed to select a number of students for experimental purposes. The 250 students accepted in these groups complete the entering class.

The selection model presented here suggests the need for the development of an interrelated counterpart, a model for the educational environment. Even without a second model, however, the strategy for selection alone has implications for the development of tools better designed for measuring potential talent and for possible modifications of the educational environment to stimulate more active cultivation of creativity.

Specifically, the model would emphasize the value of developing depth of knowledge as well as general proficiency, and depth of knowledge is often prerequisite to creative contribution. At the pre-college testing level, emphasis would be placed on the development of measures of specific abilities, from which would follow the possibility of a greater range in our definitions of talent. Secondary school personnel, seeing the importance of superior performance in one area, would be alerted to the promotion of single abilities where they exist, as well as the multidimensional talent sought today.

At the college level, the model would relate selection procedures to the current departmental structure of liberal arts colleges, for it is within departments that the specialists are available to capitalize upon and to help nurture potential creativity. Given the kind of class the model would produce, colleges might try offering greater flexibility in their curricula, allowing some students to penetrate areas of study in considerable depth, in keeping with their interests and in harmony with their developmental patterns, before attempting to interrelate areas of study at a more general level. Faculties might attempt to grant more explicit recognition to talent through a grading system that gave special premiums for highly creative performance. In addition to providing these potential areas for environmental manipulation by college faculties and administrations, the model would produce a class composed of some individuals with peaks of talent. Students could then perhaps educate one another more effectively than in today's classes comprised of students of more homogeneous abilities.

If colleges were to undertake a systematic delineation of their selection programs, such as that proposed in the model, better continuity between schools and colleges could be effected, to the advantage of our national talent resources. More specific information about admissions goals and practices could be made available for the guidance of students from secondary school to college, and the secondary schools would be able to achieve better and earlier identification and training of talent, as well as to provide more accurate information for improved college placement.

The selection model has within itself the potential for continuing evaluation by faculties and administrative officials, so that its effectiveness in identifying creative individuals and providing colleges the opportunity to nurture them would come under constant scrutiny. In a sense, each class would be viewed as an experiment. As information was gathered on the class's performance in college, the model could be changed in desired directions. It would not become static, but would continue to be a dynamic means of systematically evaluating change and improvement. (A counterpart model for the educational environment could be similarly dynamic.) Each college could undertake a partial evaluation of proposed alterations in its selection process prior to the implementation of changes. For example, changes in the quotas assigned particular classifications or the introduction of new classifications could be simulated with data already available from previous classes; and the resulting simulated composition of the class could be observed and compared with its composition under previous actual conditions.

Depiction of the admissions process in multidimensional terms perhaps describes what some colleges are now groping toward in a less structured fashion. The model proposed here would not cure all selection problems, nor would it assure the identification of all talent for creative roles. The model does, however, suggest certain practical means of utilizing the selection process in conjunction with the educational environment in order to enhance opportunities for the identification and cultivation of creativity.

PHILIP H. ABELSON

Relation of Group Activity to Creativity in Science

BRAINS ARE our greatest resource, but we use them ineffectively. Few men and women develop more than a small fraction of their potential. When inspired, individuals can often do in a week what might require months at their customary pace. The discovery of ways to improve the use of talent would be one of the most important advances that science could make.

This challenge has recently elicited noteworthy contributions from a number of sources, including groups at the University of Utah and at New York University. Creativity, however, is a comparatively elusive target, and an understanding of the circumstances producing optimal creativity is still at a primitive stage. As creative insight is attainable only by individuals, most discussions of creativity focus on the individual and his mental processes. But in the realities of today's world, scientists who are creative rarely live and work in isolation. To some degree, all receive stimulus, information, and help in making judgments from others in their immediate environment. These interactions are highly important and, with the evolution of science, are becoming even more so. As a prelude to a discussion of the role of group interactions, I shall first review some of the steps leading to creativity in the individual.

The usual discussion of creativity follows Graham Wallas in presenting it as occurring in four stages. Herbert Fox has set them down in condensed form:[1]

1. *Preparation,* involving thorough investigation of the problem by reading and experiment.

2. *Incubation,* involving a conscious and unconscious mental digestion and assimilation of all pertinent information acquired.

3. *Illumination,* involving the appearance of the creative idea, the creative flash.

4. *Verification,* involving experimental testing of the creative idea.

Recently Harold Hughes has added two steps which should be included.[2] His list is (1) interest, (2) preparation, (3) incubation, (4) illumination, (5) verification, and (6) exploitation.

In discussions of creativity most authors emphasize what is often the spectacular phase—illumination—perhaps because people are fascinated by the spectacular or possibly because of Poincaré's dramatic description of his own experiences. Though it is familiar from frequent quotation, a brief excerpt seems appropriate. Poincaré had worked fruitlessly for two weeks on the theory of Fuchsian groups and Fuchsian functions. Then, he says, "One evening, contrary to my custom, I drank black coffee and could not sleep. Ideas rose in crowds; I felt them collide until pairs interlocked, so to speak, making a stable combination. In the morning, I had established the existence of a class of functions. There remained merely to set down the results and that was done in a few hours."[3]

Major creative flashes have been noted by many great scientists; undoubtedly they constitute an important phenomenon. Nevertheless, dramatic illumination, though representing a culmination, is for most scientists only one part, perhaps even a minor part, of creativity. The other five steps outlined by Hughes are also essential. Without the first three, interest, preparation, and incubation, there can be little illumination. In our generation the first two stages have assumed ever-increasing importance.

To be creative in science today, one must stand on the shoulders of giants. Many geniuses have already delved deeply into nearly every aspect of knowledge. As further opportunities arise, many fine minds quickly turn to exploit the new phenomenon. The probability that an unprepared mind will have a flash of illumination is practically nil.

The crucial element in creativity in science today is not dramatic illumination; it is judgment. When an experimental scientist seeks to be creative, he must make and implement a series of judgments. The complexity of his needs can be seen by looking at some of the prerequisite steps. First, he must decide upon an area to investigate. Obviously, this choice is crucial, for diligence which may be expended fruitlessly in one area might be richly rewarded in another. Having selected the major topic, the investigator must decide what to read, and how intensively. Some research scientists get lost in the morass of the literature, unable to make proper judgments about what to read, what to skip, what to believe, what to be skeptical about. Next, the scientist must decide what approach to take. Again, judgment must be applied, and even some creativity, for a uniquely good method is often the real key to major discovery.

Once he begins to experiment, the investigator faces more judgments. Are his methods really sound, or are there hidden defects in his procedures? Chance observations may suggest tantalizing byways; should he pursue them? Sometimes results that initially seemed valid are not satisfactorily repeatable; should he build a new, better apparatus to pursue his original goal, or should he turn to another problem? The creative scientist is daily faced with major and minor choices. Either he makes good choices as a result of deep thought and the use of every available aid of consultation, or he makes bad choices by default.

Only rarely is good judgment readily available. It requires a weighing of obvious alternatives and even the invention of new alternatives. Usually the best judgments come after wrestling with a problem in an environment free from distractions. In today's world, judgment and reflection are often crowded out by activities that represent more fun for the scientist—more experiments, administrative matters, committee work. In the face of the sharp competition of distractions, few scientists exhibit as high a quality of judgment as they potentially could. To exert good judgment requires self-discipline, which, in turn, rests on adequate motivation.

Motivation is essential to creativity; without it, even the best minds accomplish little. With adequate motivation comes the self-control necessary to draw on inner resources. Creative effort differs from most other activities in requiring unusual discipline. People in other walks of life may go for long periods without exercising much self-control. But a creative scientist must take himself in hand. The initiative must be his. No foreman call tell him how to think or what to do next. He has to do his own thinking and make his own judgments. Therefore he must organize himself and his activities. If he fails to exercise proper self-discipline, the deficiency may not be immediately obvious to others. He may appear for work at the usual hour, go through all the accustomed routines, attend seminars, read the literature faithfully, and give the appearance of creative effort. But, if his mind is elsewhere, his activity may be only a façade for inertia.

Related to the need for self-discipline are qualities of patience, courage, and willingness to take the punishment of disappointment.

In the present era of science there is pressure to build extensive bibliographies. The easy way to do this is to carry on research that is merely a small extension of what is already known. Then the scientist does not have to think very deeply; he can let a technician perform the work; and at the same time he feels some security as a contributor to science. Little creativity emerges from such a procedure. The path of courage lies in choosing a difficult but fundamental problem and working on it even though the walls of confusion seem insurmountable. The person who undertakes such a task must be capable of living with disappointment. He must be able to cope with the unhappiness that follows failure of what seemed to be promising approaches. Even after an extended period of work from which there is no obvious accomplishment he must be able to summon the stamina necessary to persist in his efforts. The inner resources on which the creative person calls in order to continue after repeated failure can be tapped only by deep motivation.

How are people motivated? To that question there is no single easy answer. First of all, the great variation in the intrinsic capacity of individuals to respond to motivating stimuli must be recognized. Little can be done with a man devoid of character. The capacity to be motivated has its roots in genetics and is nurtured by environment. The contribution made to motivation by the home environment in early childhood is well known. Many, perhaps most, creative scientists come from families in which the father engages in professional activites. Obviously, the children in such a family are reared in an atmosphere in which knowledge has a high value and excellence is considered a way of life. Another stimulus can come from a teacher who inspires an enduring love of knowledge and an insatiable thirst for learning.

Experiences that enhance motivation do not stop with formal schooling. One of the most effective agents is mutual stimulation arising from the interaction of two or more individuals. Given the right circumstances, human beings can interact in extremely constructive, helpful ways. Interactions can produce enhanced motivation; they can also provide other factors (judgment, for example) that are essential to the creative scientist.

Some of the benefits to creativity arising from group interactions have been reviewed by Likert.[4] Although his book was concerned mainly with means of improving management of commercial and business activities, many of his ideas nevertheless seem at least partly applicable to scientific creativity. For example, he emphasizes the potential helpfulness of the group in providing motivational support. The role of groups in scientific creativity does not seem to have been probed frequently or deeply. Accordingly, I shall present some anecdotal material which indicates the high importance of human interactions in creativity.

For years I have been impressed by the enormous scientific contributions of three Hungarians—John von Neumann, Eugene Wigner, and Leo Szilard. Since all came from Budapest, I recently asked Professor Wigner about possible interaction among them. He told me that there was a strong mutual stimulus. Wigner and von Neumann had known each other during high school days in Budapest. Later they had both gone to college in Berlin. Being foreigners, and not feeling part of the social structure, they became especially close. Professor Wigner had told me earlier that he learned more from von Neumann than from any other man, and though Wigner would be modest in his estimates, I am sure that von Neumann learned a great deal from Wigner. Later these two became associated with the highly imaginative and stimulating Leo Szilard, and the three were very close. They found excitement in ideas and mutual stimulus in arguments and discussions with one another. Finding their surroundings uncongenial, they discovered in creative science a perfect vehicle for escape from the rest of the world and, at the same time, a wholly satisfying common ground for excitement.

Dr. Wigner, in discussing the matter of creativity with me, emphasized this matter of discontent, of the importance of not quite fitting into the environment. He also suggested that perhaps the success of two Nobel prize winners, Lee and Yang, resulted from a relationship similar in pattern to that of his relationship with von Neumann, and Professor Yang has confirmed the surmise. Lee and Yang had known each other in China during the forties. They reestablished contact at Chicago in the late forties. There was an intense interaction, which was later noted at Princeton. It had a highly constructive influence and contributed much to their subsequent success.

Another famous example of constructive interaction involved Enrico Fermi and a group of physicists in Rome during the late twenties and the thirties. Fermi first began his work in Rome in 1926 shortly after obtaining his doctoral degree at Pisa. In the preceding generation there had been no first-class physicists in Italy. Yet in a few years there gathered around Fermi men who were to gain reknown. Fermi himself, moreover, was to become one of the greatest physicists of all time. When the group began to interact there were only a few indications of future greatness. Fermi had already shown signs of being an extraordinary man. His first associate, Franco Rasseti, even in graduate school showed a touch of genius. However, Emilio Segré, who was later to receive the Nobel prize, was still an undergraduate, as was Edoardo Amaldi, now one of Europe's leading physicists. Fermi, of course, was the leader of the group, but there is little doubt that he was stimulated by the others and that they in turn benefited from association with him. The group was much stronger than the sum of its parts. Moreover, the stimulus of working together for a time had a permanent beneficial effect on all the members—an effect that lasted long after the vicissitudes of politics and war broke up the close interaction.

In this area I have had three personal experiences. On a lesser scale, they nevertheless had considerable effect on my life. During my childhood I lived in an area of the city that for years had not produced a college graduate. A group of my playmates interacted most favorably with one another. We had science projects in an era when almost no one paid any attention to science. We engaged in friendly rivalry to outdo one another. All the group went to college —not to do so would have led to unthinkable loss of face. And all have achieved considerable success. One of the men is a leading cancer surgeon and regent of a state university; one has won national recognition as an architect and heads his own company; and another is chief mechanical engineer of a petroleum company.

A second experience gave me a chance to contrast some aspects of individual and team research. I spent four years (from 1935 to 1939) at the Radiation Laboratory at Berkeley as a graduate student in physics. To this laboratory came a score of some of the best young scientists of that day—Luis Alvarez, Edwin McMillan, Glenn Seaborg, Emilio Segré, and others who have had fine careers. At that time probably no laboratory in this country had a more talented group. Professor Ernest O. Lawrence, the director, had two goals: to develop his cyclotron, and to encourage exploitation of its potentials in research. Development of the cyclotron was a task requiring a team approach, and Lawrence was captain. The rest of us, particularly the graduate students, were just so many pairs of hands. While working on the cyclotron we had almost no opportunity to be creative. Indeed, innovation on the part of graduate students was often detrimental to the team effort. Altogether, the experience in the Radiation Laboratory would have been miserable and stultifying had it not been for Lawrence's second goal of encouraging research employing the cyclotron. In this area, organization of the effort was entirely different. Lawrence was enthusiastic and encouraging in his support of research by the staff, but he made no effort to go beyond giving helpful suggestions. The experimental activities were largely conducted by individuals or by pairs. New results were greeted with enthusiasm by all the laboratory personnel. The eager group of physicists present provided helpful suggestions, judgment, taste, and knowledge of the literature and technics. In the hours when an individual was free to conduct his own research, the laboratory was an excellent environment for creative effort. The contrast in the creativity of the men while engaged in team research and in individual research could scarcely have been greater.

As a result of this experience I became wary of team research. Observations during twenty-five years have not caused me to alter my attitude. Team research is useful when specific goals can be outlined in advance. A team effort may be the most effective approach when only a few members are capable of creative thinking and they are responsible for directing the work. In the exploration of the unknown, however, teamwork usually suppresses initiative. Prolonged experience as an underling on a team contributes little to the development of an individual and may even be harmful.

A later experience of group interstimulation proved very valuable for me. Shortly after World War II, three other nuclear physicists and I joined with a biologist to form a biophysics group at the Department of Terrestrial Magnetism of the Carnegie Institution of Washington. The physicists knew no biology and almost no chemistry, and it was ridiculous to attempt biophysics research in a department devoted primarily to geophysics. Professional biologists and biochemists who learned of our activity felt free to make caustic comments; in fact, one distinguished biochemist was heard to describe us as "a group of wistful physicists contemplating the mysteries of biology." At the same time our former colleagues in nuclear physics shook their heads sadly at our insanity in abandoning an established professional position to embark on such a foolish venture. The semi-hostility of the outside world helped knit the group together. Naturally, we were under all manner of pressure to establish a niche for ourselves and to win the respect of a new body of professional colleagues. Embarking on a course of self-education, we taught each other physical chemistry, biochemistry, and microbiology. Our conversation and our thoughts were centered on the experimental work we were doing and on its interpretation. While each usually worked on his own individual projects, all helped one another in many ways—with suggestions, enthusiasm, and judgment. We gave mutual support by fostering the concept that all of us were doing important, exciting, and significant work. We felt lucky to be having so much fun while being paid for it. Soon we were pioneering in studies of biosynthesis in microorganisms, and in a few years we were making worthwhile contributions. Our book entitled *Studies of Biosynthesis in Escherichia coli* came to be regarded as an outstanding text for students of microbiology.

These examples of mutual stimulus could be multiplied. Most of us are responsive to our environment, and group stimulus seems to be one of the best means of enhancing creativity. In the examples I have cited there are several components that I believe to be essential. First, there is a banding together of individuals to create a microenvironment which offers intellectual satisfactions to those within the group and which also meets the need for human fellowship. It is then possible to adopt the attitude that the value system of the rest of the world does not really count, that a common interest in advancing an area of science is the most important and only tenable activity for the members of the group. Moreover, if an individual temporarily loses his élan, he can soon regain it, for at all times there are some present who are brimming with infectious enthusiasm.

Judgment can usually be sharpened through group interactions. Related to this is the matter of "blind spots." A man may think deeply about a problem but fail to solve it because he lacks some small crucial idea—an item of knowledge, perhaps—or makes a slight error in analysis. Discussion of the problem with others can provide the single item that opens new vistas of comprehension.

Bringing a group together does not invariably produce this favorable mutual stimulus. Men who have the capacity to create must have their share of pride and egotism. In a closely knit, tight environment, tensions and rivalries are always latent. Indeed, the greatest hazard in group activity is internal dissension. When tensions begin to rise, creativity is brought to a standstill. A person engaged in a serious personal clash of wills invariably gives first priority in his thinking to the matter at issue. All too often the conflict escalates to implacable hatred, to the detriment of the individuals directly involved and all those around them. The carping critic, the jealous troublemaker, often destroys far more than he creates, and his evil influence can wither the creativity of many around him.

The tendency toward dissension can be countered in various ways. It is necessary that the individuals become so desirous of accomplishing common goals that they suppress their natural egotism, or, alternatively, each must receive so many benefits from an association that he believes self-interest requires a smooth relationship.

One clear-cut example of a common goal is seen in wartime, when national energies are concentrated to meet a common foe. Those who worked in the great wartime laboratories remember that the activities were relatively free of the usual frictions. In some of the examples of interaction previously cited there was a common element of group unity in the face of an unfriendly or drab environment. Rivalry between institutions can be another healthy way of promoting internal accord and common purpose.

An effective means of ensuring peace within a small group lies in the choice of its members. They should be people whose background and temperament are different. One, for instance, may be a skilled experimenter, and another a great enthusiast who spouts ideas. A third may have excellent judgment and the ability to recognize what leads are likely to prove valuable and to dispose quietly of the trivial, unsound, or sterile ones. It is usually desirable that the group contain a compromiser or peacemaker, as well.

It is also desirable that the various members of the group have somewhat differing bodies of knowledge so that they can teach one another. By assembling people of sufficiently different competence, almost encyclopedic knowledge can be provided in even a small group. Individuals having different talents and knowledge are intrinsically less competitive, for each has the security of knowing that he has a special contribution to make from his own particular area of strength.

I should like to touch on another mode of group stimulus that has proved effective, namely, the small, interdisciplinary, closed symposium. In an ideal arrangement, some twenty individuals meet for three days at a secluded spot where the rest of the world cannot intrude. The topic of the meeting should be an important one which draws on a number of different areas of knowledge. The key to success in such a meeting is to place individuals in close and agreeable contact with other creative scholars whom they have not previously met and to facilitate the juxtaposition of ideas in combinations that have not been made before.

The problem of achieving stimulus from larger group interactions among scientists has become progressively more acute. Large national meetings have ceased to fill the role they once had. Attendance at a huge gathering generally brings neither satisfactions nor effective transfer of ideas. To maintain the health of science we must find means of restoring the stimulating quality of interactions among larger groups. I believe that special symposia are one of the best answers to this need.

The general quality of the intellectual atmosphere of the community environment may also have a considerable effect on a scientist's activities. There is a marked variation in this factor. I, for example, find the intellectual atmosphere in Boston stimulating. New ideas are in the air, and they are received with enthusiasm. On the West Coast there is also a favorable climate for innovation. The midcontinent is not nearly so receptive or interested in intellectual matters. New York resembles Boston, but Philadelphia seems fragmented by rivalries and antagonisms. Intellectually, Washington seems to me curiously dull—sometimes apathetic.

I have mentioned some nearly ideal situations in which highly motivated individuals like Poincaré have succeeded in tapping the subconscious, or geniuses like Fermi have achieved great things, and persons associated with them have received a life-long stimulus. These ideal situations come rarely, and most individuals receive lesser stimuli from their environments. Even so, some constructive steps can be taken and some pitfalls can be avoided.

Highly intelligent, highly motivated individuals with natural good judgment can probably attain creative insights in almost any environment. Most people, however, are much influenced by surroundings and the circumstances under which they work. In any research effort there are usually periods of relatively routine work, and often they are essential. The crucial effort, however, is that which goes into judgments of interpretation and decisions of what to do next, especially the decision to embark on innovation. The quality of such decisions is highest when they evolve from intuitive insights. Every man I have known who is markedly creative has devoted a substantial part of his time to thinking about his work. The really good men achieve some of the total immersion that Poincaré cited. I believe that such complete immersion in a problem, at least periodically, is essential to developing a person's best potential.

In our efforts at organizing research we probably make our greatest mistakes in failing to provide for the need for total immersion in creative thought. In choosing group leaders, section heads, and others higher up on the administrative ladder we select men who have demonstrated ability as creative scientists. We then saddle them with the need to make a continuing series of major and minor decisions, and provide them with an ever-ringing telephone and a chattering distraction for a secretary. In the process we destroy most of their potentiality for creativity.

From my personal observations I would suggest that research administration be organized so that all creative individuals have frequent opportunities to attain total immersion in technical problems. Administrative responsibilities, if they have them, should be attended to periodically but with free spaces in between. Creativity should not be thwarted by incessant petty distractions. Also, for many individuals, there is a seasonal variation in creative capacities. During these periods they should try to avoid making interfering commitments and devote as much time as possible to laboratory work.

Many scientists find it useful to have two or three deadlines to meet each year. At our laboratory we have an annual report that we take very seriously. The report, a technical discussion of all work that has made substantial progress during the year, is sent to more than two thousand persons and establishments throughout the world. When the deadline for it approaches, our staff puts on a tremendous spurt of effort to complete studies for inclusion in the report for that year. Another type of deadline occurs as the staff prepares papers for technical meetings. On these occasions there is another burst of effort, and men turn out several times more work than is their usual custom.

I have discussed some of the factors that go into making a creative scientist and providing him with a favorable environment. Some of the factors are genetically controlled. Others depend on family background and early training. In choosing staff we want to recognize men with brains and character who are motivated to achieve. Then we must do our part by providing a combination of challenges and deadlines coupled with periods in which there is freedom from distraction, preferably for weeks at a time. Finally, we must endeavor to provide the kind of climate in which negative aspects of group interaction are suppressed while new ideas and contributions are received with enthusiasm. We should seek a situation in which the individual has maximum opportunity to tap his own resources but in addition is helped and sustained by the stimulus of close associates and the broad environment.

REFERENCES

1. H. Herbert Fox, "A critique on creativity in science," in Myron A. Coler and Harold K. Hughes (eds.), *Essays on Creativity in the Sciences* (New York, 1963), pp. 123-152.

2. Harold K. Hughes, "Individual and group creativity in science," *ibid.*, pp. 93-109.

3. Henri Poincaré, *Science and Method,* translated by Francis Maitland (London, 1914), quoted by H. Herbert Fox, *op. cit.*, p. 127.

4. Rensis Likert, *New Patterns of Management* (New York, 1961).

NEVITT SANFORD

The Human Problems Institute and General Education

OUR SOCIETY needs not only creative scientists but also people who can recognize and appreciate them, create conditions favorable to their work, and make judgments about what they ought to do. We need not only scientists but people who can make contributions in various fields of human endeavor; we need not only leaders, but people who at various levels of talent and responsibility can be useful in our complex and troubled society.

The focus of this paper will be upon the role of undergraduate education in the production of better scientists and better people, upon how the potentialities of entering freshmen may be developed by educational procedures. This is in keeping with the tradition in American higher education that assigns to the college the task of developing the student's intellect and sensitivities, of freeing and individualizing him, and to the graduate or professional school the task of training, that is, giving the individual the skills and knowledge in respect to which he resembles all others in his chosen field.

I shall not be concerned with the discovery or selection of unusually promising young people. At a good college today all entering freshmen will have obtained high scores on tests of ability and of academic achievement. It is not possible, on the basis of further examination of these students, to tell which are likely to be creative or productive and which not.[1] It is not possible, therefore, to design special programs for especially promising students. The only recourse is to offer all students at a given institution the best possible education for developing their potentialities.

Even if unusually promising students could be identified, it is hard to see how or why they should be treated differently from the others. It is true that success in the academic world is associated with performance in high school (adaptation to this culture begins early) but this does not hold for success in broader spheres of life. Special programs for the "gifted" within an institution have met with some success, but this may be due to the fact that being labeled gifted helps some students to live up to the high expectations that are held for them. By the same token, being labeled "not gifted" or mediocre, which happens to thousands of excellent young people in our best colleges every year, does a great deal of harm— as is known from our studies of students at Stanford and at Berkeley.

On the other hand, we do have some evidence that the qualities that distinguish creative people who are performing as professionals in various fields have very much in common with qualities that distinguish college seniors from college freshmen. MacKinnon and his colleagues at the Institute of Personality Assessment and Research at Berkeley[2] have shown that the most creative people in architecture, literature, mathematics, and engineering science are distinguished from less creative ones by, among other traits, their greater flexibility of thinking, breadth of perspective, openness to experience, freedom of impulse, breadth of interest, autonomy, and integrity. Our work at Vassar College[3] showed that all of these qualities increase during the four college years and can be understood as effects of education rather than as correlates of increasing age. The argument from this is that, in general, the creative person is above all a highly-developed person, and that educational programs can have an effect on such development in college.

Observational evidence suggests that outstanding work in many areas is favored by breadth of education. Creativity is little understood, but it seems to be in considerable part an ability to combine ideas from diverse areas of experience, and thus connect things that are ordinarily treated separately. This would seem to depend heavily, at least in fields such as literature, psychology, and social science, upon breadth and richness and complexity of personality and background. This may be why it is that in psychology we find so many men in the first rank, men like Köhler, Tolman, Boring, and Murray, who made radical changes in their fields—from physics, engineering, or biochemistry to psychology. This is not to mention the case of Freud, who was a physiologist and then a practitioner of medicine before he became a psychologist and whose greatest love was for archeology and general theory. It is risky to constrict or to speed up liberalizing education in the interest of hastening a student's ascent of a professional ladder, and it may well be a good idea not to discourage students who want to change fields at a comparatively late stage of their training.

The Current State of General Education

Education to produce good scientists and good men, men who possess qualities such as those that distinguish seniors from freshmen and creative professionals from less creative ones, that is to say, education that is aimed at developing the individual's potential as fully as possible, is, in the best sense, *general education*. Introducing the student to a range of subjects and ideas, as in survey courses, is not the essential aspect, though this may be a useful instrument, of general education. Developing the generalist approach to inquiry, the synthetic function, is closer to the mark, and so is involvement in significant experiences with people and things; but this is by no means all that is required for a person to be a productive scientist, or a leader in society, or even a useful citizen. General education aims at development toward full humanity, and all the resources of a college should be organized to this end.

However we may view the resources of a college, it is to be seen clearly that the teacher is central. Whatever curricular reforms may be instituted, whatever changes in the organization of teaching or in the social life of the college may be made, whatever schemes might be concocted or gadgets contrived, nothing very good can happen unless there are teachers with some enthusiasm for educating the undergraduate.

This is a cause of great dismay among those who have responsibility and concern for American higher education. The Carnegie Corporation[4] reports grimly that there is no significant increase in the proportion of new Ph.D.'s going into college or university work (45.2 per cent in 1954-55, 46.7 per cent in 1961-62) to meet the dramatic increase in the proportion of young people of college age who are entering college. And this is only part of the problem. Faculty members of our colleges and universities do less and less teaching— as Federal expenditures for research and development increase (over two hundred times between 1940 and 1964). Most serious of all, from the point of view of one interested in education for individual development, much of the teaching that is done is specialized and preprofessional and thus not well calculated to induce developmental changes in students.

Declining interest in teaching undergraduates is part of a larger picture of decline of the liberal college. This has been eloquently lamented by numerous university leaders such as Barzun,[5] Brown,[6] and DeVane.[7] It has been shrewdly, but less passionately, analyzed by Kerr.[8] The college is being "squeezed," according to these writers, between the high school and the graduate school; the former is tending to do what the first two years of college used to do, while the latter is extending its ways of doing things onto the last two years of college. Owing mainly to the prestige and power of the graduate schools, which are increasingly specialized as well as endowed with research funds, there is great pressure upon the university man to define himself as more specialist than intellectual, more researcher than teacher, more a teacher of graduate students than of undergraduates. Knapp[9] has supplied documentation for this point; but to the college or university man of today this state of affairs seems as real as the new freeway through his district.

The kind of specialization of which we have been speaking is embodied in its purest form in the research professor working on the frontiers of knowledge with advanced graduate students and postdoctoral scholars. He provides the ideal for the rest of the faculty who fight for conditions of appointment that will come as close to his as possible. The undergraduate is left out not only because the faculty's interest is elsewhere, but because the specializations of knowledge and professional language require a long, often dull period of mastery before the student can share the professor's concerns. The opportunity to work creatively on the forefront of knowledge has to be postponed to later and later years, even beyond the Ph.D.

Specialization has even deeper implications for the student; it tends toward the fragmentation of *him*. When everything in nature is conceived as being susceptible to abstraction from its context for purposes of intensive study the student himself does not escape; he too is conceived as an aggregate of part-processes, such as intelligence, sex, creativity, and motivation—the usual psychological model—each of which can be studied separately from the rest, and each of which is to be dealt with by special machinery set up for that purpose. If a teacher has this conception of the student it is easy for him to say that he is interested only in the student's intellect, which is categorically separated from the rest of him; or, it may be the other way around; if one insists that education is only a matter of transferring specialized knowledge and skills to the student, then the student comes to be viewed as the embodiment of bits of knowledge and particular skills. With no instruction in how to integrate the knowledge he acquires or how to protect his self, the student—unless he rebels—begins to live according to the prevailing conception of him, and eventually he identifies himself with the system. Thus the students, successful and unsuccessful ones alike, become reflections of the system in which they live for four years.

The problem is how to enlarge college and university faculties and how to persuade more of their members to take an interest in general education. It is usually supposed that this can be done either by love or by money.

The love is there, but it is inhibited. For an academic man to take an interest in his students as developing individuals is to be regarded by his colleagues as weak, or neurotic, or—what is worse —anti-intellectual. Even so, many teachers are still responsive to the call of students for some attention; often they are persuaded to take part in arrangements for improving faculty-student relations or offering students something fresh and interesting. But initial enthusiasm soon fades, and after a while the project is abandoned. Incentives are not sufficiently real or enduring.

Money seems at first glance more promising. But the big money goes for research; and even if substantial sums were poured into undergraduate teaching it would be filtered through the existing university apparatus, with the great likelihood that most of it would wind up in the budgets of departments eager to install new courses at the frontiers of their disciplines.

Need for Reorganization in the Search for Knowledge

The educational problem is deeply embedded in social dynamics; and efforts at reform must be directed to the real seat of the trouble: the way in which the search for knowledge is organized and the effects of this structure upon both society and education. It will be argued in this paper that specialization in inquiry and in teaching, while necessary, has led through its very success to the creation of new human and social problems, to a serious neglect of the generalist approach in science, in addition to a misconception— even a misuse—of the student. Then it will be proposed that a solution to our current dilemma will require the restoration of the generalizing and synthesizing function to its proper place in science, and that this can be the basis for an approach to teaching that recognizes and nourishes the humanity of the student.

The dynamics of specialized knowledge and consequent hu-

man problems. The potentiality for creating fresh human problems is inherent in the dynamics of specialized knowledge, whose sudden thrusts within a limited sector of a social system create imbalances in the whole. For example, the great effectiveness of specialized scientific inquiry is evident in the success of medical science in reducing rates of mortality; but the resulting "population explosion" has had to develop to the point of imminent world catastrophe before the need for a proportionate reallocation of resources to the resulting problem could be seen as a matter for serious scientific attention. The long delay between the creation of such knowledge-consequent problems and the slow, cumbersome organization of the means to meet them, as in this case, often spells human tragedy on a large scale. The apparatus originally set up for coping with particular problems, having generated momentum and built into itself self-perpetuating mechanisms, continues to operate along the same lines as before. Thus the university structure of departments, schools, and research institutes is exceedingly difficult to change, even though the problems they help create do not fall within the domain of any one of them nor lend themselves to attack by their favored methods.

The need for generalists in science. New problems, or old problems that have been neglected because they do not fit into the existing apparatus, have to be approached in the first instance with the use of generalist methods, the neglect of which is at the heart of both our human and our educational problems. This neglect at the present time is due not so much to the requirements of scientific inquiry as it is to the special dynamics of the present organizational structure of inquiry in universities and to a national system of rewards that make specialized approaches self-perpetuating.

A generalist approach requires, first, a recognition that problems arising as a result of social changes constitute new ranges of empirical phenomena. They are not at the frontier of any science, even though they may be in the forefront of the ordinary citizen's attention. They cannot be attacked with the most advanced methods or the most sophisticated concepts of existing disciplines; instead they call for exploratory or qualitative study, study directed to their proper definition, to the understanding of their connections with other problems, and to the generation of new concepts and methods.

A generalist approach also interprets inquiry to mean not only the discovery or demonstration of facts, but also the organization and interpretation of them. If knowledge is to serve human purposes, if it is to develop into wisdom, facts from various fields of specialized inquiry have to be brought together and evaluated in relation to the new problems that emerge as a consequence of applications of specialized research. Such continually new organizations of knowledge require a capacity to draw from several existing fields cutting across departmental divisions which have grown up around advanced specialties. If this is not done we shall continue to be faced with enormous human and social problems while in the midst of an "explosion in knowledge," that is to say, a proliferation in knowledge and a contraction of understanding.

The need for a new addition to existing institutions for specialized inquiry. There is an urgent need, then, for an institutionalized agency that can quickly bring knowledge and skill to bear upon problems that arise as consequences of social developments. Because this agency has to use a generalist approach to understanding, it can serve as a counterforce to the present heavy accent on specialized inquiry.

It is proposed that universities and colleges set up such multidisciplinary institutes for the study of pressing human problems. Such an addition to existing departments can radically alter the relation of a number of our scholars to their field of inquiry and to their undergraduate students while leaving departments to continue what they do best: the advanced education of the professional specialist.

The Human Problems Institute at Stanford

An example of what is proposed—the beginnings of a model—is the Institute for the Study of Human Problems at Stanford University. This Institute was started in 1961 with two research grants, one for studying and making policy recommendations affecting problems having to do with alcohol and alcoholism, the other for studying how students develop as individuals as they go through college and how they might be induced to develop more fully. The staff of the Institute soon embraced at least one person trained in each of the following fields: psychology, sociology, anthropology, political science, social welfare, psychiatry, education, law, literature, public health, philosophy, and bio-statistics. This group has worked closely together for four years and most have experienced a gradual loosening of their disciplinary ties. New projects and new staff members have been added. Although the Institute began without any plans for teaching, beyond providing places for research assistants, and although most of the staff have been full-time researchers, it is significant that most have been drawn into undergraduate teaching. This has been mainly informal, or less formal, or somewhat special teaching: senior colloquia, independent reading and research, a course in higher education—with special reference to the local scene—for selected student leaders, serving as resource persons for a group of seniors who were promoting and trying to organize an "intellectual community" of freshmen, taking part in a set of lectures, with discussion, on sex, sex relations, and sex roles on the campus, for forty student "sponsors" (seniors who are available as counselors and friends to freshmen) and other student leaders. All members of the staff, including young men and women who have yet to establish themselves in their careers, have said they would be happy to teach in an undergraduate general studies program while doing the same kind of research as at present, provided that the program was new, interesting, and well-conceived, and provided there was reasonable job security.

Another example is the Center for Research on Conflict Resolution at the University of Michigan, where multidisciplinary research and the training of graduate students have proliferated into undergraduate teaching.[10]

A Model Human Problems Institute

In the remainder of this paper I would like to suggest what might be the ideal role of the "human problems" institute in research and action, something of how such an institute might operate, and what might be its best role in teaching. At the same time I can indicate what some of the problems—and some of the promises—are by references to our experience at Stanford.

Choice of problems. Problems might be selected according to four main criteria: whether the problem is of deep human concern, whether it requires for its solution the resources of several disciplines, whether it is being neglected by those who have the capacity to solve it, and whether it is possible to get financial support for work on it.

"Alcohol problems"—problems related to the use of alcohol in our society—qualify very well according to all of these criteria. Alcoholism is a major health problem, and it ranks high among the problems dealt with by a variety of welfare and law enforcement agencies. According to all present indications, this condition is a result of an interplay of biological, psychological, and social factors, and an understanding of it will be attained only through the close collaboration of researchers from several disciplines. It is partly because of the complexity of the problem that it has been so badly neglected; there are various reasons for the unpopularity of alcoholism as a phenomenon to study or to treat; but because it has many facets and can be viewed in different perspectives, it has been easy for university departments and schools and various professional groups to pass it along to someone else. Yet, from the point of view of policy-makers at high levels of government, the problem is so serious that ample funds for research are available— far more, in fact, than can be allocated.

The study of individual development in college also meets all the criteria listed above. Although the development of young people is the main, though often unexpressed, concern of parents who send their sons and daughters to college, and although knowledge of how students change under the influence of educational procedures must be the basis for educational policy, this whole area has been neglected by psychologists and educational researchers because it does not lend itself to investigation by the more specialized methods of these disciplines. The field has in recent years begun to receive some attention from researchers. Now that students have at last found their voices there is new ground for hope that a major effort will be made to understand their experience and needs and how they might best be educated.

There is no lack of problems: war and peace, economic planning, the improved working of democratic institutions, race relations, poverty, rehabilitation of the culturally deprived, the deterioration of our cities, the swelling population, the alienation and demoralization of youth, aging and longevity, air polution and other environmental hazards to health, addictions of various kinds, conservation and land use, and so on. Problems in any one of these areas might well be made the focus of study in a multidisciplinary institute. These problems are highly salient today, and funds are being poured into efforts to solve some of them. It is almost universally assumed, however, that the existing structure of professions and university departments and schools will be adequate to these challenges. Yet, when one considers the rapidity of change in our time, this structure seems to have been designed for a different age. One is forced to conclude that there should be institutes for the study of universities.

Problems such as these affect the whole society, involve powerful interest groups and passionately held belief systems; hence particular approaches to them are favored or disfavored in different political climates and stages of social and economic development. In 1950, for example, it was virtually impossible to raise funds for the study of the effects of racial segregation; in very recent years the problem has been to find the manpower to work in what has become a popular area. The current accent on doing something for the great mass of our people seems to have caught almost everybody unprepared; apparently few believed in the possibility of the radical shift in ideology, at high levels of government, that has come about—the shift from an accent on equal opportunity to an accent on preparing people so that they might take advantage of the opportunities offered them.

The new institutes should work on several different problems at the same time. There are highly important scientific reasons that the institute should work on several problems at the same time. It is just this kind of exposure to differing problems, and the accompanying association with colleagues from different disciplines, that serves to educate the staff in the generalist orientation. Little would be gained if a scientist gave up a disciplinary specialty only to become a specialist in some particular applied area. Work on different problems at the same time would also lead the staff to look for underlying affinities among them, for processes central to a diversity of surface phenomena, and then to make advances on the conceptual and theoretical front.

In beginning our work at Stanford we considered it very important that research on alcohol-related problems go forward in a setting that favored close association between the staff of the alcohol project and the staffs of other projects. This was partly to lend status to what has been a low status field, but it was mainly to combat the tendency to make of "alcohology" a specialty that could be kept out of the main stream of science and practice, with the consequent development of outgroup attitudes among the "alcohologists." We wanted to insure that alcohol problems were viewed in new perspectives, and that the empirical phenomena of the field were connected with those of other fields.

The fact that people of different disciplines work under the same roof and have the same general research interests and ideology does not mean that their collaboration will be very close. The pull of the specialty is strong. Scholars, typically, are reluctant to burden others with their highly specialized concerns, and usually they are under such pressure to meet their writing deadlines that they are not very eager to learn the details of work in fields other than their own. The shared problem provides the basis for close collaboration across disciplines. If a group of scholars and scientists are required to make recommendations for action with respect to an important problem there is a strong tendency for them to pull together—if they stay together at all.

To consider an example: should the age at which young people are permitted by law to purchase or possess alcoholic beverages in public places be held at twenty-one, as it is in most states, or should it be lowered to eighteen, or dispensed with altogether. Our "alcohol staff" has the obligation to work out a defensible position on this question. It seems that in order to do so we need a great deal of knowledge about the nature and determinants of different patterns of drinking among young people, and about the implications of particular patterns for the later development of the individual. What is true for the individual is also true for the social group. A change in the law of which we are speaking would amount to a change in our culture. Various groups and institutions in our society have a strong interest in the matter, and any judgment of the feasibility of such a change would have to be based on an appraisal of the climate of opinion in these groups and institutions and in the population generally. If a change were actually made, various segments of our society would be affected, particularly all those that have some responsibility for youth.

To organize knowledge around problems of this kind, to confront the various issues of value that are involved, to lay plans for studying the consequences of actions require the closest interdisciplinary collaboration. In our experience, the representatives of the various disciplines mentioned above have been fully challenged, and we have felt the need to draw upon other disciplines as well. When scholars and scientists work on problems of this kind, all become highly stimulated, communication becomes very free and is carried on without benefit of specialized terminology. Each member of the group is grateful for the contributions of various disciplines, and he becomes appropriately realistic about what his own group has to offer.

The same kind of close collaboration has been attained by the psychologists, psychiatrists, social workers, and educators who are studying student development with attention to educational policy. But the same circumstances that created a maximum of cross-disciplinary fertilization and intellectual companionship among the alcohol staff on the one hand and the student development staff on the other tended at the same time to draw the two groups apart—and this despite the fact that the two staffs overlapped to some extent. This is testimony both to the power of the shared problem to pull people together and to the difficulty of researchers being generalist when they work on sponsored projects and are under pressure to meet deadlines. Even so, the alcohol and student development projects have interpenetrated one another in fruitful ways. The study of students has contributed directly to our knowledge of drinking among youth, and the study of drinking patterns and liquor control policies on the campus—in important ways a microcosm of the larger society—has aided our efforts to formulate general policy. At the same time it has been discovered that a student's approach to alcohol, his way of drinking or not drinking, his relations with drinking subcultures are very significant expressions of his personality and the developmental changes within it. Such interaction among our projects has been favored by the presence of several visiting scholars who have had the time and freedom to move among the several projects.

The Scientific Importance of the Human Problems Institute

To accent social need is not to say that the problem-centered institute represents "applied science" in the ordinary sense of this term. There are, of course, institutes of applied science deliberately organized, and staffed by "practical" men, to exploit knowledge created by university departments and research institutes. To some extent the human problems institute participates in this kind of applied work, but the study of new problems that arise as a result of social change broadens the empirical base of the component sciences upon which the institute draws and leads to the creation of new concepts. A well-constructed idea always has a definite relation to the empirical events it seeks to conceptualize. If the observational base is narrow the concept can have little generality. An observer who studies his subjects in an extended environment, as the problem-oriented researcher must usually do, will invent different concepts than will an observer who confines himself to laboratory or clinical situations. The study of college students, for instance, has shown that considerable change in personality takes place during the college years. This could not be seen in a clinical situation where the therapist-theorist usually worked with adults who were still caught up in continuing childhood conflicts. Thus the notion that personality development takes place very largely in childhood has had to be revised, and new concepts for dealing with the conditions and processes of change at later stages have to be developed.

To be practical, the psychological and social sciences must deal with long sections of behavior and with large areas of the person and of the social system. They must also do this in order to be good sciences. The processes of nature are not first of all isolated objects of inquiry waiting to be observed and then synthesized; they exist, instead, in contexts of other processes and are to be fully understood only when seen in their natural setting. Although inquiry proceeds by analysis, and by the intensive study of part-processes that have been abstracted from the wholes in which they are naturally embedded, the wholes must be reconstituted if they and their parts are to be known well. It seems then, that knowledge of how things cling together is at least as important a part of science as is knowledge of how things may be analyzed.

This last is freely admitted by most scientists, but the objection is often made that complex wholes and wide ranges of variables cannot be studied by existing scientific methods. The answer is that we *must*, sooner or later, study complex and wide-ranging phenomena if our sciences are ever to become fully developed. The suggestion here is that one way to be holistic, comprehensive, and generalist in one's approach is to be practical. This is a key conception in the human problems approach. In thinking comprehensively and holistically about human or social problems, the scientist must use gross units of analysis; and he must content himself with rough estimates of the variables he studies. He cannot hope to achieve the refinement of conceptualization and the precision of measurement that is achieved by the laboratory man, but this does not make him any the less scientific—not so long as he suits his instruments to the task at hand and makes sure that his gross categories are not inconsistent with what is known at lower levels and lend themselves to reduction and systematic treatment.

There is another way in which the human problems approach is to be distinguished from applied science: in the former, the scientist does not accept the surface definition of the problem; instead, the definition of the problem becomes a part of his inquiry. When he is called upon by individuals or groups to help solve a problem it almost always turns out that they have a narrow view of what the trouble is and an unrealistic conception of what they desire. The scientist cannot be content to bring his expertise to bear on such problems as how to keep school children quiet, how to forestall Civil Rights demonstrations, or how to prevent eighteen-year-olds from drinking. This would be unscientific, as well as unhelpful to those who sought counsel. When a scientist concerns himself with matters such as these, the most useful thing he can do is help define the problem and to bring about a fresh consideration of goals. By starting with the assumption that practical problems are complex, interwoven with other problems, and tied to long-range human and social goals he initiates a process of inquiry, in which his clients become involved, and in the course of which he may ask questions of general scientific interest. Most often the question will take the form of how might individuals or social structures be changed in some desired way. The phenomena with which he has to deal in working on a particular problem can almost always be regarded as a special case of something more general, and thus he has an opportunity to contribute to systematic knowledge while aiding in the solution of practical problems.

To be immersed fully in the realities of a problem situation and concerned with bringing about some desirable change is to be in a situation that is very favorable to the creation of ideas. It is a significant fact that the most important concepts for the understanding of the individual personality have been produced by men who were engaged in the practice of psychotherapy. The development of a social therapy whose aim it was to overcome failings of social systems could be equally productive of ideas for the understanding of social processes. The individual scientist who engaged in this activity would be fully challenged; he would be concerned as well as curious, and this would favor his success. He might, when the demonstration of hypotheses was the order of the day, allow a part of his scientific conscience to dominate his work, but for the most part he could function as a whole human being, whose nature it is to inquire.

Some contrasts with traditional institutes or centers. The idea of a multidisciplinary institute devoted to current human or social problems is not new. The Yale Institute of Human Relations and the several institutes of child welfare established in the 1930's had this general purpose. But history records that there is a strong tendency for such institutes to transform themselves into centers for specialized sciences. It has proved to be very easy for scientists to work in these centers without surrendering any of their disciplinary concerns or professional identity. And departments, it seems, have always known how to utilize such institutes for their own purposes —purposes such as bringing in a new man without having to use departmental funds. The institutes being discussed here cannot be creatures of the departments. Although various kinds of mutually beneficial patterns of collaboration can be worked out, institutes and departments are fundamentally different, and they may easily become rivals.

Finally, the human problems institute is different from all those centers where scholars and scientists of different disciplines come together just to exchange ideas, or to generate ideas from the armchair. It differs also from centers in which various activities are located for administrative purposes, or because on some preconceived principle or another they can be said to belong together. The kind of institute being advocated here is multidisciplinary because the problems with which it is concerned can be attacked only in this way; and in this institute all staff members engage in research, though they need not—and preferably do not—do so exclusively.

The Institute's Potential Role in Teaching

At a time of a great shortage of teachers, college administrations might well look to the staffs of various types of institutes as a source of talent. It seems highly likely that such staffs include many scholars and scientists who, though their research is highly specialized, have generalist inclinations and could be recruited for special programs in general education. Staffs of human problems institutes, who are generalists in their research, can also be persuaded to take part in various kinds of general education programs. If, indeed, they lose so much of their professional identities that they are not wanted by departments it is hard to know where else they might teach. Today, when there is a great deal of discussion of innovations in general education, and experimental programs are actually being set in motion, it is almost universally assumed that the teachers will be borrowed from their departments for a while or that they will be allowed to keep one foot in their departments while giving themselves wholeheartedly to the new venture. No one claims that these arrangements are altogether satisfactory, and there is reason for grave doubt about their effectiveness in the long run. The establishment of problem-centered institutes can help to sustain educational innovations, for the general education program, especially if it is new and challenging, is a natural base for the teaching activities of the generalist researcher. More than this, if staff members of problem-centered institutes were affiliated with undergraduate teaching programs this would help to maintain the stability of these institutes. It may be added also that college teachers, or teachers in university general colleges, who do not have adequate opportunities for research might well organize, or have organized for them, multi-disciplinary institutes of the sort being advocated here.

But over and above these practical considerations is the argument that the problem-oriented generalist may be, or may become, uniquely qualified for a particular kind of undergraduate teaching, and that this kind of teaching is especially valuable to the undergraduate. The generalist researcher *needs* the undergraduate, and the undergraduate needs him.

The researcher on human problems has to proceed in an exploratory way, and he cannot rely on the technical terms of his parent discipline. He is in a poor position to talk to graduate students, who often seem to know everything already, or even to those undergraduates who know what they want to do and are in a hurry to envelop themselves in the cloak of a specialty. The open-ended, curious undergraduate is a natural audience and companion; and men who are engaged, as men and as scientists, with pressing problems about which little is known and who are generating ideas *do* need an audience.

The fact that the problem-oriented scientist works on problems about which little is known is of great benefit to the students he teaches. It means that they can reach the frontier early and begin participating creatively in the search for knowledge. Through being given a chance to use their minds actively at the beginning of their careers students may "learn how to learn"—the most essential ingredient of general education—instead of being required to devote themselves exclusively to mastering set fields of knowledge that will shortly be outmoded.

The entering freshman is a natural generalist. Often he thinks that a college professor can talk on any subject, and in his questioning he leaps from topic to topic although they are somehow related in his mind. It is only later, probably just a few weeks later, that he discovers that different questions have to be asked of different people and that he himself must learn to keep his knowledge in separate compartments if he is to be a success in college. How may the freshman's generalist tendencies be nourished? A minimum strategy, surely, is to expose him to a range of subjects. Teaching based in a problem-oriented institute would do this by bringing into the discussion material from the several fronts on which the institute was engaged. And since these fronts were at a relatively early stage of development, the student would be returned to a situation not unlike Newton's day, when an educated man could learn all there was to know in several directions. But generalism is not primarily a matter of breadth. It is inconceivable today that a scholar can have any sort of grasp of the sum total of knowledge. If mastery of a range of knowledge were the sole criterion of generalism we should have to conclude that the scholar who wished to be a generalist could only be so in a specialized way! Generalism, most essentially, is a form of inquiry, and a set of attitudes toward knowledge. The generalist accents the synthetic function; he is out to connect things that have been isolated; but most of all he is impressed by the complexity of things, and he seeks to understand them in their context. There are many ways in which things cling together, and ways in which they can be brought together intellectually. A fundamentally important sort of cohesion of diverse factors is that which is exposed by the human problems type of inquiry. It is this that should be put across to students, in the interest of their general education.

It follows from this that students may best acquire a generalist orientation in the same way that the mature scholar does, and that is through direct involvement with human and social problems. Institute-based teaching would bring directly to the student some of the phenomena of life, in all their complexity and immediacy, and the work of conceptualization would be performed, as it were, before his eyes. The institute could help to provide, in fact, the functional equivalent of the physical scientists' laboratory. Students could take part in some of the institutes' field studies and integrate their experiences with their didactic work. More than that, students could find in the institutes' teaching program an intellectual and theoretical context for the field work that they do in the normal course of events. They would then discover—what never becomes clear to many college students—that liberal education does not need to be divorced from life.

There are questions about the place of this kind of experience in the overall undergraduate education of the student. How much should there be and at what time? One proposal would be that the student take course work in each of several problem areas, these courses substituting for that part of his studies that would normally meet the requirements of a departmental major. On the other hand, as indicated above, there is the task of nourishing the generalist tendencies of the entering *freshman*. If he were introduced to the human problems orientation it might influence in a favorable way the remainder of his college career; the experience might involve him, win him to the educational enterprise in a way that courses introductory to the disciplines often do not; he would be offered some protection against premature commitment to a vocation, and some insulation against all the forces of specialized inquiry that he will encounter later.

Graduate education. We supposed in the beginning that whereas undergraduates and post-doctoral students might very well spend some times in our Institute and receive instruction at the hands of our staff, it would not be a very good place for graduate students. Under pressure to meet the requirements of their specialized training programs and eager to establish their professional identities, graduate students would be impatient with our generalist orientation and would not find within our policy science and long-range studies suitable topics for Ph.D. dissertations.

We had some research assistantships to offer, however, and since 1961 fifteen graduate students have worked at the Institute, some from its beginning. It seems that we overestimated the problems and dangers. These students say that they have enjoyed and benefited from their Institute experience, particularly from being members of a relatively small community or household, without being handicapped in their pursuit of the degree. By the end of this year four of these students will have had their Ph.D. theses signed by members of the Institute staff.

We have changed our minds about graduate education. This has been not only because of our experience with students at the Institute. We have been increasingly impressed by the nation's need for psychologically sensitive social scientists who have the basic intellectual tools for action-oriented inquiry, and we have become increasingly acquainted with the job opportunities for people of this kind. Most important of all, we believe we have acquired some understanding of graduate students in general. A great many of them —in this age of the Peace Corps—are very unhappy with the constraints of their professional training and with the prospects that lie before them; they would gladly add two years to their period of training and invite an uncertain future in order to be able to work, now, on important human and social problems. (One does not dare encourage them too much in this last.)

In an ideal arrangement graduate students who worked at the Institute would take part in the teaching of undergraduates who enrolled in the field-oriented courses organized by staff members. These graduate students would be helped to realize that it is undergraduate teaching that holds the university enterprise together, that generalist teaching is the best expression of their membership in the university community, and that they have an important role as makers of undergraduate culture.

Conclusion

Although this paper is concerned mainly with the improvement of undergraduate education, a large part of it has been devoted to presenting the idea of a multidisciplinary, problem-oriented institute. This was made necessary by the basic assumption that the existing pattern of undergraduate education in America cannot be changed, fundamentally or enduringly, without change in our graduate schools, which determine what is done in the colleges. The great need is for change in the way the search for knowledge is organized. Under present arrangements the college or university teacher is virtually forced to be a specialist, both in his teaching and in his research. There is no apparent way to reward generalist teaching, which is what the undergraduate needs most, well enough so that the scholar will put this ahead of his specialized concerns. The institute proposal is designed to promote generalist research and thus to produce generalist scholars who can integrate their research and their teaching in general education programs. This idea is fundamental; it therefore has been necessary to show that the institute, which chooses problems primarily because of their deep human concern and works on more than one problem at a time, really represents a change in existing arrangements: that it is not a research institute of the usual sort, not "applied science" but a center for pure science of a particular kind, and not merely an arrangement for paying lip-service to the idea of multidisciplinary collaboration. It has been necessary to show, too, that such an institute can work and that it can be established within existing university structures. This last is particularly important. The present organization of the search for knowledge is very resistant to change. Universities and the major agencies that support research are, essentially, parts of the same apparatus, which has no built-in mechanism of change. In general, proposals for real change cannot be supported; if a proposal for change is supported one may be reasonably sure that it does not involve real change. If one is seriously bent on change the wisest course is to secure funds for other purposes, and to make of change-inducing activities an additional enterprise while faithfully achieving stated purposes. It may thus be possible to initiate change on the fringes of the structure, with some hope of a deeper penetration later. But one would not hope for lasting change unless the innovation was in line with developing social forces. Here there is ground for optimism today. Universities and funding agencies do change—if almost never according to plan. They adapted themselves to the requirements of the Cold War, and they move according to the demands of a technology that nobody controls. They are beginning now to respond to public demands for attention to some of the vast human and social problems that have been created, including that of how to get better teaching, and to an increasingly widely felt desire to break loose from the bonds of technology. This last is expressed in the attitudes and longings of the students— graduate and undergraduate—who come out of the society and into the university. To know these students well is to realize that the period of over-accent on specialization and abandonment to technology is nearing an end. There are many indications that the best students of the present generation, unlike those of the generation that now mans the establishment, want to be educators and social reformers. They want to nourish their humanity and that of others. The conflict of the generations is, in fact, a powerful force toward change. We of the Stanford Institute for the Study of Human Problems believe that, for once, we have correctly anticipated the course of events; we hope to do something that will help shape it to human ends. We do not advocate any radical reduction in specialized inquiry, but only its removal from its position of domination over all higher education. Problem-oriented institutes would not by themselves accomplish this objective, but they could be the beginning of an effective counterforce.

REFERENCES

1. David C. McClelland, "Encouraging Excellence," *Dædalus* (Fall 1961), pp. 711-724.

2. D. W. MacKinnon (ed.), *The Creative Person*, (Berkeley, California, 1961).

3. N. Sanford (ed.), "Personality Development during the College Years," *Journal of Social Issues*, Vol. 12 (1956), pp. 1-71.

4. Carnegie Foundation for the Advancement of Teaching, *The Flight from Teaching* (New York, 1964).

5. J. Barzun, "College to University—and after," *The American Scholar*, Vol. 33 (1964), pp. 212-219.

6. J. D. Brown, "The Squeeze on the Liberal University," *The Atlantic Monthly*, Vol. 213 (1964), pp. 84-87.

7. W. C. DeVane, "The College of Liberal Arts," *Dædalus* (Fall 1964), pp. 1033-1050.

8. C. Kerr, "The Frantic Race to Remain Contemporary," *ibid.*, pp. 1051-1070.

9. R. Knapp, "Changing Functions of the College Professor," in N. Sanford (ed.), *The American College* (New York, 1962).

10. Center for Research on Conflict Resolution, *Review of Program, 1959-1964* (Ann Arbor, Michigan, 1964).

DOCUMENTS

CARYL P. HASKINS

The Changing Environments of Science

DURING THE year just past, a new and immensely powerful source of radio energy was discovered in the heavens, in observations made with the twin ninety-foot dishes of the radio astronomy observatory of the California Institute of Technology at Owens Valley. When the object had been brought within the optical field of the great Hale telescope on Palomar Mountain, the spectrum of its light exhibited a redshift so great as to mark it a new outpost of our reach into the universe. So distant is it that exact specification of its remoteness is not yet possible, because the conditions of space itself are still insufficiently understood. But it is evident that the light that reached the Hale telescope this past year to bring the image of the new object had left its source when our universe was hardly half its present age. This immense penetration into space that the year has brought, which is thought to reach over a large fraction of the entire radius of the universe itself, climaxes a long train of triumphs in astronomy which within little more than twenty years has increased our view into space by easily a factor of ten, changing distances thought of less than three decades ago in terms of hundreds of millions of light years to reaches now reckoned in the billions. Even a decade ago, we could not have remotely imagined what we know today.

During this same year, a new and striking method has been perfected in analytical genetics at the molecular level that has opened the widest and most exciting potentials for the further extension of our understanding there. It makes possible the direct comparison among different organisms of the actual ordering of the nucleotide bases on the chromosomes—the ordering that constitutes the "language" in which the information of heredity is coded and stored from generation to generation in all plants and animals and in man himself. The method allows the comparative examination of genetic codes among organisms far too distantly separated biologically to permit the use of ordinary genetic methods. It suggests extremely broad and novel ideas about evolution at the level of the genetic code itself. It adds a powerful new experimental tool to aid in deciphering the very processes by which the hereditary information stored in the chromosome can determine the constitution—biochemical, physical, nervous—of the developing body whose nature and shape it directs. It bids fair to shed new light on the structure and function of microorganisms vital to man's welfare, including some viruses that appear to be concerned with cancer. The new concepts that this advance suggests, and indeed the very ones upon which it is based, would have been well-nigh unimaginable two decades ago.

In 1963, nearly two and one-half million specialists were at work in the United States. They comprised almost four per cent of all those employed in the nation. Included among them were a million and a quarter or more scientists, technicians, and engineers. Nearly three in every five were engaged in projects supported or sponsored by the federal government, or located within the government itself.

During 1963 the Swedish nation established a science advisory council, chaired by the prime minister and including five members of the cabinet. Thereby it joined the United States, the United Kingdom, France, and Canada and Australia, India and Pakistan and Turkey and Thailand, to name but a representative sample of nations where official actions taken within the last few years have reflected a striking and important development of our time. On both national and international scenes, over the years since World War II, science in its relation to affairs has become significantly transformed from the *instrument* of public policy which it has long been to a new and subtly but significantly different position—that of an *object* of public policy. The consequences of this shift could be considerable in the years to come. The shift itself is diagnostic of changes in the relationships of science to the societies which support it and of which it has become an integral part that may run deep.

It would be hard to assemble four more divergent arenas of thought and action than are represented in these four great developments, occurring over the span of little more than a single year.

They hardly seem linked at all, save in their common emphasis upon vast and wind-swift growth in the substantive range and power and penetration of the science of our day, on the one hand, and in its sheer massiveness and complexity and the extent and the degree, as well as the kind, of its social impact, on the other. Yet joining these diversities, and underlying them, there may be at least one set of common themes that deserves a close reexamination in the context of our day. They link three apparently dissimilar elements that yet may be closely related—the processes of planning both in and for science, the complex of contingent choices by which that planning is brought about in practice and through which both the shape and the functions of science are constantly being mediated and determined, and, finally, the role of the qualified and prepared individual who in all the aspects of science itself and of activities affected by science must make such choices.

There is a related point that also challenges examination. When the early scientific associations came into being in Europe, the first Industrial Revolution had not yet begun, and their initial relations were with an essentially preindustrial society. When they were first founded in America, it was a rural and primarily agricultural society, not an urban and industrial one, that they early served and where they matured—a society which at the national level called upon the aid of science primarily in relation to agronomic matters.

The original social environs of science have changed profoundly in the years between, in this country and abroad. As Geoffrey Vickers has penetratingly remarked:

Rapid industrialization, as we see it today, is certainly not a cross section in a linear progress of indefinite duration. On the contrary, it is probably a rapidly passing phase, in which signs of self limitation can already be clearly seen. Yet ephemeral though it may be, it is of critical importance in two ways. For first, it involves the irrevocable commitment of resources, physical and human, in ways which may determine the pattern of life for many generations to come. And secondly, during its dominance, insights won over the last two thousand years, virtually the whole of our accumulated knowledge of value, will be either confirmed in a form profoundly changed or lost, for some later age painfully to discover.

What have been the effects both on and for science at the national and international levels of its activity, and how are they related to the subtle shift of science in its public context from instrument to object of policy?

The influence of science and technology upon our nation is as old as the history of the nation itself; a good case could be made, indeed, that it is considerably older. An important part of that influence, of course, has been and continues as never before to be exercised through the products of science and technology. But it is important to remember that it is a very different aspect of the scientific way which throughout our history may have exercised the deepest and most important influence on that profoundest of all our national concerns—the molding of our national character. It may well be that a half century from now we shall conclude that the social significance of science has less to do with the products that it has inspired, with the control of the material world which it has placed at our command, with the physical power that it has aided us to subsume from nature, important as these are, than with its inner and guiding philosophy; with an ethos involving an overriding personal commitment to enduring values and a high personal discipline in fulfilling them.

In a historical and evolutionary sense, science lies at the very heart of western society. Both were born in the common philosophy of the Enlightenment. From the beginning they shared basic principles. For our wider society, as for science, the search for truth is an overwhelming value, however that truth may be defined. From that commitment to the search for truth flow our concern for originality, our maintenance of an attitude of skepticism, our protection of and our heavy reliance on the processes of pluralism in all we undertake, our defense of argument and dissent. These are the values that give to our society and maintain within it the continuing power to evolve.

Perhaps most significant of all, this ethic of the search for truth inherently gives special honor to the place of the inquiring individual. Historically, we have always depended on him heavily to preserve and implement our values, and as a principal bearer of this vital social responsibility we have esteemed him accordingly and have consistently protected his freedom and provided for his continuing flexibility of action. So if one were to choose among the common themes that at a deeper level bind together these four disparate developments of the year, the most fundamental would surely be that of the individual, and especially the individual deeply concerned with science, whether in a strictly professional role or as guardian or implementer or observer. What is his place in a scientific world so different in its substantive scope and richness and complexity from that of his grandfather as hardly to be recognizable, and so different in its social impact from that even of his father as scarcely to be the same in kind? Is he still truly relevant? Or have his functions now been subsumed collectively by the great teams and the great organizations of our time, scientific and social alike? If he still is truly relevant and vital, is he being adequately prepared, today, to comprehend the newer aspects of his multiple roles? Is he being trained in sufficient numbers to properly serve an extended and immensely evolved science, serving in turn, in a multitude of ways, a vastly expanded and elaborated society?

In a recent and penetrating essay on the emergence of Darwinism, commemorating the centenary of the concept of evolution, Sir Julian Huxley posed a question of striking concern for our time. What would have happened to Darwin as an individual scientist if he had been born a century earlier, or a century later? The essayist speculates that if he had been born in 1709 he might have gone down to posterity as a sound, and perhaps a brilliant, amateur naturalist, possibly somewhat like his grandfather Erasmus, whose own philosophy, however, Darwin so strongly rejected. It is easy to forget that Erasmus was an ingenious and even a brilliant thinker. Yet his notions never really stimulated the development of modern concepts of evolution—indeed, they may actually have retarded it. Did this reflect on his innate capacities? Or was the failure instead akin to that of Edward Blyth, who a generation later, but still well in advance of Darwin's publication of the *Origin*, evolved a concept of natural selection that was essentially correct, yet used it to reinforce the idea of the fixity of species that was still a dominant concept of the time? Was the overarching structure of scientific thought simply not fitted, in Erasmus Darwin's day, to accommodate a modern theory of evolution?

A Charles Darwin born two centuries later, Huxley surmises, would today at fifty-five be a respectable, indeed, perhaps an eminent, contemporary ecologist, but little more. As a modern disciple of evolutionary thinking, conceived as laboring with the same methods and orientation as the original Darwin but deep in the shadow of his achievements—or, if the original Darwin had never existed, then in the shadow of some near-contemporary who inevitably would have proposed the theory—this hypothetical modern Darwin would hardly be a revolutionary world figure in today's structure of scientific thought. Earlier, the time would have been unripe for his actual greatness; later, it is far overripe.

Few speculations indeed can be more fascinating than this of the probable career of a Darwin displaced forward or backward by a century. And few could be more relevant to our own time. For it emphasizes strikingly how rapidly the whole conceptual structure of even one sector of the scientific environment has changed within a hundred years, and how important and how different this environmental challenge may be to the individual of Darwinian quality and kind who would enter it today. It also poses several penetrating questions. When a field of thought has become both far advanced and highly elaborated, are its new frontiers still within the reach of individuals, however gifted? And if they are, what is the relative significance, in the minds of those individuals, of innate quality and of environmental influence? Would Darwin's specific aptitudes, his specific fields of interest, his specific modes of approaching the world, have persisted more or less intact had he been born in 1709 or 1909? If so, were there research questions truly relevant to those talents great enough and near enough the surface in the two hypothetical life periods to have engaged his interest and proved his genius? Is it possible that a mind of such lofty stature, and gifted with such an immense capacity for plumbing the underlying verities of a very special sector of the natural world, was by those very circumstances deeply and irrevocably committed to the arena where it chose in fact to work? Was the actual timing of Darwin's life, then, one of those rare near-miracles?

On the other hand, would a mind of such native originality and power, given the appropriate training and opportunity, have chosen quite different areas of inquiry in the different periods—areas more accessible in the one case, areas involving new unanswered questions of comparable magnitude and novelty in the other? Is it not true that in any age of science issues of the power and the generality with which Darwin dealt lie below the surface, too deep perhaps for ordinary men to perceive, but still accessible to individuals of Darwinian penetration, still ready to be detected and revealed by such vision—as indeed is happening in adjacent areas of biology at present? Would Darwin's particular kind of genius burn as bright at any period in the growth of scientific thought about the natural world? Or must new kinds of scientific workers, of ever-changing tastes and talents, be available in each generation to man the frontiers of a constantly changing and elaborating science?

Some of these questions are clearly unanswerable in the present state of our knowledge. Some may not even be real. Yet they bring home with force the profound issue of the nature of the influence

that existing scientific environments have exercised in each generation on the whole scientific career of those who have entered such
environments most sensitively and powerfully. And they underline
the unprecedented quality of that environmental challenge in our
own day and in the future, posed equally by the complexity of the
vast, interconnected, organism-like webs of theory and fact, of concept and projection, that collectively make up the vast texture of an
age of advanced scientific scholarship, on the one hand, and of the
very different but equally complex organizational environment
embracing the formal structuring and implementing of science in its
relationships to the greater society that it serves, on the other. The
sheer magnitude, the intricacy, the power, and the pervasiveness of
those two environments in our time must profoundly condition the
philosophy and the orientation of every individual entering upon the
scientific way. Moreover, in their headlong future evolution, these
environments must in the nature of things constantly place new and
ever more importunate demands upon him—demands that occasionally, in a very general fashion, we can foresee, especially in the area
of scientific scholarship, but of which, often enough, we have little
inkling.

Many challenges to our understanding and action are limned
here with special clarity. A particularly important one concerns the
quality of this relationship between native intellectual orientation
and the capacity for sensitive and discerning reaction to the contemporary scientific environment in molding the effectiveness of the
young research worker. Closely related is another, equally arresting,
question. How can the young individual of potentially great stature,
entering the complex scientific environment of today, best be prepared to seek and to uncover and to pursue the issues that tomorrow
may have major significance? How can he or she learn to recognize
them amid the random noise of the vast and varied contemporary
scientific scene?

At least two points of major relevance are here emphasized. The
first is the cardinal necessity for breadth and flexibility and a fundamental quality in preparation—breadth and depth and generality in
substance to minimize the perils for the entrant too specially trained
that can inhere in the rapid exhaustion of specific fields so characteristic of modern research; flexibility of outlook so that the multifarious
relationships of science to the larger society will not be foreign to
him in principle. The second point is involved with that curious and
elusive quality perhaps best called the power of penetration—the

Darwin-like quality displayed by true scientific genius in every generation—the power to discern key issues too securely hidden to be detected by ordinary men and to generalize from them broadly and effectively. An important prerequisite for this quality, as we have long recognized, is the ability to keep many things in mind at once, to experiment and play with a multitude of permutations and combinations. This power to retain many things simultaneously at the forefront of attention has always been an outstanding attribute of individual genius in securing scientific advance. In the future, it must be taxed ever more severely as the reach required to generate novel insights at the frontiers of many fields inevitably increases, as the challenges to significant generalization grow. Will the time ever come when the number of elements which must be held and considered simultaneously in order to achieve truly great new insights exceeds the capacity of even the greatest single mind? Have we any effective working tools to increase our powers of penetration further while retaining the freedom and flexibility of the individual? Or, in a time of massive science, highly organized both within its own complex structure and in its even more complex relationships to the rest of our society, has the role of the individual actually lost the significance that it had a generation ago? Is the challenge too complex to be met effectively except by massive human constellations?

In its every aspect, a continuing exploration of the role of the individual, of his tasks, of his preparation, in the changing scientific environments of our time, is of far more vital concern to us than ever before in our history. For we live today with the very real danger that the special power inhering in that role, its unique relation to creative effort in whatever setting, could easily be lost in a perspective, all too compelling, which could confuse the nature and purposes of organization with actual processes of advance. In such an exploration a first concern must be for those environments themselves—the environment provided by the structure and discipline of substantive science; the related but yet different environment of science in its role of public servant.

When scientific scholarship is compared with scholarship in other fields, or with the arts, it sometimes appears to be distinguished by an important difference of kind. It seems to be additive in nature, to grow as the sum of facts accumulated by a multitude of workers and piled up from generation to generation like the fabrication, brick by brick, of some massive wall. Other kinds of scholarship, and the arts, do not seem to be cumulative in precisely the same sense. This distinction, indeed, has an element of validity. As discoverer, collector, and arranger of new facts about the world, science is indeed an activity of accumulation—sometimes even of simple summation. And when one looks at the explosive rate at which that activity has accelerated in our own nation and over much of the globe since the second world war, it is tempting to regard accumulation as a preeminent characteristic of scientific endeavor.

Many factors, of course, have contributed to this explosion in the unearthing of new data about our universe. The very storehouse of facts already won can accelerate exponentially the uncovering of new facts in contiguous areas, so long as those areas themselves remain potentially fertile for further discovery. Again, the range and power of the highly sophisticated scientific tools developed so conspicuously in this generation—and often employed to illumine fields far distant from those for which they were originally designed—constitute a most significant factor. Electron microscopes and electron probes and techniques of gas-liquid chromatography have opened new areas not only in physics and geology and geophysics. They have nearly revolutionized some aspects of quantitative and molecular biology as well. Spectrophotometric techniques of interest to the astronomer are also of interest to the student of photosynthesis in green plants. Means for measuring the flows of small currents with minute electrodes and of amplifying and displaying the results which are vital to parts of electronics have also proved powerful tools in investigating phenomena of the living brain. Advances in the sensitivity of photographic plates have been of profound importance in extending the reach of the great telescopes of the world.

Finally, the rapid increase in the numbers of those trained in science and active in scientific research in the last decades, though actually inadequate to growing opportunities, has been an extremely weighty factor in this context, especially in our own country. In 1940, for example, approximately one and one-half per cent of the working population of the United States were classified as technical specialists. Since then, according to a number of demographers, the population of the nation as a whole has increased at an annual rate also of about one and one-half per cent. But during the same time the numbers of those engaged in scientific and technical work have been expanding at an annual rate of roughly five per cent. By 1970, it is estimated, some four and seven-tenths per cent of all those employed in the country may be comprehended in such specialist occupations. Small wonder that the accumulation of scientific and technical facts should proceed at an explosive rate, or that the additive property of science should impress us so greatly!

But if this additive and cumulative aspect of scientific scholarship were a true measure of its inner structure, the concepts of our universe would have changed in no such dynamic way as they have even over the last two decades. A hypothetical Darwin born in 1709, or reincarnated in 1909, would have encountered relatively familiar scientific environments instead of ones that, as we must imagine, would have been or would now be very strange indeed. And if the collection of facts randomly unearthed were the only, or even a dominating, factor in the evolution of scientific scholarship, there might well be no such pressure as now exists to further expand the numbers of scientists in our society.

For, in a profound sense, the structure of science is no more that of an assemblage of facts, brought together in simple additive arrays, than is the living body a simple assemblage of cells, coexisting without interaction or integration. Rather, like a living body, the body of scientific scholarship is a highly organized entity. Its multifarious parts, to be sure, are sometimes so diverse and so separated in their various specializations that it is often difficult to recognize them even as components of any organized whole. Yet so long as the parts are developing dynamically, the essence of an integrated relationship is maintained through the whole vast structure of science. The intensity or the importance of the reaction of one part of the body on another seemingly far distant can never be foreseen, from one year to the next or even, sometimes, literally from day to day. But it is a permanent potential of health and vigor.

Furthermore, this interlocked character of scientific scholarship, across fields and over generations of workers, makes it far more than simply a static organic whole. In a very real sense it is a living and evolving organism. Its growth over three centuries has been marked, as in so much of actual organic evolution, by movement from the simple to the vastly more complex and at the same time by a correlated knitting and integration, transforming initially loose assemblages of hypothesis and theory and fact into more tightly woven, more inclusive, more efficient—and often superficially more simple —tools to achieve new orders of understanding.

As in organic evolution, moreover, the evolution of science is irreversible. In any literal sense, scientific scholarship can never go back. One thing must follow another: it cannot precede it. Without the work of Newton, the work of Einstein would have been impossible; even if it had been accomplished, it would have been irrelevant to the stream of our understanding. Without Gregor Mendel's demonstration of the individuality and the integrity of the elements of inheritance, the demonstration of the linear arrangements of genes in chromosomes by Morgan and his school, three-quarters of a century later, even had it been possible, could have had little meaning for us. Without Robert Brown's recognition of the nucleus and the cytoplasm of the cell in 1831, without the proof of the physical existence of chromosomes in the nucleus by Anton Schneider in 1870, neither the work of Mendel nor that of Morgan would have carried the meaning that it did. Without all these discoveries and the characterization of "nuclein" by the Swedish biochemist Miescher almost contemporaneously with the findings of Mendel, without modern developments in physical chemistry and information theory and much else besides, the notions that have revolutionized our thinking about the molecular nature of heredity over the last decade would surely have been unattainable. Modern physical theories of solids could never have been developed apart from the work of molecular chemists accomplished two or three decades earlier. And this work in turn could not have been accomplished without the conceptual structures of the quantum theory, yet a decade older.

As it has been in the past, so, clearly, will it continue in the future. In many new areas it is possible to anticipate even now the outlines of future conceptions. A deeper comprehension of the behavior of gas plasmas may prove directly relevant to a fuller understanding of conditions in interplanetary space. And as the structure of the interplanetary medium becomes clearer, concepts about the outer layers of the solar atmosphere will be elaborated and refined. These in turn must bear heavily on our understanding of the energy balances within our own terrestrial system.

There will be many instances not only where specific information gained in one area will prove directly relevant in very different ones, but where major conceptual structures too will be found to underlie fields apparently very disparate. Concepts of evolution today illumine the natural world far beyond the aspects for which they were originally designed, coloring our views in fields as remote as the formation of the elements or the transformations of stars. But here, particularly, careful and critical judgments of those most capable to take them are vital to the sound extension of any conceptual system beyond the boundaries for which it was designed, even though the extension in itself may seem quite trivial. The vast advances in our understanding of the genetic code which the decade has brought will surely invite us to apply those hard-won notions in other fields where they may or may not prove relevant. The visualizing of mental processes in molecular terms, for instance, clearly offers one of the most exciting challenges, and one of the greatest areas of opportunity, for a new generation of investigators. We shall certainly be tempted to think of the mysterious processes of memory at the molecular level in terms analogous to those in which we have come to conceive the recording and the operation of the information of heredity, in terms perhaps of a ribonucleic acid-mediated mechanism, sensitively affected by environmental influences acting on the nerve cell. Whether any such conceptual bridge can be valid, given the durable and highly invariant nature of the genetic mechanism as we now know it, is a vital question which in the future must demand one of those key judgments so crucial to scientific scholarship.

As in organic evolution again, the tempo of scientific progress is highly uneven, and also varies greatly from place to place within the framework of science. Periods of gradual and hard-won advance may be punctuated by occasional swift bursts when new insights accomplish rapid and major transformations. The general profile of the growth of scientific scholarship, indeed, may in one sense be likened to that of beads on a chain.

Finally, once again as with organic evolution, the overall tempo of the evolution of science accelerates as evolution itself proceeds. This combination of increase in magnitude and acceleration in tempo has confronted each scientific generation with an ever more severe challenge. When Gregor Mendel's great work was recovered in 1900 there was a vastly insufficient reserve of those whose talents and taste and training equipped them to exploit quickly and to the full the advance for the new opportunities that it offered. Since then, the number of first-class minds in the world that have been oriented and trained in the science of genetics has vastly increased. Yet they may still be quite inadequate to take advantage of all the scientific possibilities laid bare by, say, recent concepts of genetic coding. In this sense there can be no doubt that each generation of research workers has been provided with a far richer scientific spectrum than its predecessors. This has been true of our own generation to an extraordinary degree. But by the same token, each generation has also had to reconcile itself to living with an ever-growing backlog of potentials unexploited.

This situation, too, has clearly reached unprecedented proportions in our own time. It carries at least three implications of signal importance. The first is that, despite (or precisely because of) the great numbers of those already working in scientific fields, we shall always feel that we require more, not only in practical terms of national needs, but in terms of the growth and vigor of scientific scholarship itself. Yet, just as we must constantly beware of attributing to organization per se properties that in the last analysis belong to creative individuals, so we must be constantly wary of the temptation to imagine that mere numbers of individuals engaged in scientific pursuits can in any real sense replace or even compensate for lack in individual endowment and quality of training in that smaller corps upon which the greatest part of real progress depends. A single genius, we must always remember, may accelerate the evolution of his branch of science more, in his generation, than a thousand less outstanding contemporaries.

Our enthusiasm for numbers, too, must be tempered on the broader front by the continuing recognition that a primary requisite for a healthy society is the maintenance of some balance in the proportions of those committed to the various functions that serve it. Gross departures from that balance can pose a serious threat to social well-being. So in any period there must be a limit to the numbers of those who can or ought to be dedicated to the attainment of scientific excellence, and we should be continuingly sensitive as to approximately what, at any given time, that limit should be. Fortunately, however, there is every indication that an appropriate limit is actually set by the natural rareness of those who by high talent and by burning inclination are destined to become dedicated scientists of the highest caliber. So there is little danger that, in terms of such men, we shall exceed prudent boundaries in the foreseeable future. Rather, our society will continue to be short of them. Nothing, therefore, can come higher on our agenda than *both* the excellence *and* the extent of the training of those among us who in future may choose the scientific way.

A second implication of the accelerating tendency of scientific evolution, though related to the first, has somewhat different practical connotations. Since it has never been possible to explore adequately more than a minute fraction of the promising leads that science has laid bare at any time, careful and rigorous choice among many possibilities has always been a characteristic and critical duty of the investigator. Just as in living nature, what we see in the evolution of scientific scholarship is in fact the result of an uncountable multitude of individual choices of the past, made among a plethora of alternatives, each winnowed and scrutinized, each put to the hard test of survival. Thus are linked two of the three themes uniting the disparate developments with which we began—choice and the individual. We shall shortly return to them and to their connection with the third—choice and the individual and planning, both in and for the scientific endeavor—a process of planning which, as we shall see, carries a very different meaning in the two contexts.

The third implication involves an obverse to this picture of dynamic growth. If there are always sectors of science that are rapidly growing and evolving, there are also, inevitably, always points of stagnation, always branches of investigation that are dying. Few research scientists today would choose to enter the field of the determination of atomic weights even though, conceivably, greater accuracies could still be obtained. The study of stable isotopes of the elements, dynamic in the first half of the century, is no longer a very active pursuit. Three decades ago studies of cosmic rays, as received at the surface of the earth, provided one of the most exciting challenges in all of physics. Today, students trained specifically in that area have at times had to turn to other pursuits, while the most exciting growing point of the field, studies of the celestial origins of the rays, has become the province of astronomy and astrophysics in its widest reaches. Whole areas of classificatory biology, and even of more conventional physiology, have been exhausted, and there is little chance, in many of them, that a revival of interest or indeed of opportunity will come.

And just as the opening of new opportunities in science is ever accelerating, so too does the tempo at which opportunities are exhausted increase. Only two years ago the spectacular discovery was made that xenon, traditionally thought to be so unreactive that it has long been known as a noble gas, can be made to react readily with fluorine to form xenon tetrafluoride. This dramatic finding opened a new chemical field of considerable dimensions. Yet so immediately and intensively was it attacked by capable investigators that already the field has been largely exhausted. Over the whole front of science, more than one student has found on completing the work for his doctoral degree that the very field of his thesis has literally disappeared while he was writing it, possibly leaving him with a frightening dilemma of career. And the menace is not lessened when the career itself has been well launched. The modern development of the computer has carried no more serious implications for the untrained worker than it has for the intensively but narrowly trained professional numerical calculator of the old school—if anything, indeed, it has been less devastating for the untrained man, who at least is generalized. The implications for breadth and flexibility in scientific training, for maintenance of the fundamentals, for the perils of too great concentration too early on too narrowly specialized arenas in the preparation of the individual who is to enter science today are all too clear. Yet even today they are not always heeded.

Thus the scientific environment per se. What of the individual and his role of judgment and choice in the forming of it? The organic quality of scientific scholarship is of course prima facie evidence that the essence of science, its shaping and its growth, lie in processes of effective integration and meaningful organization of information that no mechanical aid yet devised and no massive effort yet known are able to accomplish. For they are deeply integral with the attainment of insights which both make our current vision of the world more comprehensive and can serve as predictors beyond the boundaries of present concepts—insights that can prepare our understanding for new adventures into the unknown. The attaining of those insights, and their validation, must indeed continue to be the work of the scientific scholar, so long as we can see into the future.

Above all, then, the primary motif of a dynamic science is that of constant and critical judgment—of making constant and sensitive choices—choices among avenues of investigation that are best pursued, choices of direction of effort, choices, above all, in the formulation of new hypotheses and in judging the relationships among older ones and their soundness and relevance and applicability outside the fields for which they were designed. These will, in general, be choices that are individual and often highly specific. Each choice as it is made will be exposed to a constant scrutiny, to a constant validation or rejection, to a constant judgment by the facts themselves and by a trained and sophisticated audience of co-workers in the field. In this pattern of achieving growth as the product of constant individual choice, science, far from being distinguished from artistic activities in the more usual sense, indeed finds common ground with them.

This process of choice through which the evolution of science takes place constitutes a very real process of planning—none the less real for the fact that it is the work of a host of contributors dispersed all over the world and through many generations. It is worth emphasis that planning in this sense veritably lies at the heart of scientific scholarship. Yet it is very different from planning as we ordinarily understand that word. Its highly contingent nature makes of it a very special kind of planning. It is planning at the level of the work, and its whole effectiveness in the past has rested on the excellence of judgment and the freedom of judgment of individuals whose abilities and preparation fitted them to make the specific choices demanded, and also to judge similar choices made by colleagues. The words of Elihu Root, written in 1918, carry a lasting and special significance: "Occasionally a man appears who has the instinct to reject the negligible. A very great mind goes directly to the decisive fact, the determining symptom, and cannot afford to burden itself with a great mass of unimportant facts. . . ." It is such minds, acting with individual freedom and flexibility, that provide the sinews of our scientific planning today, as they did a half century ago, and as they surely will into an indefinite future. It is not, and it inherently cannot be, the function of the great organization per se, or of planning as ordinarily understood.

But if the investigating mind should not be burdened with a mass of unimportant facts, it still cannot discover or test potentially significant relationships without taking into account a plethora of collateral evidence which, though less salient to the principal lines of reasoning, is yet contributory to it. Consciously or not, the individual pioneer must have access to a wide range of facts and hypotheses as he ponders new combinations. Outstanding ability to hold such a store in mind is indeed one frequent attribute of genius, and is commonly prerequisite to original and penetrating thought. Today, with the frontiers of science become in many areas so wide and many-faceted, this individual ability in even its highest expression has become hard pressed. In some areas it may even have become limiting. And so we return to that insistent and urgent question of whether there are possibilities of structuring the scientific effort to provide the pioneering individual with more powerful investigative tools without at the same time submerging his identity or limiting his initiative.

There are such means, and in principle they have had a long development. The inherent limitations posed to even the greatest minds by the vastness of the subject material with which they must deal are surely part of the reason that individuals in science have always, and characteristically, sought to form unusually intimate working communities, tightly constructed about their disciplines, however widely physically separated their members might be. In our own day, such communities have on occcasion evolved further, to form deeply intimate associations, working so closely over long periods on matters of common concern that the group may ultimately become truly greater and more powerful than the sum of its parts—truly a "thinking organism" in its own right. In many fields such intellectually close-knit, concentrated teams have become identified with some of the most significant conceptual advances in the science of our time, comparable to and often reminiscent of the kinds of advances achieved in another age by the individual genius of a Heaviside or a Pasteur—such groups as those within the Pasteur Institute itself, of the Lawrence Radiation Laboratory, of the Bell Telephone Laboratories, of the British Medical Research Council's Laboratory of Molecular Biology at Cambridge, of the Carnegie Institution, to cite but a representative handful. Indeed, it is possible that if one looks to those larger and apparently unitary organizations where scientific frontiers are being most spectacularly pushed back today, and examines them in close detail—in industry or government, within private research institutions, and even to a considerable extent within universities—it will be found that in a great number of instances those conquests depend in the last analysis upon the work of such relatively small, close-knit, and concentrated teams harbored within them.

A particularly powerful quality of teams of this kind lies precisely in their compatibility with the play of individual genius. It seems clear that in the ideal research group of this sort not only are the unfettered freedom and individuality of each of its key members carefully guarded as a factor vital to success but also a major function of the group is indeed to provide an environment where such individuality will be enhanced and stimulated to the utmost, fired by common concern and common sympathy, given access to a stream of ideas and a collection of facts broader and deeper than any individual alone could reach, exposed to resources of criticism far more apposite and stringent than could be experienced in solitude. Such groups may indeed offer particularly relevant and powerful reponses for our time to the encompassing issue of how we are to devise effective means further to increase our powers of penetration into the unknown, and of the place of the independent investigator in them.

By all the evidence, then, it seems abundantly clear that the role of the individual in the processes of very special substantive planning through which science advances, of the individual whether working alone or in small, unfettered teams, continues as indispensable in our own time as it has ever been. Its importance needs repeated emphasis. For it is easier than ever today to forget this cardinal truth, or to lose it in the obscuring image of the giant scientific and technical organizations with which we live. It is natural, but gravely misleading, to regard such organizations as monolithic entities, failing to discern in their finer structure the congeries of close-knit groups of individual investigators that bring them their vitality and effectiveness in research.

Such misconceptions may be perilous. They could exacerbate a trend, already evident and probably destined to become more conspicuous, that can easily dominate the climate of thought and feeling in a technically advanced society—a trend toward a progressive secularization of the search for new knowledge, and especially of knowledge related to scientific and technical discovery: the taking-for-granted both of knowledge won and of the processes of winning new knowledge that is so apt to cloud our horizons. What happens to the emotionally compelling quality of great new conquests of nature, of great new technical developments, of comprehensive new systems of ideas, as the impersonal concerns of large-scale integration displace those of discovery itself, with its early wonder? What may happen, not only to quality, but also to standards of quality? How often may the temptation that is no stranger to us today seem wholly logical and even efficient, the temptation to substitute money or sheer volume of numbers for hard thought, often enough not in sophistry but in what is actually much worse, honest self-deception of a peculiarly insidious kind?

Such dangers pose important challenges indeed. For it may be deeply characteristic of the human mind that, as the organization and the systematization of knowledge proceed, the color and the vividness that surround the acquisition of new knowledge become progressively more difficult to maintain. Yet it is just as this point in our history that those elements become most vitally important. Verve and style and deep individual involvement are indeed inseparable

241

from quality, and from the adequate making and the adequate monitoring of those perpetual and myriad individual choices upon which the progress and the final shape of science ultimately depend. The significance of their maintenance must become increasingly pressing with the years. By the standards of training and of work, through the great unities of approach and of preparation that bind those dedicated to the scientific path: the requirements of verifiability; the discipline of parsimony; the constant emphasis on the significance of individual effort with its exacting demands of originality and imagination, of the maintenance of style, the individual scientist, so long as he remains conscious of the weight and seriousness of his personal responsibility, can do much to preserve those priceless qualities, so often confused and threatened with destruction in a contemporary crowded world. No era to which they have been lost can be great, whatever its other assets. The responsibility to conserve them is a major one indeed. And it belongs supremely to this generation.

So much for the processes of substantive scientific planning, for planning in science and its relation to choice and to the ultimate importance of the individual. What then of the different question of planning *for* science, in its effects on and its relations to our greater society? With science as substantively immense and intricate as it now is, with science as demanding as it has become in terms of the material and the human wealth of nations, with science, in short, so overwhelming a social force on both intellectual and material fronts, can we longer say that we can allow it to proceed without a measure of planning from without? And, if we must affirm this, what do we mean? Is the process of planning *for* science remotely like that of planning *in* science? Is the planning for science, like that of planning in science, intimately linked still in our day with the work of individuals, or is it, in its vastness, subject only to the influence of relatively impersonal organization?

Were a Darwin, miraculously reborn in 1909, observing us today, he would find the landscape of science vastly altered from what he knew in features quite other than the richness and the diversity, the sophistication and the complexity of its inner substance. One touchstone of its accompanying outer transformation would surely be the vast increase in numbers of those engaged in it. Another, and one yet more poignant in this context, would be the spectacular growth in public expenditures in scientific and technical fields. Among all the industrial nations of the world that increase has been explosive. It has been especially vividly illustrated in our own country during the postwar period. In 1950, for example, our national expenditures for research and development amounted to about 3 billion dollars. By 1960 they had grown to 13 billion, averaging more than a doubling for each five years. In the current year the appropriation exceeded 15 billion. Such a rate of increase is to be set against a rise of only about 3.5 per cent in the gross national product of the nation. If we were to project both rates unchanged to 1973—an unlikely hypothesis but one underlining strongly the drama of the situation—our national expenditures for research and development would comprehend no less than 10 per cent of our gross national product.

And the share of this burden carried by the federal government has grown formidably in the last years. In 1940, the federal government spent about $74 million in research and development. By 1960 it supplied about 10 billion dollars, as against $4.7 billion provided by private industry, while colleges, universities, and private scientific institutes, still probably the primary *producers* of research, *supported* only about 3 per cent of the total. By 1963, when the total expenditure for research and development in the nation had reached almost its present level, the government had come to support more than two-thirds of it, at an annual rate greater than the total sums it had committed to research and development from the time of the American Revolution to and through World War I. It comprehended 15 per cent of the total federal budget, and about one-third of the part not already absorbed in fixed commitments.

At fifty-five, a reborn Darwin would indeed work within a science which, over all the industrialized world, had changed greatly in the character of its relationships to societies and to governments. To be sure, the original Darwin must have been very familiar with the beginnings of organization at the interfaces of science and of society at large. He was just twenty years old when James Smithson died, leaving his bequest of half a million dollars for the further promotion of American science. He was thirty-nine when the American Association for the Advancement of Science was organized in Philadelphia. It is easy to imagine how familiar in type such private organizations designed to promote the service of science to society would have seemed to him, and how much they might have recalled some of the contemporary and parallel work of corresponding bodies in Great Britain. He was fifty-four when the National Academy of Sciences was organized, and one can imagine how comprehensible such a systematized organization of science in the public service would have been to him, and how logical it would have seemed.

But within three-quarters of a century after Darwin's death three important developments had occurred to fashion in the social landscape of science a topography so different as to be, in essence, new in kind. The first has the longest history, and has always been the most obvious. The precipitate rise of industrial power, and the critical place of both science and technology in evolving and maintaining it, were ultimately to bring to both a new kind of social significance. The second development, which has dominated the last quarter of a century, was the recognition brought by three great wars of the indispensable role that science must play in defense and in the maintenance of military capacity. The third, taking its root in the first two, is embodied in the final conviction of our day that contemporary science and its associated technology have become in themselves major forces changing the very face of society. Associated with all these developments, but most particularly with the last, has come an increase in the public expenditures for science in many lands to the point where they constitute major items in overall national budgets.

These transformations of position and of attitude, subtle but surely profound, have brought yet another in their train. With science of such an order of importance for societies and for nations, with science supported at such a level of public expenditure, science must henceforth be as directly accountable to its supporting public as any other activity of like social impact. In this context, science is a public activity of major importance—public and major, and so, inevitably, political. And in this context it may not be generally visualized as the private exercise of great intellects in the exploration of the universe. It may not, indeed, be generally thought of as an activity of individuals at all.

This orientation would surely have seemed very unfamiliar to Darwin, though its beginnings in our own country can certainly be traced at least as far back as his lifetime, in the philosophy and the organization and the conduct of the Department of Agriculture itself. But, spurred by the great shifts in the center of gravity of the large-scale practical implications of technology from agriculture to such immediate life-and-death matters as national defense and military power, and to the equally vital arena of the transformations of industrial societies, the change in our own country has accelerated with astonishing rapidity. Indeed, the full change has actually been surprisingly recent. As late as 1938 one-third of all the federal money committed to research and development was expended by the Department of Agriculture, and the Departments of Commerce and of the Interior combined accounted for approximately another fifth. The entire military budget of the Departments of War and of the Navy consumed only a fifth. Only fifteen years later, in 1953, nine-tenths of the entire federal budget for research and development was to be devoted to military or military-oriented research, expended largely through a group of giant federal or quasi-federal agencies. Within that period had come the second world war, and all that it brought in knowledge of the power of science in national defense when appropriately organized and conducted at the federal level.

All over the globe since World War II the effects of these powerful influences to make of science a major object as well as a major instrument of public policy have been signalized by the formal organizational relationships of science to government which have been architected in many nations. In the United Kingdom a Ministry of Science and Education was created not long ago. And currently, in the Zuckerman Report, the Trend Report, the Robbins Report, and in a plethora of public discussions, national issues related to this change are being explored with unprecedented range and thoroughness. In France a General Delegacy for Scientific and Technical Research has been established, directly attached to the office of the Prime Minister and supporting an Interdepartmental Committee of Scientific Research composed of eight Cabinet Ministers and chaired by the Prime Minister. A consultative Committee on Scientific and Technological Research has also been set up in France to assist the Interdepartmental Committee, consisting of twelve senior professional members, and there is also a National Center for Scientific Research. In Belgium there is a National Council for Science Policy, in Norway a Government Council for Applied Research. And now in Sweden, as noted earlier, a Science Advisory Council has very recently been established. In Canada the National Research Council and in Australia the Commonwealth Scientific and Industrial Research Organization have assumed tasks of new magnitude in linking science and national policy.

Such developments, moreover, are by no means confined to Western Europe and North America. Turkey, Iran, and Pakistan already have, or are planning, National Science Councils, and Pakistan, among a number of bodies concerned with science, has a vigorous Department of Scientific and Industrial Research serving a national function quite similar to that long served by the department of the same name in Great Britain. Indonesia has recently appointed a Minister for Science, and Thailand, with the help of Australia, is currently setting out on the same general road.

When scientific goals and activity assume such proportions in the lives of nations as at present, when science has become so significant an element in public policy, administrative centralization of the conduct of science within government clearly becomes, in one sense, a wave of the future. So obviously adaptive is it that all industrial nations are sure to face continuing pressures to evolve ever further in that direction. Such trends will inevitably be additionally emphasized by the ever-mounting economic pressures that a growing public science and technology must continue to impose, further increasing the concentration of support and control in central governments.

Although it is only rather recently that we have felt the full weight of this problem, in its essence it has been with us for longer than Darwin's lifetime. In a historical sense, we have been exceptionally fortunate in meeting it. For not only did our pragmatic American temper secure a firm conjunction between science and more general aspects of government policy early in our development. It also achieved that participation in a very "plural" way, at a variety of levels and through a variety of devices that were ultimately to proliferate into an extraordinary panoply of departments, bureaus, special working groups, special advisory bodies. Moreover, many of the individuals who initiated or early participated in these activities in government retained throughout their official service the closest of professional connections with their colleagues in private scientific bodies.

Throughout our history such circumstances have brought to our conduct of science in government a curious and probably unique balance between pluralism and centralization. In times of military or economic crisis in the nation, when the great issues were intensified and sharpened and simplified, we have always tended to concentrate our administrative concerns for science at the national level. In times of lesser national stress, with the issues of the country far more diffuse, our modes of meeting them have also been much more diverse. This quality in our relationships of science to national affairs is deeply rooted in a characteristic of our approach to policy formation in general which stems in turn from the dominantly pragmatic orientation toward affairs that we have had from the very beginning. More than a hundred years ago Alexis de Tocqueville, who knew us so preternaturally well—often so much better than we knew ourselves—emphasized that an especially striking quality of the American ethos was our strong penchant for solving the practical problems that we encountered each as it presented itself, each as it occurred, in its own way. This strong predilection for approaching our problems of policy on an essentially contingent basis has persisted through all our history, and is undimmed with us today. It has had an especially strong impact upon the whole character of the relationships of our science and technology with government and its influences on governmental policy, and indeed upon the whole cast of our thinking about the place of science and technology in our society in the broadest sense. As in the progress of science itself, the contingent mode of planning confers a special flexibility on all our thinking of the relationships of science to our society and it has allowed us over the years to change and modify our policy with unusual swiftness and ease as conditions and demands were changed.

But we have to remember that this pragmatic style of contingency, when overemphasized, can also exact its own price. We are traditionally excellent at individual scientific and technical tasks, often of the highest difficulty. But we have likewise often been indifferent at broad planning for science. Clearly such indifference is no longer admissible. For not only are the concerns of science and technology now important objects of national policy. Not only are they virtually omnipresent, affecting almost every other aspect of our national life. Their very demands, not only of material wealth, but especially in terms of the lives and fates of men and women, have become so great that, were we to attempt to satisfy all of them indiscriminately, we should so overtax both our material and our human resources as to risk serious social imbalances. Currents of such magnitude and import as those now sweeping science and technology on their courses, if allowed to flow undirected, if left to the whim of the winds, could easily wreak great damage. So we are irrevocably brought face to face with a grave conclusion. In our day, planning *for* science, though very different from it, may become as inescapable a necessity as planning *in* science has always been. Upon how wisely and well we learn to do it, indeed, much of the freedom and vitality of substantive science itself will depend. Skillful and effective planning for science can enhance the freedom with which active scientists can choose and shape the direction of their research. Unskillfully attempted, it is capable of restricting that freedom dangerously.

Now planning for science, too, is clearly accomplished as the sum of a multitude of choices, and of choices made by individuals. But how much more difficult, and in many ways how very different, these choices often are! Not only may the immediate social impact of any single decision be much greater. Its effective verification—the possibility of determining whether it has actually been good or bad—may be much more distant in time. Circumstances apparently quite foreign to the choice yet actually vital to it may change while it is being made. And choices of such magnitude cannot be easily altered or rectified if they have initially been unwise. Moreover, decisions so important to the whole life of the nation must inevitably be taken publicly and be made only with public consent, given or withheld by a public who may or may not be prepared to really understand the content and to project the consequences of the choices involved.

This necessary circumstance in turn involves two further hazards. One is that many decisions concerning science and technology inevitably must critically shape the world in which a subsequent generation—perhaps unborn at the time that the decisions were taken—will live and carry on its work. How is public choice or public consent to bear effectively upon a situation of this kind? A related hazard is that since popular expectations of the power of science have grown so immensely in our time, and since such expectations must inevitably play a dominant role in governing decision, there is the grave danger that when public attention becomes focused upon the practical benefits of science, real or potential, anticipation which is sometimes unrealistic may father belief, and may, in the absence of wise counsel, lead to serious distortions of scientific choice. Spectacular enterprises may find favor at the expense of less conspicuous but basically more significant elements; the immediate may take precedence over the long range.

It is not only in the weight of decisions taken and in the methods of validating and implementing them that planning for science differs from planning in science. It can also be far more complex in a substantive sense. The farther planning for science in the service of public affairs is removed from regions where objective verification is possible, the farther, as it were, it is removed from the workbench, the more difficult judgments become, and the more unreliable they tend to be if taken in a purely scientific context. Indeed, the virtual impossibility of planning large-scale scientific or technical enterprises—and particularly of choosing wisely among a group of such large-scale enterprises that compete for common and limited supplies of money and above all of men—on the basis of objective scientific considerations alone poses a critical kind of dilemma with which we have lately become thoroughly familiar.

In the processes through which the evolution of the body of scientific knowledge takes place, the elements judged at each point of choice can commonly be compassed within a relatively straightforward hierarchy of values. The construction of such a hierarchy, to be sure, may be a difficult process, often requiring as much skill and effort as the final act of judging itself. But one of the accepted and understood challenges to the research worker is precisely to accomplish such a reduction, however diverse his subject material, so that ultimately the values to be weighed are in a real sense commensurable. In the more detailed ranges of planning for science within a public context it may be possible to preserve this commensurability to some degree, and clearly one of the important administrative tasks for those dealing with scientific affairs in government at more specific levels is this kind of ordering.

But however much we are aware of this need, and however excellent the skills that we develop to accomplish it, judgments made at the highest ranges must continue to be taken among elements which, in any basic scientific sense, will always be intrinsically incommensurable. How is it possible, for example, to determine on a purely objective basis the relative priorities in public encouragement and support to be given in the field of oceanography as against that of mental health, of molecular biology against geophysics or atmospheric research, of physiological psychology against organic chemistry? At the most obvious level, no observer or judge, regardless of how expert he may be in a particular scientific area, is likely to be able to effectively assess in detail the relationships of all the multifarious factors involved in fields outside his own or to understand specifically their significance for the future. But the real difficulty goes much deeper. For, regardless of the extent of scientific knowledge and the wisdom of any observer, at this level of decision there can be no single criterion of choice. By the very nature of the situation, the orders of merit in such a hierarchy of preference must always be plural and often enough inchoate. And they will depend in turn upon a broad and complex range of factors. Some factors will be principally scientific. But many will be intimately tied to a wide variety of other bounding conditions, peculiar to the time and place of the decision and varying constantly.

It is particularly difficult for us to fully recognize and accept the reality that there are reaches of decisions involving scientific matters —and often among the most important in our day—where the choices to be made must remain forever incommensurable. With our long conditioning, we may tend to respond negatively to the challenges that this cardinal fact imposes, and in ways that can be dangerous. We may deny this inevitable incommensurability, insisting that choices of such nature can always, with sufficient effort, be ranked in a single overall "order of merit." Such an error can easily result in undue focusing on a few elements of a great problem to the detriment of the whole, bringing about distortions of judgment of a kind that we have not been stranger to in recent years. Another reaction epitomizes the opposite extreme: to conclude that, since choice must always be multiple and must often be made among elements that cannot be weighed objectively, planning for science is itself a deceptive and inadmissible activity.

But we have no option. For the abjuring of planning is in itself a decision of the most significant kind, and a potentially disastrous one. We have no escape from the conclusion that, the weightier scientific decisions become, economically and in affairs, the more they demand judgments of just this plural kind, as sensitive to social context as to scientific content. The greater the decisions, the more it is incumbent upon those who take them to combine with keen scientific judgment the broad, intuitive, socially based wisdom that is so universally needed elsewhere in great affairs.

The whole process through which the entire modern fabric of scientific thought has come to being has clearly been the resultant of a plethora of individual choices. Its effectiveness has always depended critically on that corps of imaginative individuals of the past and the present who, in the quality of their training, in the nature of their dedication, in the high order of their capacity, have by their collective decisions carried science forward. We are beginning now to see that the great future task of planning *for* science, which in some measure we cannot escape, must, in similar fashion, depend on the collective choices and judgments of individuals as highly qualified. Who will they be? Where will they come from? How will they be trained? How shall we recognize them?

It is abundantly clear that the scientific and technical skills and knowledge and judgment that are brought to the service of the nation at governmental level are not only plural in the points at which they enter and the avenues through which they serve. They are also, in a deeper sense, multiple in kind. They range all the way from those adapted primarily to providing the most practical and straightforward technical services to those particularly qualified to formulate far-ranging policy involving scientific parameters, but including much else besides. It is surely important to draw distinctions among these skills and functions, for men and women of very different abilities and temperament and training are—and in the future even more will be—required to implement the various sectors.

In the realm of policy alone, one can, by greatly simplifying the picture, distinguish at least four general kinds of function. They might be described as the execution of policy involving matters of science and technology on the domestic front of national affairs; the corresponding function in relation to our foreign policy; and, on both foreign and domestic fronts, the making of those great and often inchoate judgments by which policy in both arenas must be formulated. Each of these classes of function is surely sufficiently complex in itself. To make matters worse, two or more may often be combined in a single demanding situation, as was the case, for example, in the extremely difficult problems posed for the members of the Geneva Conference in 1958.

These more or less artificially distinguished levels of function must find their counterparts in the kinds of background and training and talents required of those called upon to discharge them. Both the formulation and the execution of what might be called "general and administrative scientific policy," for instance, must surely demand, among other things, constant determinations of the distribution of national emphasis among broad sectors of the scientific and technical effort. It must include vital considerations of the preparation and the distribution of the nation's precious asset of scientifically trained men and women. In such a context it must be concerned with how an adequate cadre can be protected and conserved for the work of preparing future trained generations, against the importunate demands for immediate service that often bear so heavily today. In every sector it will be constantly involved in judging issues similarly related, sometimes apparently only distantly, yet actually subtly entwined. This is not a "creative" activity of science as that word is commonly understood. But it may surely be far more difficult to fulfill than some major "creative" tasks. And it entails responsibilities for those involved that are serious and major. For upon how well such policy judgments are made may depend much of the freedom and the flexibility of creative scientific activity in the future. Surely, therefore, due attention must be paid to this capacity for judgment among incommensurables in those who will serve on such frontiers, and some training for wisdom in this kind of choice must be reflected in their selection and their preparation.

Difficult as such judgments are, they do involve the kinds of decisions that are regularly undertaken, even though on a less massive and complex scale, by able, bold, wide-visioned administrators in industry: the presidents of large industrial corporations or their vice presidents for research. Extensive and intensive scientific training is of the highest importance for such men. But it must be combined with administrative judgment and acumen in their most comprehensive sense. Scientific originality in its more strictly substantive context may be less essential. Surely we should look importantly in the future to our existing reservoirs of such talents and training and experience to implement these frontiers of planning for science in the national service.

Most difficult of all the functions, of course, is that field of planning where the choice of general political course in a scientific climate is involved. This is the field of the individual significantly related at high policy level to projecting the development of science at home, or of the drafter of some new Truman-King-Attlee declaration, or of the negotiator at some Geneva Conference of the future. Those who patrol such frontiers will need to have the broadest kind of scientific competence. Further, they should, if at all possible, have to their credit personal scientific achievements of significance, not only as preparation for comprehending the substantive aspects of the questions with which they will deal but also to enable them to command the respect and the service of men of science of the caliber who must be their advisers. At the same time, they must possess a fundamental understanding both of public policy and of the modes and patterns of public representation and negotiation.

Such men and women are rare among us. How rare they have always been is vividly evidenced by the cruelly heavy burden that the few have had to bear in every major emergency. There may never be a large number in our society who are endowed with the capacities demanded in such a role, who can through their native gifts and backgrounds assume the responsibilities imposed by it.

But, if we have always been short of such men and women, their paucity is uniquely critical today. And it can be expected to become ever more critical in the future. Don Price has expressed the requirements with extraordinary clarity and vividness:

What is needed is a corps of men whose liberal education includes an appreciation of the role of science and technology in society and whose education has not been a narrowly technical or vocational one, but has treated science as one of the highest intellectual endeavors of men who also have the responsibility of free citizens.

Among all the demands of our day in the field of science and national policy, the challenge of finding those who are equipped to work in this most exacting arena, and of properly preparing them to assume their tasks, stands preeminent. In the breadth and balance of taste and preparation between scientific matters and wider and more general concerns that it demands, it parallels the contemporary need for appropriate balance in taste and training between specialized and more generalized subject fields which is such a vital requirement in our time for those destined to enter substantive science. Both requirements present very special challenges to education in its widest and deepest reaches. How well they are acquitted in the years to come will determine in no inconsiderable measure the future of America.

If Charles Darwin stood among us today he would indeed find the superficial features of the landscape of science—the landscape that he knew and loved so well—immensely changed. In its substance, he would find conceptual structures, even in the areas that he knew best, so advanced in sophistication, so enormously elaborated, so greatly enriched in new points of growth and challenge, so altered in its emphases of old ones, that he would surely stand bewildered. And in the broader reaches of the relationships of science to society he would find a context so altered and enlarged, so different in the order of its implications and of the immanent demands pressed upon it, as to be virtually new in kind.

But perhaps he would not long remain wholly puzzled. For permeating the evolution of the whole fabric of substantive science, and of the newer fabric of planning for science in the large as well, he would surely discern a critical and invariant theme that would be thoroughly familiar to him. It would indeed be that permanent theme of the work and the essential place and function of individuals—dedicated individuals upon whose myriad and collective shoulders all those patterns of critical choice have rested and must rest which, at the level of planning in science, have preserved soundness and guided the course of its evolution, and in the province of planning for science must in future determine the breadth and the soundness and the relevance of its relations to the whole social fabric. Upon that myriad corps of individuals, upon the adequacy of their preparation, upon their capacity for continued and growing vision, the health and the effectiveness of our science must continue to depend absolutely. Today the challenges are far more complex, more multifarious, and often even more difficult to define, than anything Darwin knew. But surely they do not differ fundamentally in kind. In the requirements of individual preparation and of individual dedication that they pose, and in the supreme demand of our time for great and qualified individuals in science and in scientific affairs, whatever their specific functions and contributions to the whole, a Darwin would surely recognize the same overriding and familiar need that dominated his own age, and to which his own life so magnificently contributed.

Such functions surely call for capacious minds and reliable powers for disinterested and fair-minded judgment. It demands the habit of curbing any tendency to reach results agreeable to desire or to embrace the solution of a problem before exhausting its comprehensive analysis. . . . Its task is to seize the permanent, more or less, from the feelings and fluctuations of the transient.

FELIX FRANKFURTER—*The Supreme Court in the Mirror of Justices*

GEORGE B. KISTIAKOWSKY

On Federal Support of Basic Research

General Considerations

THE QUESTIONS posed by the House Committee on Science and Astronautics require us to look into the future and recommend certain congressional actions with respect to science that will advance the welfare and ensure progress of the United States sufficient for maintenance of leadership. This cannot be done with precision; all one can do is study the recent past, and the present, and draw inferences for the future. As to the recent past, we have overwhelming evidence that scientific research, translated into technological innovations through the media of organized applied research and engineering development, has had a dominant and beneficial effect on the welfare of advanced nations, thus adding health, military, and economic values to its intrinsic cultural worth. Our entire civilization is based on technology, and one may with some confidence predict that further progress will be as dependent upon technological innovations as upon educational and other social factors. Indeed social adaptation to technological change requires continuing technological innovation. The impact of such innovation on the lives of individuals and on the fate of whole nations is far too broad to be measured by economic indices alone, important as these are. What is the economic measure of a radical change in the balance of international power resulting from the utilization of scientific discovery of nuclear fission? Or what is the economic value of research to nearly a million people in the United States who have been saved from cancer and now lead useful lives? Or to people who, though living far from our cultural centers, are enabled to share in their activities by advances in communications and transportation?

Despite the numerous well-known examples of technology built upon scientific discoveries, resulting from seemingly unrelated research not motivated originally by practical aims or planned for specific purposes, the public tends to forget this crucial feature of technological progress. To illustrate, there is a great deal of public pressure, quite correctly, to direct large sums of money toward the solution of the problem of cancer. Great strides have indeed been made in preventing and curing cancer in its early stages, and it is interesting to examine the history of the successful methods that are now available. Surgery and chemotherapy (themselves results of research) are very important, of course. In addition, as is well known, X-rays and rays from radioactive substances play a major role. If, at a time before these two phenomena were known, a large-scale planned effort had been made to discover a cure for cancer, it is perfectly obvious that no money whatsoever could have been directed specifically toward the discovery of X-rays or radioactivity, since no one had the slightest inkling or suspicion of their existence. They were discovered because there were social mechanisms for supporting basic research over the whole domain of scientific subjects, in a manner that permitted individual investigators to follow up interesting ideas or interesting observations on their own initiative.

A serious danger of the present situation is the increasing spread, among those not fully familiar with the way in which basic science must operate, of the idea that basic science can be planned in detail and that money need be allocated only to specific topics to provide the necessary scientific knowledge for the advance of technology. Unfortunately, it just does not work this way. For instance, no committee of skilled administrators, or of highly competent scientists, could have made a plan for the discovery of catalysis, which by now has found hundreds of key industrial applications, including high-octane gasoline, synthetic rubber, many plastics, and a great variety of other essential chemicals. Discovery of catalysis was essentially accidental. Thus Sabatier was experimenting on metal-carbon compounds (carbides) and, in studying reactions of acetylene with various metals, discovered hydrogenation catalysis. To take a very different example, Hopkins believed that life could be maintained in higher organisms on a diet consisting exclusively of proteins, carbohydrates, and fats. His experiments designed to prove this thesis convinced him that he was wrong, and out of this seemingly disappointing result grew the realization of the indispensable health function of vitamins.

Such examples abound in the past; moreover, we do not have to go very far into the past to find them. A very recent one is the discovery of the laser and maser. Many millions of dollars are now being expended annually on their development and use. The maser (as a part of a complex system) is making possible trans-Atlantic satellite communications, for which a stock issue of $200 million has been eagerly bought by the public. And yet, the maser and the laser are descended from a long line of totally impractical scientific investigations beginning with Einstein's work on the quantum theory of radiation in the early 1900's and extending through many basic investigations on the response of solids and gases to optical and microwave radiations. All these investigations provided the background that made the maser invention possible. Its immediate occasion was a study of the microwave spectroscopy of the ammonia molecule. The study was a small part of a broad program of basic research supported by several science agencies in the Department of Defense. It would have been quite impossible to demonstrate in advance that these investigations would lead to satellite communication systems, and yet they have.

The point that requires repeated emphasis is that closely defined mission-oriented research has value but, by itself, is insufficient and incapable of developing really new ideas and new principles on which each particular practical mission will ultimately find itself based. If the social climate and the support mechanisms are not such as to encourage the free exploration of new ideas rapidly and effectively, our technology will die on the vine because, in the absence of the results of new, undirected basic research, applied work tends to become more and more confined to increasingly expensive refinements and elaborations of old ideas. Perhaps one reason the United States didn't develop the turbo jet engine prior to World War II, although it was spending a great deal of public money on aircraft power plants, is that the power-plant work in the National Advisory Committee for Aeronautics was organized in accordance with the design criteria of piston engines. Administratively, there was no provision for work on really new ideas.

Being a chemist I would like to mention two more examples illustrating specifically the connection of chemical research and the welfare and the position of leadership of the American nation. Past development of genetics, which provided new hybrid and mutant varieties of plants and animals, had an extraordinary impact on the broad field of agriculture. In recent years, however, this classical field has taken on new vigor by merging with chemistry in what is known as molecular biology. Thus far, no practical applications are in sight or being planned. But those familiar with the field are confident that revolutionary developments will follow. For instance, some day it will be possible to create new variants of living organisms by a controlled chemical process, instead of waiting, as now, for random mutations.

In my next example the practical results are already largely in hand. It is only some forty years ago that basic scientific research began to attack the problem of what are now called polymeric molecules. Some chemists explored their structures and showed them to be giant chain-like molecules. Others investigated the kinetic mechanisms that lead small molecules to join into these almost infinite chains, and in what orientation. Still others, including pure theoreticians using methods of statistical mechanics, explored the connection between the molecular configuration, the length and bridging of the molecular chains, and the physical properties of the resulting substances. Out of these researches, partly quite recent, grew the present tremendous industry of plastics, artificial fibers, and synthetic elastomers (rubber). The impact of the availability of these comparatively inexpensive materials upon the standard of living of society has been immeasurable. The impact is so great because, in addition to creating new devices and materials for our civilization, we are also reducing the cost, in terms of human labor, of a great many already-existing things, thus making them available to multitudes of people when once they were accessible only to a wealthy few.

It may well be asked whether the rate of increase in scientific activities and hence in their financial support must continue at a faster pace than, for instance, the growth of our gross national product. It cannot continue at such a pace indefinitely, of course. On the other hand, it is the nature of technology not only to solve human problems, but also to generate new ones. Thus it is hardly likely that sometime all our problems will be solved and we can sit back in a static world and enjoy the fruits of our efforts. We live in a dynamic situation of growing population and depleting natural resources in which problems are attacked and solved by scientific and technological means, and inevitably the changes that are thereby brought about introduce new problems that must be attacked and solved in turn. Furthermore, the solutions of many human problems generate the need for faster solution of others. These problems are in part social and in part technological. For example, the fact that the western democracies have achieved a very high standard of living for most of their citizens creates much stronger pressures for the solution of the problems of internal poverty and for the up-lifting of the economic well-being of the rest of the world. As long as nearly everyone on earth was poor, people regarded poverty as inevitable; but when many have abolished poverty, the others will no longer wait for indefinitely delayed alleviation of their distress. Millions of underprivileged who once lived in isolation and accepted poverty because they knew of nothing better now learn of the true possibilities of life by means of modern communications and transportation. Thus it is the technology of advanced nations that has created in other nations the "revolution of rising expectations," and this in turn places more and more demands upon technology.

The same is true for questions of health. On the one hand, spectacular improvements in public health over wide areas of the earth have so reduced mortality that we are experiencing a world population explosion; thus means must be found for control of population growth. On the other hand, having seen the conquest of many diseases, the people are dissatisfied with delays in the solution of other health problems. A careful study, endorsed by a government agency, has demonstrated that cigarette smoking is dangerous to health, and yet a large part of our population continues to smoke. A scientifically developed elimination of this hazard, rather than prohibition of smoking seems called for. Technology resulting from science has made possible modern industry and the concentration of population in great urban complexes, but these in turn have created problems of environmental pollution and deterioration for which science and technology must furnish solutions. These are only a few of a vast number of examples of the modern world's need for more and more science and technology, even as its older problems are solved. In many cases, the solutions will turn out to be the result not of patient, planned investigations along well-charted lines, but of new ideas that arise from the efforts of scientists to understand nature better and to solve abstract scientific problems that suddenly appear soluble in the light of the existing state of knowledge.

It is quite certain that the solution of the major problems of humanity by technological innovations alone is impossible. Educational and other social progress is probably more important, but I am not qualified to judge what specifically needs to be done in these areas. However, observing how widely different are the opinions on what

259

should be done in these areas, I conclude that we need better understanding of relevant social and behavioral problems. This will require more and better research in social and behavioral sciences. Modern technology, by means of computers, new techniques of information-processing and analysis, and so forth, is involved increasingly in such research, and the research methods approximate more and more closely the experimental methods of the natural sciences. The results of such research will enable us in turn to utilize and modify existing technology (for instance, to improve education by audio-visual aids) to achieve further social progress. The main point is very clear: we must not commit the error of those in England in the early 19th century who resisted the Industrial Revolution. Progress of human society cannot benefit from the cessation of technological innovation; indeed, it must be based on social change keeping pace with technological progress.

Some Comments on Research and Development Statistics

There is a great deal of discussion about the rate of growth of research and development in the United States. The total is now estimated at nearly 20 billion dollars, including both federally financed activities and those financed by state, local, and private sources. This figure is quite irrelevant, however, to the discussion of pure science, since about 90 per cent of the total is being spent on efforts to achieve clearly specified practical objectives, so many of which are related entirely to the military and space programs. Basic research, even after counting in many activities that are hardly relevant from the point of view of pure science, accounts for only a few tenths of one per cent of our gross national product. The number of scientists engaged in basic research (calculated on a full-time basis) is less than 100,000 compared to the total technical community of some 2,000,000 engineers and scientists. . . .

The House Committee on Science and Astronautics has posed two distinct questions, one dealing with the requirements for over-all support of basic research, the other with proper balance of support among the several sciences. In the following I shall attempt to give a partial answer to both questions, but shall use a modified approach, breaking down basic research not into several sciences, but into organizational forms of research and organizational environments in which it is done. I shall thus divide basic research into four categories. The first category has been called by others "little science," somewhat inappropriately, because it is not small either in total investment or in the results achieved. It is, however, characterized by the small size of the autonomous research units that comprise it. In contrast, "big science," the second category, involves large coordinated effort and usually involves very costly research facilities. Both of these categories are mainly identified with academic institutions. The third category is basic research in mission-oriented government establishments, and the fourth is basic research in industrial laboratories.

The reason for choosing this approach is that the available information on the current investment in several sciences, and on the scientific opportunities and material requirements of these sciences, is so inadequate as to make projections for a break-down by separate sciences well-nigh impossible. A start toward analyzing opportunities and requirements of particular scientific areas has been made by groups of experts in planning reports for oceanography, high-energy physics, atmospheric sciences, and space sciences. These reports have been used by federal agencies as a partial basis for allocation of resources, but this experience indicates that the earlier planning reports need extensive revision. Hopefully, the expert groups now working on such reports (ground-based astronomy, computer sciences, physics, chemistry, and others), which are financed mainly by the National Science Foundation and supported by the Committee on Science and Public Policy of the National Academy of Sciences, will benefit from past experience, and their reports, when available, will make further valuable contributions to decisions affecting broad allocation of national resources to various sciences. In all cases, one must be careful to regard these planning reports not as exact blueprints, but as carefully reasoned guesses regarding future scientific trends and requirements. Their value is unquestionable, as indications of what science may bring and what it requires; yet one must always bear in mind that scientific progress is intrinsically unpredictable and that too detailed centralized planning can be harmful to that progress. The purpose of planning for science is not to "master-mind" its detailed development, but rather to chart in advance the evolution of a scientific environment and climate in which innovation and creativity can flourish.

Criteria for Fiscal Support of Scientific Research in Four Categories

The first category, "little science," is in the main an integral part of our universities, "educational institutions proper" in the language of federal statisticians. How have such revolutionary discoveries as radioactivity, X-rays, vitamins, antibiotics, masers, and the mechanism of genetic inheritance been made in the past? What were the system and organization of science that were favorable to such discoveries? Overwhelmingly it was the pattern of the university professor doing the teaching and working with his graduate students and postdoctorate assistants in fields chosen by him exclusively for their scientific interest and because they presented problems that were capable of solution. In the past, these men were supported by their universities, or sometimes by private foundations; they were free agents able to shift their attack from one day to the next as the state of knowledge developed and it became apparent that a given problem could be hopefully attacked, or as ideas suddenly came to individuals working in a given field. This category of scientific research has been considered at length in a recent report of the National Academy of Sciences, entitled *Federal Support of Basic Research in Institutions of Higher Learning.*

Today this research is largely (approximately 57 per cent) supported by research grants and contracts from the federal government to universities. The rest comes from state, local, and private sources. The total amount of federal money being expended on "little science" annually is comparable with the capital being put into the single enterprise of constructing a world-wide satellite communication system, an enterprise that would have been impossible without the discoveries of "little science" in the past. Reckoned on a full-time basis, there are substantially fewer than 100,000 people involved in this kind of work. I believe that it is a very important component of our scientific effort; it is responsible for great contributions to scientific knowledge and so to our scientific world leadership. Characteristically, these contributions cover the entire spectrum of scientific fields because individuals are free to choose the subjects on which they want to work, and hence select the most promising and most exciting fields. Frequently in the course of their lifetimes they move from one field to another as new opportunities and new challenges offer themselves.

This segment of the scientific community is responsible also for the training of most of the new scientists—the some 7,000 science Ph.D.'s now being produced annually, a number that is growing at the rate of 6 or 7 per cent per annum. The new Ph.D.'s constitute a group that is completely indispensable for the future technical progress of the United States; the responsibility of "little science" for the training of most of them sets it apart from other categories of science, as being especially vital to the nation. Only a fraction of these research-trained Ph.D.'s stay in the universities to teach our youth and to engage in basic research. Others staff industrial laboratories, in which they translate basic research results into technological innovations; still others staff government laboratories and management organizations that are responsible for the many technical and military programs of the government. On the basis of extensive personal experience and observations, I believe that education and research in basic science form the best base from which young scientists can develop their skills in applied work. I might also note that many of the senior people have themselves established active contacts with industry and/or government and have thus added to the insight, inspiration, and guidance in activities that are applied in character. Perhaps the most striking example of this contribution was the impact of American scientists on the evolution of military technology during World War II.

As noted earlier, the federal support funds are largely in the form of research project grants and lump-sum contracts, which are discussed in the National Academy of Sciences report referred to earlier. A not insignificant fraction of the investigators working in "little science" do research under group contracts and grants in which several tasks are specified, each being the responsibility of one senior scientist. Whether or not a given project is given support by a federal agency is frequently influenced by referees chosen from among the active scientists to evaluate the scientific merit of a proposal. In other words, the scientist is judged by a jury of his peers. This system is not only democratic but also scientifically sound; even though it demands a good deal of the time of scientists, it is hard to think of a better one, although some refinements would be desirable.

It has been estimated by the National Science Foundation that the average cost to the federal government of a senior researcher, including his part-time salary, technicians' help, scientific supplies, travel, and other pertinent expense items, is $20,000 per annum; that of a post-Ph.D. research associate is $15,000, and that of a graduate research student $3,500. Allowing for indirect costs, purchase of special equipment, and depreciation of general laboratory facilities, I *estimate* that the total annual cost of research averaged over all these people is under $20,000 per annum per man. Of course, the annual value of some project grants and contracts is much larger, because each is supporting the work of a whole group of graduate students and Ph.D. research associates under the leadership of a senior man.

Contiguous to "little science" is a very wide variety of research activities more or less intimately connected with the universities. Not really distinguishable from "little science" are various research laboratories and institutues, which bear such names largely because, for local reasons, the old accepted form of departmental organization was unsuitable. Many of these establishments perform essentially the same functions as those performed by the traditional departments. One must recognize, however, that some of the best scientists are not interested in, and some not capable of, effective teaching and training of young scientific personnel. Such scientists tend to segregate themselves in research institutes which sometimes are unrelated to universities. To deny them research support (and I am thinking here still in terms of support on the scale indicated above and applicable to "little science") because they are not engaged in the production of scientific manpower would be exceedingly unwise. But (although this cannot be put in precise quantitative terms) more should be expected from them in scientific output if they are not contributing to the training of new manpower.

In some cases, financing of the work of institutes takes the form of single large contracts or block grants covering the whole establishment. In some respects this form of government financing is extraordinarily attractive, since it reduces bookkeeping chores and other administrative problems for individual investigators and makes money more readily available for exciting and unforeseen research than do project grant funds. On the other hand, these large contracts and grants, because of the way they are awarded, have the serious weakness that distinctly second-rate and poor research can be more easily hidden and protected by the good work of a few leaders. For budgetary purposes some of these establishments should be included in "little science." Some others, even though they lack a unique costly research facility characteristic of "big science," which I shall consider next, should be included in that category. The dividing line is far from sharp and could not be drawn solely on the basis of the magnitude of the supporting grant or contract. The nature of the activities involved is more important and should be considered in each case—those being similar to "little science" being included in that category, and those involving highly coordinated group effort, i.e., acting as a single scientific task force, included in the category of "big science."

On what basis can one decide what the total amount of money expended on the "little science" category of basic science should be? There appear to be several bases for this decision. In the first place, it has been recognized on the basis of past experience that rapid fluctuations in support cause long-lasting damage to scientific progress. Hence continuity is important and what was *effectively* expended in the past year should be a major factor in deciding what should be expended in the next year. This historical base can be improved by determining the growth rate from recent history and extending it into the immediate future. The second, very vital, consideration is assurance that students of tomorrow who have scientific aptitudes will be given the opportunity to learn productive scientific research. Scientific talent is scarce now, and to do less than educate all those who want to and are capable of being trained for creative scientific work, regardless of geographic origin or economic status, would be most unwise. The third consideration is the level of support in the rest of the world, since I believe that our country should strive to maintain its status as scientifically the most advanced. When calculating the expenditures of other countries, some adjustment factors must be introduced because many undertakings are more expensive in this country than in others. Nevertheless, relationship to national income or gross national product is probably as good a criterion as we have, and certainly the United States, with the highest per capita income in the world, is justified in spending a larger fraction of its income on research than do other industrial nations. The amount of money that can be spent efficiently in a given area of science should provide another reasonable limit; estimation of this should be greatly improved with the availability of the reports on opportunities and requirements of several sciences, which I have referred to previously.

The costs of scientific research are steadily increasing because of ordinary inflation, rising scientific salaries, and, most important, because the problems of science become more difficult every year, so that the time and equipment required to solve them become more expensive. With the efficient instruments we now have, problems that appeared very formidable many years ago can be solved in a matter of days instead of years, and thus much more cheaply. Thus, a century ago Adams spent approximately five years of work on making orbital calculations which led to the discovery of planet

Neptune. Recently, this calculation, including programming, was redone in a matter of weeks on a computer at the Smithsonian Astrophysical Laboratory. Moreover, we are not concerned today with problems of the same nature as those that concerned us many years ago, but with much more difficult problems. These require the full efforts of our investigators aided by the most modern instrumentation. It is the solution of the easy problems and the necessity for facing more difficult ones that makes research more expensive each year. Science planning reports will provide the relevant data on this aspect of research for budgetary considerations.

The ideal way to decide on the proper size of the budget for pure science would be in terms of material requirements of the nation, but this is extraordinarily difficult without factual knowledge of the relation between scientific research and material progress. We do know that we are not making sufficient advances in many scientific areas as a potential basis for technological application. For example, we are not solving the problems of cancer and heart disease sufficiently rapidly; the control of insects has gotten us into very serious difficulties with no clear way out; the economical extraction of pure water from salt or brackish water, though making good progress, is still in the future; the discovery of methods for the control of excessive population increase and acceptable to all religions has become a very urgent problem; the problem of employing usefully the fraction of the population that seems to be incapable of procuring employment in our highly automated society is not yet solved; the psychological problems of delinquency and crime have no obvious solutions. It is highly likely that the ultimate solution of each of these problems, even the social ones, will stem, in part, from some scientific advance in a totally unexpected area.

It is clear, therefore, that we need more basic research across the whole range of scientific fields, including the behavioral sciences. I doubt very much that the availability of qualified scientific personnel is the limiting factor in the present rate of progress. An indication of this can be seen in the numbers of contract and grant proposals that various federal agencies have been unable to support. Substantial percentages of these have been rated as worthy of support and yet the funds are not available. There is some duplication in proposals, and this must be allowed for, but studies indicate that this probably pertains to less than 5 per cent of the total of all applications and hence does not alter the main conclusion.

Making allowances for the growing number of graduate students, for the need to give them more extended training (often beyond the Ph.D.) because of the increasing complexity of science, and for rising costs of research due to more sophisticated instrumentation, I arrive at a very tentative figure of 15 per cent for the overall annual growth of "little science" for the next five to ten years to meet the objectives spelled out in the questions posed to us. The National Science Foundation calculates that in 1963 the federal support of *basic* research at educational institutions proper amounted to approximately $450 million. A large percentage of this and comparatively little from other categories of federal support should be classed as basic "little science." To arrive at the total, one must also add a rather small, but currently not known, relevant fraction of the $160 million in federal obligations for the research and development plant at educational institutions proper. Also, the value of fellowships to students, pre- and post-doctoral, in "little science"; that is, a fraction of the $330 million obligated by the federal government for fellowships, traineeships, summer schools for high school teachers, and similar training allocations. The total for "little science," I estimate, was not far from $600 million in 1963 and, at 15 per cent per annum, it would double in five years.

The dollar figures given above refer to basic research. The totals going to educational institutions proper are at least twice as large, the difference being defined as applied research and related expenditures. Much of this applied research (e.g., in biomedical sciences) is not substantially different from basic research in "little science," and should perhaps be included in it for budgetary purposes. On the other hand, the objectives in supporting applied research—while certainly as valid as those relating to basic research—are different. Moreover, applied research is mainly concentrated in professional schools—medical, engineering, public health, for example—while basic research is typical of faculties of arts and sciences. On the whole I believe that separate budgetary planning for basic and applied research has some advantages in view of the differences noted above.

The practical budgetary problems of maintaining a steady growth of "little science" are far from being simple. For instance, the long-range commitments of several federal agencies to "big science" projects have currently led to an actual contraction of "little science" budgets in several scientific areas, because the total scientific budgets did not increase as fast as expected by agency planners when the commitments were made. Another difficult problem arises because much of the "little science" is supported by agencies with practical missions (e.g., the Department of Defense, the Atomic Energy Commission, and the National Institutes of Health) and is therefore, in principle, "mission-oriented" research. The breadth of definition of what basic research is relevant to the practical mission varies greatly from one agency to another, and also changes with time, and this creates difficulties. For instance, the Department of Agriculture does not support broad-based research in plant sciences in the way that the National Institutes of Health supports research in other parts of biology, or the Atomic Energy Commission supports research in high-energy physics, but the National Aeronautics and Space Administration appears to be relatively indifferent to astronomy beyond the solar system; and so on. These difficulties are made more serious by changes in policies defining what is mission-oriented, reflected, for instance, in a recent decrease of support of "little science" in universities by some research offices of the Department of Defense. To cope with these situations and trends, which may be wholly justifiable from the point of view of mission-oriented agencies but which can be very harmful from the national point of view, I see but one procedure. It is to set the research budgets of the National Science Foundation so as to allow for budgetary trends in other agencies and thus to ensure the overall growth of "little science" that has been decided upon. At the same time, the mission-oriented agencies should be discouraged from abandoning basic research, since otherwise the federal system will become too centralized.

So much for the problem of gross allocation. There remains the problem of detailed allocation to individual problems. Here, I strongly believe that every effort should be made to avoid overly detailed centralized planning and control. No man was wise enough in 1900 to foresee that the Curies would make a major contribution to the cure of cancer. Similarly, no man today is wise enough to know from what field will come a critical discovery that, directly or indirectly, will solve the problem of the control of insects. Will it be new chemical discoveries, the use of radioactivity, as in the case of the screwworm fly, or sex attractants, or some idea that does not now exist in any man's mind and therefore cannot even be guessed, much less incorporated into a planned program of research?

How, practically, can we be sure that freedom of scientific enquiry will always be carefully considered and protected in the allocation of funds? As far as "little science" is concerned, this can be assured if allocations are guided by the requests for funds from individual investigators. Does chemistry have a large number of worthy grant or contract proposals? Are the funds for chemistry sufficient to cover these? Naturally any such device can be distorted, by padding proposals and other obvious means. Federal agencies are and must be constantly on the watch for distortions. The reports on opportunities and requirements of particular sciences should be of major help in determining broadly what is important and possible. But in specific cases it is only the investigator working closely in his field who knows what is possible, and he is constantly on the alert for problems that are both important and soluble. Similarly, research students, free to study what they wish, tend to move into scientific fields with the greatest intellectual opportunities. The detailed allocation of support should therefore be based, democratically, on the multitude of the individual choices made by individual investigators. This is the basis of the flowering of science, and hence technology, in the twentieth century.

Prior to World War II, basic science seldom made use of costly research equipment, almost the only exception being astronomy. Since World War II, because of federal support, the use of costly research facilities has been growing very rapidly and has led to the establishment of a new category of basic science, which I will call, following others, "big science." The organized teamwork that is usual with these costly research facilities has opened completely new fields to scientific research and greatly advanced our knowledge of the world we live in. This "big science" is as indispensable to world leadership and the continuing progress of the United States as is "little science," but from a fiscal point of view it presents different problems. In appreciating these problems one needs to bear in mind that the transition from "little science" to "big science" is continuous and far from sharp. However, a somewhat arbitrary boundary might be defined in fiscal terms. I have estimated above that one man-year of research in "little science" costs under $20,000. This included the annual cost, per researcher, of general laboratory facilities, which are useable, of course, for many years. The boundary of "little science" could be drawn by defining "little science" as limited to annual costs of this order of magnitude. Where special research equipment or facilities are costing much more or a major research establishment involves a centralized task-force effort, one might speak of "big science." For instance, a research facility initially costing $12 million, whose annual operating cost is $3 million and which becomes obsolete or requires major reconstruction after six years, would cost about $170,000 per scientist-year if 30 scientists, including post-Ph.D. fellows and graduate students, were using it. The costs of individual projects in this category have been rising very rapidly since World War II (perhaps by a factor of 100 in 18 years), and there is no natural upper limit to such costs. "Big science" is fiscally open-ended because the commitment of *scientific personnel per project* is rising comparatively slowly and the costs are concentrated in the engineering effort of constructing the special facilities and their maintenance, operation, and improvement. To illustrate, it has been reported in the newspapers that Project Ranger has already cost $200 million. It has yielded very significant detailed pictures of the moon surface which are being studied by astronomers and will advance our understanding of the moon. The overwhelming fraction of the money has gone, however, into the engineering of the space probes, the manufacture of the rocket boosters, the construction and operation of the launch facilities, and similar items. Our engineering resources are so great that it has become *technically* feasible to engage in individual projects costing in the range of hundreds of millions of dollars (e.g., the proposed nuclear-particle accelerators) or even many billions of dollars if Project Apollo is regarded as scientific. The essential point is that technically such projects are not limited by the supply of scientific talent in the way "little science" is, but only by the (much greater) supply of skilled engineering manpower.

Currently this "big science" is composed mainly of a rather large group of establishments for basic research that are built around expensive special facilities and are normally fairly closely connected to universities. As examples, I might mention the nuclear-particle accelerators, large radio and optical telescopes, oceanographic research vessels, the National Primate Center, and special ventures like the Mohole, Project Ranger, and scientific satellites. Some of these activities are not managed by individual universities, but by groups of universities, as the Brookhaven National Laboratory, the Kitt Peak Astronomical Observatory, and the National Center for Atmospheric Research. Still others, like Projects Ranger and Apollo and the Mohole, are managed directly by federal agencies. The financial characteristic of these operations is that the cost to the federal government per active scientist and per unit of scientific knowledge, as measured by scientific papers, is very much higher than that in "little science." Where a scientific paper may have cost the federal government $20,000 in the domain of "little science," a similar scientific paper based on research with a large nuclear-particle accelerator may cost half a million dollars, because of underlying engineering and logistic costs. About the same ratio of costs probably applies to the training of new scientific personnel in these establishments, and it is questionable whether individual training costs of such large magnitude can be used to justify the operation of these establishments. In fact, they usually depend for most of their personnel on people who were scientifically trained in "little science." The student training they do should be seen as a secondary aspect of their activities, and their support should be justified mainly on the ground that *they provide scientific results that cannot be obtained by any other means* and are important enough in at least one of the ways defined below to justify the cost.

Realistically, we must think in terms of a limited total national scientific budget, and then, because of the absence of natural limitations to the costs of individual "big science" projects, the question of financing them acquires a special perspective. Although an accurate figure is difficult to arrive at, I estimate that in the United States today considerably more money is going into these establishments and projects than into "little science." Thus the space sciences budget of the National Aeronautics and Space Administration, of which a large fraction is in the category of "big science" as defined above, alone amounts to nearly half of the $1.6 billion classified as total federal basic research in fiscal 1964.

It is my belief that in order to maintain our world leadership we should continue to support "big science," and support it on a broad front, but the determination of the proper growth rate requires different considerations from those advanced earlier for "little science." In seeking to determine what factors should be considered in determining the financing of the projects and establishments of "big science," I found the considerations developed by Dr. Weinberg in his article in the magazine *Minerva* (Winter 1963) very helpful.

Before discussing them, however, I wish to emphasize another factor. Before weighing seriously the comparative value of a new project in "big science," it is essential to ascertain two factors: (a) it must be feasible technically in the judgment of engineering experts; (b) it must be backed by a qualified group of scientists who consider it important enough to make firm personal commitments to it if undertaken. The latter point is essential to ensure scientific success of the project.

One factor considered by Dr. Weinberg is the impact of a given type of research on related and significant branches of science. With respect to this factor, he has given a low rating to high-energy physics research on elementary particles. The contribution of this factor can be determined in detail by consultations with people who are not themselves involved in the research in question, but who are active in adjacent scientific fields and hence can sense the impact on their sciences of the special programs and projects considered.

A second factor, useful because many of these projects are of somewhat programmatic nature (and hence of somewhat predictable outcome), is the impact of the results of scientific work on practical applications. This is related to Dr. Weinberg's social-value criterion. For instance, the drilling of the Mohole will undoubtedly advance oceanic drilling to shallow depths, which may be of importance for oil and other natural resources. Much oceanographic research has clear, practical implications of a number of types, including military. Atmospheric research has obvious practical importance for weather prediction, and possibly ultimately for weather modification. These considerations must be developed for each establishment or project, and weighed.

The third factor is one of national prestige and international influence, the significance of which, of course, is strongly dependent on the general world political situation. There is no doubt that space explorations by means of satellites and deep space probes have a substantial international impact, improving the apparent stature of a nation, even though their scientific results are of interest only to a very limited audience. High-energy physics research seems also to be a matter of some national prestige. Oceanographic research, by showing the flag, as, for instance, in the case of the current expedition to study the Indian Ocean, certainly has a major international impact.

The last factor, which is probably least susceptible to quantitative evaluation, is the broad cultural impact of scientific research, satisfying the age-old urge of humans to understand the world and themselves. Three scientific areas impress me as having now probably the greatest human appeal and grandeur in this respect.

They are galactic astronomy, probing the structure and the origin of the entire universe; molecular genetics (now part of "little science"), advancing the understanding of the origin and evolution of life; and high-energy physics, exploring the elementary particle structure of all matter.

To sum it up, when engineering feasibility and adequate commitment of scientific talent are assured, there remain four main considerations that have to be carefully weighed and put together, and on that basis it should be possible to arrange the existing and the newly proposed projects in an order of preference. If one restricts consideration to projects whose initial costs are in the millions and operating costs (including scientific activities) are correspondingly high, the total number (excluding establishments whose main function is applied but including the previously mentioned "single-task" research institutes not attached to a unique facility) would be only in the hundreds, so that an ordering of priorities on the national level is wholly feasible. Since these ordering judgments are fallible, I would not advocate dropping a particular type of activity—for instance, deep earth drilling—as totally worthless. The judgment is not between "black" and "white," but in terms of various degrees of value. Here also some "planning reports" on the opportunities and requirements of particular sciences will be valuable, because their authors, who are experts in the field, identify the most promising new research facilities in their scientific fields and assign relative priorities to them. After a decision on a total federal budget for all "big science" ventures in the light of available fiscal resources and needs of the government, it should be possible to allocate the total available funds among the different enterprises—existing and proposed—according to the judgments developed above. Because of inaccessibility to me of all relevant information, I am unable to conclude whether the total budget for "big science" should grow more or less rapidly than that of "little science," but it certainly should not grow *at the expense* of "little science," for the reasons already developed. A poor nation that would still profit greatly by nurturing "little science" may not be able to afford "big science." (Note the recent openly acknowledged decision of the Soviet Academy of Science not to "compete" except in selected areas of "big science" because of limitations of their national resources.) On the other hand, "big science" generates effects of international import and provides some scientific knowledge that "little science" cannot.

The third category of basic scientific research to which I turn my attention is some of the work done in government laboratories, other government technical establishments, and contractor-operated federal research centers. Included in this category are all those that were established to achieve practical goals within the broad mission of the government agency financing the establishment. They are numbered in the hundreds. Careful studies of the optimum conditions for effectiveness of such establishments have led to a consistent conclusion (see, for instance: *Strengthening American Science*, Washington, 1958, a report of the President's Science Advisory Committee) that they should incorporate in their activities basic research related to their practical mission, i.e., mission-oriented research. Such in-house activity provides a bridge between the contemporary science and the applied effort and assures a continuing forward-looking posture of the establishment. This general requirement, I believe, is absolutely essential to ensure the viability and worth of such establishments, but its details—that is, the definition of the scientific scope of mission-oriented basic research and the division of funds between such basic research and the applied work—should be very largely the administrative function of the sponsoring agency and the management of the establishment, subject, of course, to the approval of Congress.° The primary concern of Congress should be to determine the total funds to be allocated to the establishment on the basis of the importance and promise of the practical mission, and on the basis of the past record of accomplishment of the establishment in the performance of its practical mission.

While thus endorsing firmly the need and value of mission-oriented research, I have reservations about the introduction of general basic research, not related to their mission, into such establishments. This creates distinct classes of personnel and is not conducive to an effective prosecution of the main objectives of the establishment. In this connection I must also note that the original practical mission of some—but certainly not the majority—of such establishments has been accomplished or lost, and no new one of equal validity has been established. The substitution of basic research for the practical mission as a justification for the growth of an establishment appears to me to be not very sound. Valid questions must be raised concerning such factors as lack of firm scientific tra-

---

° Needless to say, the use of competent "outside" scientists in assesing the scientific worth of proposed basic research would be as valuable here as it is in categories 1 and 2.

dition in management, comparative isolation, high costs and inability to educate new scientific personnel, as well as scientific productivity. If the answers are unfavorable, clearly the establishments should receive low priority in the allocation of funds for scientific research. While abrupt discontinuance of support of these establishments would be harmful and disturbing, if their scientific productivity were recognized as satisfactory, essentially fixed budgets seem to be the most that can be recommended, except where research is of outstanding quality. In effect, the fixed or decreasing budgets would be equivalent to "mothballing" an establishment in order to have it available for an unanticipated new practical need.

My reservations about the introduction of general, non mission-oriented basic research into the in-house establishments are the same in principle as the objections to the creation of career research personnel, not related to teaching, in universities. Basic research in universities, seen from the point of view of the government agencies, is also mission-oriented, the general mission being the training of new scientific personnel. Of course frequently there is also a connection to the particular practical mission of the supporting agency, such as the AEC, etc.

The fourth category is basic research financed by the federal government in the research laboratories of profit-motivated (and some rather similar "non-profit") private corporations as distinguished from wholly government-financed federal contract research centers included in category 3. This fourth category includes basic research done under contracts aimed at practical objectives, some of the so-called independent research financed partly from the overhead of procurement funds (ASPR 15, amounting to about $1 billion in 1964) and separate contracts and grants for basic research.

The principles developed above for category 3—the government laboratories—are, I believe, applicable to category 4 also. When the profit-motivated organization is engaged in an applied practical task under contract to the government, the government agency and the contractor must determine whether related basic research by the contractor will expedite the accomplishment of the mission. If so, they must also determine what constitutes mission-oriented basic research. It should also be mainly an administrative function of the agency, in consultation with the contractor, to decide on the division of funds among the various activities of the contractor. The Congress, on the basis of the importance of practical missions and records of progress achieved, should, of course, decide on the total funds to be allocated.

Most of the funds under ASPR 15 are given in support of applied research. Where these funds are used to support basic research, the principle now in force, I believe, is that the work is intended to increase the contractor's value to the government, and is therefore to be related to the contractor's existing practical capabilities. This principle appears sound to me and requires no modification, but perhaps a more consistent application is called for.

The contracts and grants for basic research by profit-motivated corporations that is unrelated to their development and production activities for the government appear to me to have little justification. Of course, there are exceptions where an outstanding scientific capability exists and where continuing creative activity is in the national interest. Where there is no solid basis for assuming such capability, the same arguments should apply, as stated earlier regarding government establishments without applied missions. The high costs of such research (see testimony of Dr. D. F. Hornig before the Subcommittee on Science and Research, May 21, 1964) militate against its expansion or even continuation.

In conclusion, I want to comment on two subjects that have been referred to in this paper only very briefly. While I believe that basic research should be supported over the whole spectrum of sciences because of the difficulties in predicting its practical value in individual cases, I am convinced that the main justification for federal support on the present scale lies in its practical applications of benefit to the nation. Hence the process of translating basic scientific findings into practice is highly important, and this involves applied research prior to engineering. The strengthening of such research in government laboratories and in profit-motivated corporations is as vital to the nation as that of basic research, mainly in universities. The former and the latter types of research involve different considerations, however, and I have not discussed the former because I consider it to be somewhat outside the specific problem posed to us by the House Committee.

Finally, I want to reaffirm my deep conviction that better education of our youth, based on equal opportunity for all who want to avail themselves of it, is indispensable to a good future for our nation. Education and research training of young scientists is but a part of this large task.

Notes on Contributors

PHILIP HAUGE ABELSON, born in 1913 in Tacoma, Washington, is Director of the Geophysical Laboratory at the Carnegie Institution of Washington and Editor of *Science*, the publication of the American Association for the Advancement of Science. Mr. Abelson edited *Researches in Geochemistry* (1959).

J. DOUGLAS BROWN, born in 1898 in Somerville, New Jersey, is Dean of the Faculty and Professor of Economics at Princeton University. He was Director of the Industrial Relations Section, Princeton University, from 1926-1955 and was co-author and editor of many reports on industrial relations and manpower. He has also written many articles on social insurance and higher education.

LOREN EISELEY, born in 1907 in Lincoln, Nebraska, is University Professor of Anthropology and the History of Science at the University of Pennsylvania. He is author of *Immense Journey* (1957), *Darwin's Century* (1958), *The Firmament of Time* (1960), *The Mind as Nature* (1962), and *Francis Bacon and the Modern Dilemma* (1962). He has also written many scholarly articles on anthropology and on the history of science.

CARYL P. HASKINS was born in 1908 in Schenectady, New York. A scientist by profession, he also has deep interests in education and government. His recently published Root Lectures at the Council on Foreign Relations, *The Scientific Revolution and World Politics*, and his Edge Lectures delivered at Princeton in 1964 deal with various aspects of the relation of science to domestic and foreign policy. He is president of the Carnegie Institution of Washington.

DAVID HAWKINS, born in 1913 in El Paso, Texas, is Professor of Philosophy at the University of Colorado. His publications include *History of Project Y*, Los Alamos Manuscript (1961), and *The Language of Nature* (1964). His essay, "Design for a Mind," appeared in the Summer 1962 issue of *Dædalus*.

PHILIP WESLEY JACKSON, born in 1928 in Vineland, New Jersey, is Professor of Education and Human Development at the University of Chicago and Principal of the University's Laboratory Nursery School. Mr. Jackson is co-author of *Creativity and Intelligence* (1962) and author of *Life in Classrooms* (in press).

JEROME KAGAN, born in 1929 in Newark, New Jersey, is Professor of Developmental Psychology at Harvard University. He is the author of *Contemporary Issues in Thematic Apperception Methods* (1961) and co-author of *Birth to Maturity* (1962) and *Child Development and Personality* (1963).

GEORGE B. KISTIAKOWSKY, born in 1900 in Kiev, Russia, is Abbott and James Lawrence Professor of Chemistry at Harvard University. His research work has been largely in the fields of kinetics of gas phase reactions, structure of polyatomic molecules, thermo-chemistry of organic compounds, enzyme catalyzed reactions, and shock and detonation waves.

LAWRENCE S. KUBIE, born in 1896 in New York City, is Clinical Professor of Psychiatry at the University of Maryland Medical School, Visiting Professor of Psychiatry at the Jefferson Medical College of Philadelphia, and Consultant on Research and Training at the Sheppard Pratt Hospital in Towson, Maryland. He is Editor-in-Chief of the *Journal of Nervous and Mental Disease*. His publications include *Practical and Theoretical Aspects of Psychoanalysis* (1950), *Psychoanalysis as Science* (1952), and *Neurotic Distortion of Creative Process* (1958).

DONALD W. MACKINNON, born in 1903 in Augusta, Maine, is Professor of Psychology and Director of the Institute of Personality Assessment and Research at the University of California, Berkeley. Mr. Jackson is co-author of *Assessment of Men* (1948) and *Experimental Studies in Psychodynamics* (1948).

SAMUEL MESSICK, born in 1931 in Philadelphia, Pennsylvania, is Chairman of the Personality Research Group of the Educational Testing Service in Princeton, New Jersey, and Adjunct Professor of Psychology at the City University, New York. Mr. Messick has co-edited *Psychological Scaling* (1960), *Measurement in Personality and Cognition* (1962), *Computer Simulation of Personality* (1963), and *Problems in Human Assessment* (1967).

NEVITT SANFORD, born in 1909 in Chatham, Virginia, is Professor of Education and Psychology, Director of the Institute for the Study of Human Problems, and Scientific Director of the Cooperative Commission of the Study of Alcoholism at Stanford University. He is co-author of *The Authoritarian Personality* (1950) and editor of *The American College: A Psychological and Social Interpretation of the Higher Learning* (1962) and *College and Character* (1964).

E. PAUL TORRANCE, born in 1915 in Milledgeville, Georgia, is Professor of Educational Psychology at the University of Minnesota. He is the author of *Guiding Creative Talent* (1962), *Education and the Creative Potential* (1963), and *Constructive Behavior: Stress, Personality and Mental Health* (1965). His research has centered largely on the psychology of stress and creative thinking.

MICHAEL A. WALLACH, born in 1933 in New York City, is Professor of Psychology at Duke University. Mr. Wallach is the co-author of *Risk Taking* (1964) and *Modes of Thinking in Young Children* (1965). He is also editor of *The Journal of Personality*.

JEROME B. WIESNER, born in 1915 in Detroit, Michigan, is Dean of the School of Science at the Massachusetts Institute of Technology. He was formerly Special Assistant for Science and Technology to the President and Director of the Office of Science and Technology. He has contributed articles to *Science*, the *Journal of Applied Physics*, *Proceedings of the I.E.E.E.*, *Physics Review*, and several other publications.

FORREST WILLIAMS, born in 1924 in Paris, France, is Professor of Philosophy at the University of Colorado. The author of numerous articles in scholarly journals, Mr. Williams has translated Jean-Paul Sartre's *The Transcendence of the Ego* and *Imagination*. He is currently writing a book on film as an art form.

CLIFF W. WING, JR., born in 1922 in Reed City, Michigan, is Assistant Professor of Psychology and Director of Student Resources at Duke University. His publications include "On Selecting a College and Seeking Admission," in *American Universities and Colleges*, edited by Allan M. Cartter (1959).

INDEX

Index

Index

Index

New World Dictionary, 17
New Yorker magazine, 8
New York University, 191
Nobel prizes, 130, 195–196
Nomothetic science, vs. idiographic, 21
Non-Euclidean geometries, 41
Non-involvement, 103
"Normal" process, in scientific education, 133
Novelty, in learning, viii, 10, 162

Oberon (Wieland), 62, 64
Oceanographic research, 272
Oedipal anxiety, 82
"Open-mindedness," 16
Originality, estimates of, 134
Origin of Species, The (Darwin), 59, 228
Orton, Samuel T., 129

Painting, representational, 42
Palomar telescope, 224
Paraconscious state, 118
Paranoia, 28–29
Parent, in child learning process, 154–155
Parnassian hypothesis, 143–144, 150
Pascal, Blaise, 103
Pasteur, Louis, 240
Pasteur Institute, 240
Peer groups, in teacher-scholar faculty, 174–175
Penetration, power of, 230–231
Perfectionism, in teacher-scholar, 171
Performance standards, in learning, 158
Personality, masculine and feminine components of, 29
Personality tests, 21–23
Personal "style," 97
Persona role, 29
Peter the Great, 113
Ph.D. degrees, number of annually, 262
Ph.D. theses, and Human Problems Institute, 220
Physiological psychology, 249
Picture Construction Test, 80–81
Planning, for and in science, 247–248
Plastics, 258
Plato, 85, 150
Poetic character, creativity and, 16
Poincaré, Henri, 136, 142, 146, 149, 200
Polymeric molecules, 258
"Pop" art, 45
Possibilities, expression of, 36–55

Postulates, in geometry, 38
Potential, tests for, 77–84
Preconscious learning, 118–123
Predictions, in scientific education, 128
Prejudice, 28
Premises, in human thinking, 46–47
President's Science Advisory Committee, 274
Problem-solving, creativity and, 74–76, 96
Proceedings of the American Philosophical Society, 59
Product Improvement Task, 79
Productivity/creativity criteria, 93, 130, 134–137
Progressive Education, 86–89, 110
Progressive Education Association, 86
Project Apollo, 270
Project Mohole, 270, 272
Project Ranger, 270
Prose writing, infra-conscious agency in, 149–150
Psychological levels, learning and, 118
Psychopathology, creativity and, 28–29, 126
"Publish or perish" slogan, 175
Pygmy culture, 104, 107, 116

Quantum theory, 257

Radiation Laboratory, Berkeley, Calif., 196–197
Radio astronomy, 224
Random association, 147
Raths, J. D., 88
Regression, psychological, 142–143
Remote Association Test, 3
Repeated Closed Figures Test, 81
Repression, 120
Research, experimental, 88; Federal support of, 255–276; scientific, 92–94 (see also Scientific research); see also Research and development
Research and development, expenditures on, 243; statistics on, 260–261
Research scientist, creativity of, 32; see also Scientist
Rewarding Creative Behavior (Torrance), 82, 86
Riemannian geometry, 39
Rime of the Ancient Mariner, The (Coleridge), 58, 62
Rivalry, 199
Road to Xanadu, The (Lowes), 61–62
Robbins Report, 245
Roe, Anne, 94

286

Index